Effective writing for social work

Making a difference

Lucy Rai

LEARNING RESOURCES
CENTRE

Havering College
of Further and Higher education

209227

First published in Great Britain in 2014 by

Policy Press
University of Bristol
6th Floor
Howard House
Queen's Avenue
Clifton
Bristol BS8 1SD
UK
t: +44 (0)117 331 5020
tpp-info@bristol.ac.uk
www.policypress.co.uk

North America office:
Policy Press
c/o The University of Chicago Press
1427 East 60th Street
Chicago, IL 60637, USA
t: +1 773 702 7700
f: +1 773-702-9756
sales@press.uchicago.edu
www.press.uchicago.edu

© Policy Press 2014

British Library Cataloguing in Publication Data
A catalogue record for this book is available from the British Library.

Library of Congress Cataloging-in-Publication Data
A catalog record for this book has been requested.

ISBN 978 1 44730 516 3 paperback
ISBN 978 1 44730 517 0 hardcover

The right of Lucy Rai to be identified as the author of this work has been asserted by her
in accordance with the Copyright, Designs and Patents Act 1988.

Cover design by Policy Press
Front cover: image kindly supplied by www.alamy.com
Printed and bound in Great Britain by Hobbs, Southampton
Policy Press uses environmentally responsible print partners

FSC
www.fsc.org
MIX
Paper from
responsible sources
FSC® C020438

Contents

List of tables and figures

Tables

Figures

About the author and contributors

Lucy Rai is Associate Dean (Teaching and Learning) in the faculty of Health and Social Care at The Open University. She is a qualified social worker and has worked in both children's and adults services. Lucy has been teaching at The Open University since 2001 and her research has focused on student and professional writing in social work.

Theresa Lillis is Professor of English Language and Applied Linguistics at The Open University. Her research centres on writing in academic and professional contexts.

Amanda Harrison is a qualified consultant social worker for Cambridgeshire County Council (Children's Social Care)

Guillermo Garcia-Maza is a qualified social worker and manager of Mental Health Support Services at Derbyshire County Council.

Acknowledgements

This book is the product of research and reflection that has only been possible with the contribution of some dedicated students and practitioners. These include social work students who participated in my doctoral research and also the practitioners who acted as co-researchers on the Writing in Social Work in Academic and Professional Domains (WiSWAP) project. We would like to thank Amanda Harrison, Iain Brown, Gillian Lucas and Richard Ganderton for their contributions to research on academic and practice writing in children's services and also the assessment teams in North East Derbyshire for sharing their time and perspectives: in particular, Peter Bunting, Tony Lloyd, Linda Morton, Liz Naylor, Linda Nixon, Yolanda Dixon and Daniel Teasdale. Our thanks to Jonathan Moore for his insightful comments on recording relating to mental health. My sincere thanks to all of those involved for their time, reflections and enthusiasm for the project.

I would also like to thank Sheila Finlayson for reading the first draft, Douglas Gray, Roshan Rai and Kal Rai for their enduring support, and my colleagues at The Open University for their patience while I took time out to write.

Writing in social work

Introduction

The aim of *Effective writing for social work: Making a difference* is to enhance practice with service users through offering discussion and guidance on academic and professional social work writing. It also aims to provide readers with the resources to think critically about the demands and expectations of social work writing in academic and practice contexts. *Effective writing for social work* is a book for anyone who is involved in social work writing and concerned with its effectiveness in practice, but it is aimed primarily at students and educators in the UK. It will also be of interest to researchers and students studying academic and professional writing. The book offers insights and strategies which will help social work students become more strategic and, hopefully, successful in their writing. For educators, it offers a different perspective on designing and assessing learning that includes writing itself as a curriculum area, or capability to be learned and assessed. *Effective writing for social work* offers explicit, grounded guidance to enable practitioners to become effective professional writers. It provides an opportunity for readers to gain an insight into their own 'writing practices'[1] and the nature and demands of writing in social work.

The book draws on recent research and my own experience, as a social worker, researcher and educator in higher education teaching student and professional writing. Specifically the book draws on findings from the Writing in Social Work: Academic and Professional Domains (WiSWAP) Project. The lead researchers for the project, myself and Professor Theresa Lillis, have been working with statutory social work agencies in children and adult services exploring academic and professional writing. The WiSWAP project has been undertaken over a four-year period during which the data that was collected included recordings of interviews and groups discussions with social workers, diaries or writing undertaken, field notes of observations of practice and also examples of authentic texts. Where data is used from this project it will be identified as being from the WiSWAP. Practice examples used throughout the book are from both published work and from the WiSWAP Project.

Effective writing for social work begins by setting out the context of social work education in Chapter One and the theoretical foundations that the rest of the book is based on in Chapter Two. Chapter Three focuses on academic writing, specifically essays and reflective writing that are both commonly used in social work assessments. In Chapter Four the focus shifts to practice; this chapter explores the writing that students undertake during their practice learning placements and introduces practice writing. Chapters Five, Six and Seven explore practice writing in more detail, Chapter Five introducing the context and some of the challenges of writing in practice while Chapter Six focuses on case recording and Chapter Seven on report writing. The book concludes with an overview of the main themes in Chapter Eight.

Writing in social work

In common with many vocational fields of study, social work is constituted of a range of academic disciplines such as sociology, psychology, social policy, law, ethics and health. It has also increasingly carved out its own distinctive academic identity, an identity that is played out through social work academic writing. This identity has always incorporated a strong ethical value base along with developing theoretical foundations, which have, over the years, included social welfare, psychoanalytic casework, empowerment and advocacy and care management. Lyons suggests that managerialism in social work also grew in significance through the 1990s, largely as a defensive response to criticisms of the profession. Bureaucratic procedures and the measurement of performance indicators or became increasingly dominant, limiting professional autonomy (Lyons, 1999: 28, 36). Managerialism is referred to throughout this book as it has had a significant influence on social work writing through, for example, the emphasis that was placed on measuring performance indicators over the discretion and professional judgement of individual social workers.

Throughout *Effective writing for social work* writing is treated as a form of communication that is embedded in social contexts and human interaction. Communication is a well-established foundation stone of social work practice, and social work educators are required to invest considerable time and resources into ensuring that student social workers develop the required range of communication skills. Effective writing, commonly discretely embedded within the capability of 'communication' (as illustrated below), is an essential but often overlooked component. It is not uncommon for writing (in education and professional practice) to only become visible when problems arise in the performance of students. At this point the focus of institutional effort is generally remedial and directed at individual writers. This book offers a new perspective on developing the effectiveness of writing in social work. It draws on broadly psychosocial perspectives, familiar to social workers, and a body of research that has investigated student and professional writing as 'social practice'. 'Social practice' refers to an approach to literacy that treats writing as communicative acts taking place in contexts that have social, institutional and interpersonal significance. It involves:

> Viewing literacy from a cultural and social practice approach (rather than in terms of educational judgements about good or bad writing) and approaching meanings as contested can give us insights into the nature of academic literacy in particular and academic learning in general. (Lea, 1998: 33)

As a result of this underpinning approach, writing is not treated here as a discrete skill, as an act of communication with all the associated complexities which are recognised in the context of communication in both social work and higher education, but which are frequently overlooked in writing. In addition, and perhaps more controversially, the responsibility for effective writing is not located solely with the writer, but is shared systemically across a network of others, both individuals and institutions. These ideas are all explored further throughout the book.

Why is writing an important capability in social work?

Social work has recently undergone significant review in England, during which writing has been under scrutiny as an indicator of suitability for training and also as a feature of professional practice. The Social Work Reform Board's initial report (2009) and the Munro report (2011) had different foci, but both made reference to writing as an important aspect of professional social work practice (Social Work Reform Board, 2009: 15; Munro, 2011: 6). Competence in writing has been identified as an important measure for entrants to the profession with a required entry minimum qualification in English, GCSE grade C (or Key Skills level 2 equivalent), or for non-native English speakers a minimum of International English Language Testing System (IELTS) level 7 as well as successful completion of a compulsory written test for all candidates set by the awarding institution (Social Work Reform Board, 2010: 44). Scotland and Wales share the requirement for English at Key Skills level 2, but there is no such stipulation in Northern Ireland. There has, however, been less attention paid to the part played by academic writing *during* social work education or indeed professional writing undertaken during practice learning placements, the assumption appearing to be that if students begin training with good basic writing skills, they will be able to perform well in both academic and professional writing. Writing as a tool to enable students to develop the skills they need to write once qualified appears to receive relatively little attention on social work programmes, despite that fact that professional social work writing is a very high stakes activity. Eileen Munro, in her 2011 report, states that:

> Recording is a key social work task and its centrality to the protection of children cannot be over-estimated. (Munro, 2011: 111)

Here Munro refers specifically to recording, but this is just one form of professional social work writing which sits alongside a myriad of text types[2] such as court reports, letters, assessments and referrals. Writing takes up more than half of social workers' time (Holmes et al, 2009; O'Rourke, 2010; BASW, 2012), and while the desirability and reasons for this are debatable, it reflects the reality of modern social work practice. Writing is a key tool for sharing information between agencies, for evidencing decisions and actions, for planning and making referrals, for accountability, for encapsulating and sharing assessments and for making recommendations to court. Writing can also be used as a tool for therapeutic intervention and supervision.

Effective writing for social work will provide students, practitioners and educators with guidance to assist in unpacking the requirements relating to writing within the standards governing training and registration. Professional writing, as indicated above, is commonly embedded within 'communication', and where mentioned more directly, it is usually referred to only in terms of either 'case recording' or 'court reports'. These two text types are undoubtedly important, but do not account for all the writing that social workers are engaged in. Recent research also illustrates that although there are common principles, for example, in case recoding, local agency or service user group requirements can differ considerably. Academic requirements rarely make direct reference to the specific forms of social work writing required during training unless in the form of a generic reference to 'report writing'.

Writing in academic and professional contexts

Writing plays an important role during professional education as a significant conduit for assessment in both the university and practice settings (Rai, 2004, 2006; Rai and Lillis, 2011, 2013). *Effective writing for social work* is concerned with all writing undertaken by students while in social work education; this includes the wide range of academic assignments used by universities to assess academic progress, and also the writing that students undertake during practice placements in preparation for professional practice.

Social work students are taught in both the academic context and through supervised experience and learning in professional practice. The standards that they are required to meet prior to qualification are taught across these domains with some resting primarily in the university (developing theoretical knowledge and scholarly skills) while others rest primarily in practice (communicating with service users and other professionals, and applying theory to make informed decisions or to bring about change). Many areas of social workers' learning, however, span these two domains and involve students learning to integrate and apply scholarly knowledge and thinking skills to their vocational context. Areas where such integration is needed can prove particularly challenging; the application of theory to practice, for example, has long been recognised within social work education as a pedagogic challenge.

Writing sits in just such an intersection between scholarly and vocational learning, but it has received little attention other than as a basic entry-level skill that can then be used as a means to deliver and assess learning and practice. Writing plays an important role during professional education as a significant conduit for assessment in both the university and practice settings (Rai, 2004, 2011; Rai and Lillis, 2011, 2013). Whether studying on a degree or master's level qualifying course, students are required to develop and demonstrate scholarship to the appropriate level. The primary medium through which such scholarship is assessed in higher education is writing, and consequently academic writing is central to scholarly success. Professional qualifications, such as social work, must also assess practice capabilities alongside relevant knowledge and scholarly prowess. Writing sits somewhat awkwardly as both a practice competence in its own right and the means through which students are assessed academically. This may in part explain why practice writing can slip into invisibility as a capability in its own right. I would suggest that although writing is an important scholarly as well as a professional practice capability, it is all too often only recognised as the medium for assessment and not as an outcome in its own right. One of the aims of this book is to make writing as 'content' or 'capability' more visible, and also to strengthen the connections between the teaching of scholarly skills and professional capabilities of writing through raising awareness of writing in social work practice and the challenges that it poses.

Rai and Lillis (2013) suggest that social work students are required to write three broad kinds of texts: academic assignments, routine or everyday writing undertaken as part of their professional role and portfolios (see Figure 1.1). Academic assignments are texts that are directly academically assessed as well as texts that primarily have a practice function. The assessment of practice competence is also generally assessed in part through a portfolio. The requirements for portfolios vary from course to course but may include a collection of texts which are collated from writing undertaken as part of students' professional role while on placement together with texts written specifically in order to provide evidence of students' competence by the student or others involved in their assessment. Academic assignments are generally undertaken in the 'academic domain' of the university, while routine or everyday writing takes place within social work agencies during practice learning opportunities. Portfolios straddle these two domains as they may include routine writing completed according to agency requirements as well as assessment documents written specifically to meet the assessment criteria of the programme. The significance of these domains is discussed further in Chapter Two.

Figure 1.1: Student social work writing

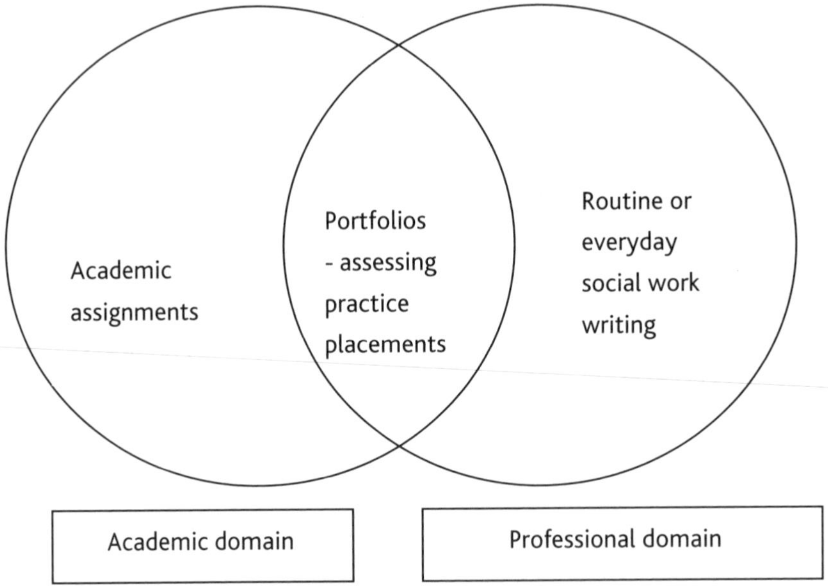

Source: Rai and Lillis (2013: 4)

Academic writing involves students in a range of assignment tasks that can broadly be described as either 'essays' or 'reflective writing'. Chapter Three explores academic writing in some detail, specifically focusing on essays and reflective writing as two key forms of assessed assignments. The broad distinction used here between essays and reflective writing is that while the essays require the development of an argument based on specified knowledge, theory or (occasionally) case studies, reflective writing requires the writer to draw heavily on their own experience (be it personal or professional) within a context of theoretical discussion. The integration of theory and experience can present particular challenges for writers:

Whilst some norms of academic writing remain, such as the use of authoritative sources and evidence, students also meet unfamiliar expectations such as the use of personal disclosure and the validity of reflection on their own practice as "evidence". (Rai, 2004: 153)

Scholarly writing as a medium for academic assessment

Writing is an essential medium for assessment in social work education, and is used for the assessment of academic and practice knowledge and capabilities. Literacy, or more specifically the ability to write, is commonly used as a yardstick to measure academic ability and the potential for success in higher education. In social work this has been demonstrated by the introduction (and raising) of the entry criteria for professional training based on literacy qualifications discussed above. Once successfully registered on a social work programme, in common with higher education generally, writing appears to be treated primarily as a medium through which the knowledge of the curriculum can be assessed. Raising entry qualifications alone, however, does not appear to prevent educators and students devoting considerable amounts of time and energy to worrying about standards of academic writing. Concerns about standards of writing are not only expressed at entry levels of higher education, however; research by Stierer in the context of education suggested that tutors report very similar concerns about the standard of writing on master's level courses being studied by higher education tutors (Stierer, 2000).

This raises the question of whether a competent grasp of spelling, punctuation and grammar alone make a successful writer. There is now a significant body of research that suggests that it is unhelpful to treat writing as a transparent method of assessment through which students, once competent in spelling, punctuation and grammar, can demonstrate their knowledge (Lea, 1998; Rai, 2008; Lillis, 2010). Writing is inextricably connected with both the subject matter to which it relates and the purpose and context in which it is written. Research that has explored academic writing in the context in which it is written suggests that although the surface features of writing (spelling, punctuation, grammar) are important building blocks, they are neither guarantees of successful writing nor necessarily the cause of unsuccessful writing. According to this research, the most common response to writing problems in UK higher education is through individually focused remedial support based on surface features of writing, frequently delivered by generic study support advisers. Research suggests, however, that addressing student writing difficulties requires a consideration of issues much broader than surface features alone, and that it is important to integrate support from 'subject' and 'writing' specialists (Lea and Stierer, 2000; Lea, 2004). Positive and effective responses to problematic student writing, however, require a holistic view of the writer and the context of the writing together with close cooperation between subject specialists and specialists in writing support.

Practice writing

Practice writing refers here to all the writing that social work students do as part of their practice, initially during placements and subsequently as qualified social workers as a routine part of their work. Some of students' practice writing is directly assessed and overlaps with academic writing, for example, portfolios, which include both examples of documents prepared in the course of practice (such as letters, case notes and supervision notes), documents contributed by third parties such as supervisor observations or service user feedback and reflections written by the student. In broad terms all practice writing is both assessing and preparing the student for professional writing that will be required of them once they are working in qualified practice. Some documents written by students will be identical to those written by qualified social workers, the only difference being that they will be written under the supervision of a qualified practitioner and the documents may be used to assess the student's competence.

Writing in professional social work practice is time consuming, complex and diverse. This complexity arises both from the range of different texts that social workers are required to write and the changing context in which they write them. Chapter Five explores the nature and challenges involved in writing in a social work context through a discussion of policy development and research findings. Hall et al suggest that writing is not merely a tool for documenting social work practice, but in common with other kinds of communication forms, the essence of what social work is:

> Daily work for social workers involved making phone calls, writing reports, talking to clients, writing, interacting and negotiating with others. These mundane features of daily professional life are not insignificant processes which merely operationalize, facilitate or frustrate evidence-based practice or critical reflection. On the contrary, the objectives of social work can only be realised through such mundane activities and these practices do not just have an influence on social work, they constitute it, they bring it into existence. (Hall et al, 2006: 10)

Over the past 15 years case recording has evolved from paper files to a range of paper and electronic documents. This development has been accompanied by increased expectations of social workers to write, or type, documents themselves as opposed to secretarial staff typing up records based on Dictaphone recordings or handwritten notes. The function of recording and documentation has also changed, with an increased emphasis on audit and accountability. The core functions of writing as a tool of assessment and decision making remain, as do the challenges of service user involvement and multi-agency communication. These themes are returned to throughout this book.

Digital technologies and social media

Digital technologies are increasingly influential in all areas of writing, including academic, professional and social contexts. In academic contexts, for example, students are encouraged not only to submit their assessments electronically, but also to interact with both tutors and fellow students through email, online forums and on some courses online synchronous or asynchronous tutorials. Universities and individual courses commonly use externally facing websites, including Facebook, to connect with current and potential students. Courses also use tools such as Blackboard to share teaching materials online and to facilitate online support through forums or discussion groups. Communicating online does not replicate the face-to-face experience, but it does provide an additional tool that facilitates communication at a distance and allows some students to study from home in their own time. Blogging (such as on Facebook and My Space) also provides a writing space for both students and academics to reflect and participate in communication with others about their learning and ideas. Blogs are a form of online journal and have the potential of offering valuable learning experiences for social work students. They don't usually generate 'visible' communities in the way that some online communities do, and are much better characterised as personal publishing spaces. Blogging has particular relevance to social work due to its potential to develop reflection in a similar way to journaling. Blogging also has the potential to support the development of literacy skills. Berman and Katoma suggest that:

> In an educational setting they provide an attractive way of honing important skills such as reading, writing succinctly, critical thinking, discussing, sharing and debate. (Berman and Katoma, 2008: 20)

Social media sites offer students a different literacy and learning experience from formal learning. Their contributions are not assessed, and may be anonymous. The posts by teaching staff do not usually represent formal teaching in the form of core curriculum, but may contribute to broadening students' engagement in public and academic debates as well as encouraging them to develop communication, reflective and analytical skills, which are key aspects of graduate skills. In terms of writing skills, social media represents another kind of literacy from academic or professional writing. The writing is generally informal and on Twitter contributions are necessarily very short and frequently contain links either in the form of hash tags or hyperlinks to external webpages. The content on social media sites also challenges students' ability to be discerning in the authority of the writer, in the same way as any website does. Unlike a published book or journal articles which are quality assured through peer review, social media offers an instant method of publishing which is not subject to any kind of peer scrutiny other than the comments made by others. Some contributors will 'claim' academic credentials by the name they publish in, which may identify an affiliation to a university or their academic status, for example, as a professor, but equally, anyone can post with or without making their credentials public.

Educators and researchers are also increasingly using social media to pose and develop key debates in social work. It allows educators to communicate with students and also with anyone interested in their subject, for example, through Twitter, blogging and online publications which set up debates on specific topical subjects. Special interest groups are becoming increasingly common. Such groups are by their nature dynamic, but current examples include Twitter sites to support induction to social learning, dissertation writing, a social work book club and topical social work chat. The breadth of access provided means that these are very powerful tools for generating debate and for building both individual and institutional profiles as well as an additional tool to support student learning. Universities, social work programmes and individual academics are increasingly making use of Twitter and Facebook as ways to reach out to students and other interested readers. Facebook provides the facility for 'closed' groups that students can use as forums to offer support to each other, but some universities and courses also use them as places where information and discussions can be shared. Twitter is developing a role as a tool to generate and contribute to social and academic debate, and in some cases offers informal teaching, support and advice to students.

The public nature of social media provides students and social workers with the opportunity to contribute to building social work knowledge that has not previously been possible. Social media has the potential to offer discussion spaces where students, academics, researchers, policy makers and indeed service users from anywhere in the world can engage in topical debates, an experience that can be both globalising and empowering. The absence of boundaries that might have restricted debate prior to online communication means that there are more possibilities for contributions from different disciplines and outside of formal academia, for example, through service user and special interest groups. Social media can also build debate from shared public experiences such as television broadcasts. There has always been the opportunity for some comment through print newspapers, but the power and accessibility of social media allows far more people to participate and effectively self-publish. Social media, therefore, offers some new and exciting ways to reach out to a huge audience, involving them in debates that have traditionally been contained within texts, and conversations that have limited access within the walls of the university, giving students (and others) direct access to academic conversations. Social media also represents yet more diversification in the possibilities for social practices around writing.

Theoretical approach of this book: social practices and academic literacies

This book draws on a 'social practices' approach to writing; this approach challenges the view that writing is based on a set of transparent, common-sense rules that once learned form a tool that, independently of culture and context, transmits ideas and information. These ideas have been applied to the context of academic writing through what is called an 'academic literacies' approach (Lea and Street, 1998) which has been developed through research into academic writing, and has recently also been applied to professional writing (Stierer, 2000; Rai, 2004, 2008; Lea and Stierer, 2009; Rai and Lillis, 2013). This approach recognises not only the diversity of writing requirements across academic disciplines and writing tasks, but also the extent to which such writing practices are local to institutions, courses and even individual tutors. An academic literacies approach:

> Views student writing and learning as issues at the level of epistemology and identities rather than skill or socialisation. An academic literacies approach views the institutions in which academic practices take place as constituted in, and as the sites of, discourse and power. (Lea and Street, 2000: 35)

One of the key features of an academic literacies approach is that it views writing as a 'social practice' or an activity embedded in social and interpersonal ways of being (Bazerman, 1981, 1988; Lea and Stierer, 2000; Bazerman and Prior, 2004). This means that it attaches particular importance to the influence of social, institutional and interpersonal *contexts* within which writing takes place. For example, 'academic literacies' has taken a critical approach to understanding the influence of both university and disciplines' specific requirements on writing. Student writing is guided and governed by explicit and implicit requirements. These requirements can be common across all universities and disciplines, but are more commonly specific to the course or programme that is being studied. Social work presents particular challenges as it, in common with other vocational programmes of study such as nursing, is a multidisciplinary subject in which writing expectations are influenced by a wide range of disciplines. On some social work programmes students may study modules taught and assessed within different schools or faculties, such as psychology, sociology or law. Consequently there may be little consistency between the expectations of scholarly writing due to differences between faculties or schools, and little explicit recognition that students are required to negotiate a path that weaves between them. Competence in social work scholarly writing therefore presents students with particular challenges, and successful writing requires students to negotiate this complex and somewhat unpredictable landscape. Baynham (1995), focusing on nurse education, suggests that new or emergent disciplines in higher education, such as nursing and social work education, require students to navigate a greater range and diversity of disciplines through their writing than single discipline subjects:

> So pity the poor nursing student, who is required to write at times like a sociologist, at others like a philosopher, yet again like a scientist and finally as a reflective practitioner. (Baynham, 2000: 17)

He further suggests that the disciplinary differences have an impact not only on content or form, but also on the way in which knowledge is conceptualised (Baynham, 2000: 21). When social workers move between writing assignments for psychology, law or sociology modules they are implicitly expected to adapt their thinking and writing as psychologists, lawyers and sociologists. Baynham's work illustrates that writing is intrinsically tied up with the knowledge base of the discipline. Writing is an integral part of the way in which discipline-specific knowledge is created and shared, in common with other forms of communication. When social workers write in academic or practice contexts, they are enacting their professional identity as social workers, and one of the purposes of student writing is facilitating an apprenticeship into this professional identity (Rai and Lillis, 2013). Throughout this book writing is theorised as a communicative act that is influenced by contextual or institutional practices (the ways in which institutions such as universities or social work employers influence writing), social interaction (communication between people and groups) and identity. Writing and social work practice is referred to in terms of 'skills' that social workers develop as they train and practice. The word 'skill' is used throughout this book as shorthand for referring to complex capabilities relating to writing. It is used, however, with the acknowledgement that the term is very problematic as it assumes a set of capabilities that can be relatively easily learned, applied and transferred. As illustrated in the discussion above (and throughout this book), this is not generally the case. Writing, as all communicative acts, is a highly complex personally, culturally and institutionally specific act.

Contextual practices

Academic writing

Academic writing takes place in the context of a discipline (social work), a university, and a particular assessment task. When students write any piece of work, they do so with reference to a range of factors that have an impact on their writing. Figure 1.2 below illustrates five layers that students need to negotiate in any piece of assessed writing, each with requirements, criteria or conventions associated with them which are more or less overt.

Figure 1.2: Layers of conventions in academic writing

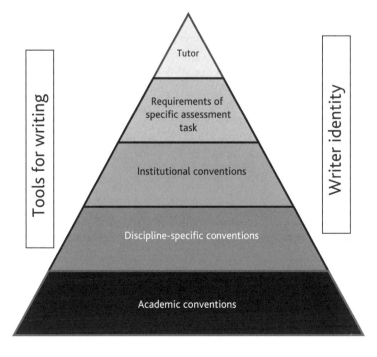

At the base of the pyramid are what are broadly referred to as 'academic conventions' that are commonly applied to all student (and scholarly) writing. There are conventions for writing any kind of text, but here we are concerned with academic texts. Conventions at this level refer to issues such as the requirement to acknowledge sources by providing references, avoidance of colloquial vocabulary and the inclusion of critical argument. These general academic conventions are mediated through the second layer, the specific discipline or subject studied which, in the context of this book, is that of social work. There has been considerable research into the significance and diversity of disciplinary differences in academic writing, and the importance of recognising such differences when providing support to student writers (see, for example, Lea and Stierer, 2000). One of the complexities introduced at this level is that the disciplinary conventions may contradict the academic conventions. One example from social work is that it is almost universally accepted that students are permitted (and even required) to use the first person singular pronoun in at least some of their assessed writing. This means that, for example, it would be acceptable to write ' I will structure this essay ...' rather than the more traditional use in academic writing of the passive 'This essay will be structured...'. This diversion from more traditional forms of academic writing has arisen due to the need for social work writers to include personal reflection and discussion of case studies within their academic writing. The third layer refers to the institutional regulations that relate to, for example, rules around plagiarism, exceeding word limits and sometimes details such as the required formatting and structuring of assessed work. Practices around plagiarism and acknowledging sources through references illustrate the three layers well. At the first level academic conventions rule that academic writers should build an argument and discussion based on references to (usually published) sources that must be acknowledged. Disciplinary conventions guide the writer as to which kinds of sources are acceptable (primary research, journal articles, books, web pages, case studies, personal or professional experience). At the level of institutional conventions students will be guided as to how to lay out and format their references and also informed of the procedures in place if breaches of these conventions occur (plagiarism). Those who have studied or been taught in different universities are likely to have come across institutional differences.

The fourth level refers to the specific assessment activity or task. This might be described as, for example, an 'essay', reflective report' or 'journal', but the specific conventions (or criteria) of the task cannot be assumed from the description given. Terms for formal assessments that are in common currency in social work education include 'essays', assignments', 'reflective journals' and 'portfolios'; all of these are codified shorthand for particular sets of expectations or conventions which are made, to varying degrees, explicit to students. The diversity of these conventions is frequently masked, however, by the common expectation that they are delivered through an acceptable standard of 'academic writing'. This is perhaps the most complex and potentially misleading layer, and one to which I return in Chapter Three. One illustration of the complexities involved in task level conventions is reflective writing, where the conventions of academic writing frequently directly contradict the explicit demands of the assignment brief (Rai, 2008). The final level is the tutor, or whoever is marking the assignment. Research has shown that students, if they have any knowledge of the marker, frequently adjust their writing based on their experience of the tutor, and also report considerable differences between the expectations of different markers (Rai, 2008). Alongside each level run the tools of writing and writer identity, both areas that are discussed in some detail throughout the book. 'Tools of writing' refers to anything from pens and paper through to software used to create texts, while 'writer identity' refers to the way in which the individual role and identity of the author has an impact on a text. The implications of these overlapping and complex expectations of assessed writing are the subject of further discussion in Chapter Three.

Practice writing

Effective writing for social work has been written to support the development of more effective professional writing. In doing so, however, it explores ways in which scholarly and practice writing can provide helpful stepping-stones. These are not always visible and are often slippery, but throughout the book I provide guidance on being thoughtful and strategic in order to negotiate an effective route through to effective writing. Practice writing shares with academic writing the complexity arising from the existence of multiple conventions which vary from document to document, employer to employer and service setting to service setting. These are set out in Figure 1.3, broadly mirroring the layers of conventions that exist for academic writing.

At the base of the pyramid, paralleling disciplinary conventions in academic writing are 'discourse conventions', which refers to the commonly accepted ways of writing and expressing ideas that are used in social work. Discourse here refers to the ways in which meaning is communicated through spoken or written forms in a specific context. Within specific contexts (such as academic disciplines and professional groups) a collective understanding (or convention) of ways to communicate particular shared meanings can develop which provides insiders to these groups with a kind of common language. Discourse conventions will include deep but sometimes implicit values and theories that underpin and define the profession. Similarly, agency

Figure 1.3: Layers of conventions in practice writing

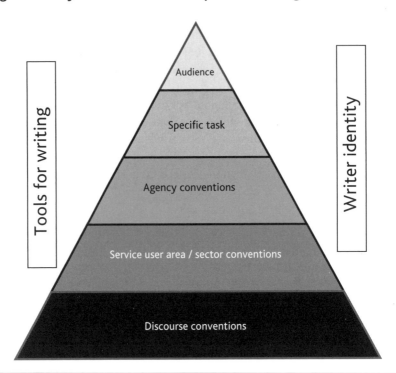

conventions can be compared to institutional conventions and 'audience' to 'tutor' in academic writing. Agency conventions (practices local to the employer) and service user group (for example, working with children and families or users of mental health services) will dictate not only the style of writing but also the theory, ethics, practices, policy or even legislation applied to a text. Agency conventions relate to ways of writing that are specific to the employing agency and frequently include local policy documents and procedures. The specific task refers to the text type and broadly equates to the 'requirements of the specific assessment task'. This would include case recording, specific forms used to record assessments, reviews, referrals, reports and also documents which do not have a specified format, including those used in the course of planning or therapeutic work with service users. The top level of the pyramid depicts audience; in academic writing the audience is relatively predictable and constant, but in professional writing social workers may be writing for diverse and sometimes multiple readers. The writing medium is a particularly important strand that is introduced below and discussed in some detail in Chapter Five. The most obvious medium for writing is the computer, but this belies the impact that software systems have on writing. New technologies also include the use of mobile and smart phones, which are increasingly used in social work. Writer identity, introduced below, includes not only those aspects of identity involved in academic writing, but also issues of professional identity and the interplay between the two. Students writing professional documents during their practice learning will need to be aware of both of these pyramids and the multiple, overlapping and occasionally conflicting demands of each layer.

Some common threads addressed through the book

So far I have introduced the main categories of writing that student social workers negotiate during their training and some of the challenges that each involves. In this final section I briefly introduce some of the issues common to all writing in social work addressed further through the book.

Writer identity

Writing is an expression of our communication as individuals and the people we are (our experiences, beliefs and values) is still relevant when we write in academic or professional contexts. An awareness of the identities that are played out through writing is an important aspect of being a reflexive practitioner. Etherington (2004), for example, suggests that reflexivity involves the ability to:

> Notice our responses to the world around us, other people and events, and to use that knowledge to inform our actions, communications and understandings. To be reflexive we need to be aware of our personal responses and to be able to make choices about how to respond to them. We also need to be aware of the social, personal and cultural contexts in which we live and work and to understand how these impact on the ways in which we interpret our world. (Etherington, 2004: 19)

The use of reflexivity is an important skill in writing as it enables the writer to be aware of their own identity in a specific context and also of the identity of their reader. The concept of identity is complex and multifaceted, and has been theorised in the fields of sociology and psychology. Goffman's sociological theorisation of identity has been applied to writing in terms of social role theory by Ivanič (1998). Ivanič draws on Goffman's dramaturgical concept of individuals' identity deriving from the diverse social roles that they play through participation in social interactions, or 'scenes'. Her theorisation of social roles in the context of writing suggests writers change the way that they write according to the social context that they write in and the role that they play in that context. The concept of identity is also developed in psychology, where areas of interest include the multiple and competing nature of identities and on people's (sometimes unconscious) emotional experiences. Throughout this book writer identity is considered in relation to both its sociological and psychological aspects.

Tools for writing: new technologies

The days of typists supporting social workers in writing up correspondence and case recording are long gone, and social workers would find their work almost impossible without a computer, mobile phone and increasingly, internet-accessible phones and tablets. Technology, which includes the software as well as the hardware used, plays a very significant role in mediating professional writing. The quality of software used by social work agencies has been the subject of significant criticism, however, and the weakness of systems such as the Integrated Children's System (ICS) has resulted in a raised awareness of how important it is to get the software right. The influence of technology raises further issues for social workers, such as selecting the most appropriate method of recording and sharing information with different service users and the impact of technology on the language used. Technology can offer great benefits, for example, the use of texting and email can create much easier and quicker methods of communicating directly with children as well as with their families.

Social interaction

As indicated above, writing is considered here as a form of communication. Communication invariably involves some degree of social interaction, even if both or all participants are not engaging in the communicative act at the same time. At times it may feel as if some documents are not written for anybody, and writing can feel like a very isolated activity, but both academic and practice writing have audiences and therefore involve the communication of information and ideas between people. The significance of social interaction may vary depending on the purpose and context of the text and indeed on the people involved, but what I want to emphasise here is that writing is a social and interpersonal act that is influenced by many factors, including the power dynamics between communicators.

Adaptability

In both the academic and practice contexts students will be required to write a wide variety of text types, each with their own layers of rules and conventions, as outlined in Figures 1.2 and 1.3. While there are some foundation stones of effective writing in all contexts, it is inevitable that both student and qualified social workers will need to remain adaptable. Change is generated not only by the nature of the text and agency setting, but also by the needs of specific service users and developments in national or local policies as well as developments in technology. Social workers will also encounter new writing tasks as they progress through their career, taking on the management role of gate keeping or quality assuring documents, or possibly undertaking further scholarly writing in the role of a researcher or academic. *Effective writing for social work* does not aim, therefore, to provide a template or guidance on writing specific documents, but to enable readers to develop the capability of becoming reflective, adaptable and creative writers who can take on new and changing challenges.

Emotion

Emotion is particularly significant in social work writing in both academic and practice contexts. Writing, as with all communication, is an interpersonal activity that involves the self, or identity. In social work the focus of much written communication is very emotive. In the context of academic writing, this is particularly true for reflective writing where the author is required to describe and evaluate highly personal issues including, values and practice experiences, in an assessment context. Emotion is not something commonly talked about in relation to academic or professional writing, but it is explored in some detail in Chapter Two. Social workers are generally well positioned to understand and make good use of reflections on self and emotion in relation to their practice generally; here, similar principles are applied to written communication.

Structure of the book

Chapter Two develops the theoretical and thematic discussion introduced here. Drawing on research and the experiences of recently graduated social workers, the key challenges are identified and a model for social work writing introduced which is applied throughout the book. The following two chapters focus on writing undertaken while students are studying, in both the academic and practice settings. Chapters Three and Four focus on student writing; Chapter Three explores academic writing through the lenses of essays and reflective writing and Chapter Four focuses on writing undertaken by students while on practice learning placements, including portfolios of evidence and first experiences of practice writing. Chapters Five, Six and Seven address writing in a professional context; Chapter Five contextualises some of the challenges and support needs of practice writers. This is then applied to case recording (Chapter Six) and report writing as a tool of assessment (Chapter Seven). The book concludes by returning to the model introduced in Chapter Two, and offers some final thoughts for practitioners and those supporting students in practice.

Notes

[1] The concept of writing practices is developed further in Chapter Two but refers to the range of physical, social and cultural factors that dictate or influence that way in which a text is written.

[2] The word 'text' is used throughout as a generic term for any kind of written product.

Taking control of your writing 2

Introduction

Effective writing for social work does not attempt to teach its readers how to write any text in any context; this would not be feasible as, even with limitless space and resources, it is not possible to anticipate the myriad of contexts and readers that may be encountered. In addition, the demands of texts for any one purpose will change over time. What is possible is for readers of this book to take more control over their writing through gaining a deeper understanding of what communicating through writing in social work involves. This chapter provides the theoretical concepts that underpin the rest of the book. Drawing on these ideas should enable the reader to think critically about any writing task in social work, and hopefully to improve their writing as a result. The chapters that follow address some specific application of these ideas to commonly encountered text types, such as academic essays, reflective writing, portfolios, case recording and assessments. Given the diversity of requirements surrounding even these common texts across universities, social work agencies and service user groups, this process can only be illustrative. This chapter develops the ideas introduced in Chapter One, beginning with academic literacies and the theoretical foundations of a social practices approach to writing.

Academic writing

Academic writing plays a central part in higher education in the UK, forming the primary medium through which students are assessed. In the context of a highly selective higher education system, the ability of students to convey their understanding through the medium of academic writing has long been a basic expectation. Concern has increasingly been expressed in the UK about the quality of student writing, which Lillis suggests can be linked to both the expanding population and widening of access to higher education (Lillis, 2001: 21). This has partly come about as a result of the development of the post-1970s universities, and partly because of a political agenda to increase the number of graduates. Despite this concern, responses to date from higher education institutions in the UK have primarily been either in the form of remedial support for individual students focused through libraries or study support centres, or where student need is perceived more broadly, through study support modules (Lea and Street, 1998, 2000; Lillis, 2001). Confidence in the existence of a universal set of transferable skills has continued to influence writing support in the UK where a 'skills deficit' or 'study skills' model, discussed below, remains influential. Such a model relies on students supplementing 'deficits' in writing skills via support offered through workbooks, toolkits, electronic skills labs and teaching which focuses on teaching the surface elements of written language, such as punctuation and spelling.

In the US, while there has been a long tradition of proactively teaching writing to students across the ability and experience range, provision has also focused on the teaching of technical skills. Targeted support for students identified as having difficulties with writing in English grew out of the 'basic writing movement', a specific kind of provision intended to meet the needs of expanding numbers of students entering higher education in the 1960s, many of whom used English as a second language or spoke a vernacular English:

> Some of the most rudimentary questions we confronted were: How do you make standard English verb endings available to a dialect speaker? How do you teach English prepositional forms to a Spanish-language student? What are the arguments for and against "Black English"? The English of academic papers and theses? Is standard English simply a weapon of colonization?… We were dealing not simply with dialect and syntax but with the imagery of lives, the anger and flare of urban youth – how could these be used, strengthened, without the lies of artificial polish? (Rich, 2001: 4)

The paper from which this quotation is taken was first published in 1973, and illustrates that issues such as the diversity of writer experiences, access and participation appeared to be recognised on some American university programmes. Shaughnessy (1977) offered the term 'basic writer' in an attempt to move away from the association between remedial classes and ability. She recognised that many students had the maturity and ability to express themselves orally that was not matched by their skills in writing within the context of the academy. The function of basic writing in the US, therefore, was to equip these students with the skills and confidence in writing to enable them to participate in higher education (Rich, 2001: 4). Those involved in the development of basic writing programmes suggested that with a universal set of writing skills, students would be both socially emancipated and linguistically prepared to participate in any field of education.

Lillis (2001), drawing on an overview of institutional responses in Australia and South Africa, as well as the UK and US, offers three common characteristics of specific writing provision. First, a shared focus on the text produced by the student as the site of concern, or 'problem' to be fixed, rather than exploring the nature of the task set, the nature of institutional or disciplinary practices surrounding academic writing or indeed, the behaviour of those responding to texts. Second, Lillis refers to the 'institutional claim to transparency', by which she means that, while the student text is made visible as the source of concern, factors arising from disciplinary and institutional practices remain both hidden and accepted as 'given'. Third, there is a belief not only that the solution lies in the student's production of the text, but also that correcting this is straightforwardly achieved (Lillis, 2001: 22).

The assumptions underpinning these three characteristics are that students' difficulties with writing will be resolved by providing them with the 'skills for the job' through either add-on study skills modules, composition classes, attendance at a writing centre or the provision of writing skills toolkits. According to Lillis (2001: 22-3), this is an unhelpful assumption. A growing body of research has developed which has questioned the helpfulness of focusing only on skill development, as characterised by provision in the UK, US, Australia and South Africa. This body of research has explored academic writing as a context-specific activity in which an understanding of social and interactional influences are essential, and challenges the transparency of institutional practices (Street, 1984; Lillis, 1997, 2001, 2010; Lea and Street, 1998; Horner and Lu, 1999; Baynham, 2000).

Research undertaken by Lillis (2001) explored the experience of 'non-traditional' student writers and introduced ideas about inequalities of access to privileged knowledge and skills. This work suggests that students' choices are influenced by their relationship to higher education institutions and by aspects of identity such as social class, ethnicity, religion and gender, which have an impact on their writing. Rai (2008) identified a close correlation between the profile of social work students and non-traditional students (Rai, 2008: 36), with a high representation of women and students with either limited prior academic experience or those who have not followed the traditional academic route to higher education. Lillis (2001) suggests that, in addition to any cultural or linguistic differences that students may have, non-traditional students may not have had the opportunity to experience the gradual familiarisation with academic writing offered to those students who have been able to progress systematically through the educational system, thus acquiring incremental familiarisation with writing skills.

Where familiarity with academic writing conventions is missing or limited, students are further disadvantaged by the implicit nature of specific writing conventions, such as 'essayist literacy'. Lillis (1997) identifies particular difficulties with what she calls 'essayist literacy'. She identifies that student writing frequently labelled as an 'essay' can disguise complex and implicit expectations of students' writing which has the effect of constraining students' meaning-making. The essay, in fact, represents a very particular way of constructing knowledge that, while frequently presented as transparent, is both implicit and complex.

> Unfortunately, explicit teaching and exploration of conventions is not common practice, one of the reasons being that within the institution, conventions continue to be viewed as appropriate and unproblematic, as "common sense". (Lillis, 1997: 186)

Lillis also highlights the importance of the power dimension in student writing, which is particularly pertinent to non-traditional students. She suggests that the sense of exclusion experienced by some students goes further than struggling to attain a particular way of writing. The power imbalance experienced by the non-traditional students in her research compounded their frustration, as they felt unable to question or challenge the implicit expectations against which they were being assessed.

Lillis' research, therefore, raises important issues, not only about non-traditional students, but also more broadly in relation to identity and writing which have relevance for social work student writers. Non-traditional students are strongly represented in social work, with Access programmes offering an important route into the profession. The highly personal, reflective nature of writing in both academic and practice contexts also makes Lillis' comments about identity particularly relevant to all social work students.

Writing as social practice

Writing support in higher education has, as indicated above, traditionally been offered in the form of remedial interventions for individual students, focused through libraries or study support centres or, where student need is perceived more broadly, through study support modules (Lea and Street, 2000; Lillis, 2001). Both of these approaches commonly draw on what has been referred to as a 'study skills' approach to student writing. A study skills approach, sometimes referred to as a skills deficit approach, is based on belief in the existence of a universal set of transferable skills in writing which students can learn and apply to their studies. Where there are gaps in these skills, this form of support encourages students to supplement any perceived deficits in their writing through the use of workbooks, toolkits, electronic skills labs and teaching that focuses on teaching surface elements of written language, such as punctuation and spelling. A skills deficit approach, therefore, individualises writing problems and looks for solutions that involve filling gaps or supplementing skills at the level of the individual student. This approach has been challenged by recent research that suggests that student writing is influenced by a wider and more complex set of factors than the mechanical skills learned by individual students. Lillis (2001), for example, suggests that the common-sense notion that writing involves the transfer of a set of unproblematic skills results in an implicit separation of 'language, user and context' (Lillis, 2001: 24). Alternatives to the skills deficit model have gained increasing influence in the teaching and, particularly, in the research of academic writing in the UK.

Lea and Street (1998) propose a 'three perspectives' model of provision of academic writing support. These can be broadly represented as study skills, academic socialisation and academic literacies (Lea and Street, 2000: 35). By study skills, as outlined above, Lea and Street refer to an understanding of academic writing as a set of transferable, generic skills and strategies that can be taught across the academy. This presupposes a focus on the acquisition of surface features of language use, treating literacy as a transparent technical skill that can be transmitted. Lea and Street's socialisation model (2000: 35) views writing and the language used to create it in terms of 'learning academic discourses'. Discourse is a term that is used to convey more than one meaning; here, it relates to the language or debates surrounding a specific topic. It could be said that there is a 'discourse of social work', but it is more helpful to think of there being many discourses relevant to social work, such as the discourse of discrimination, of childhood or of poverty. These various discourses relate to the broader subject of social work. In Lea and Street's socialisation model the student becomes an apprentice to the culture of a specific subject (or set of discourses) and the related ways of learning and associated ways of writing. Lea and Street's focus here is on enculturation within the university, but these ideas also apply to wider discipline communities such as social work practice. An academic literacies model also recognises the importance of institutional practices through its focus on broader social practices influencing writing:

> It [academic literacies] views student writing and learning as issues at the level of epistemology and identities rather than skill or socialisation. An academic literacies approach views the institutions in which academic practices take place as constituted in, and as the sites of, discourse and power. (Lea and Street, 2000: 35)

Lea and Street (1998) suggest that each discipline has particular expectations about how to write, which are familiar to those who are within that discipline. Students gradually learn these ways of writing as they progress through their studies, but essentially these expectations are implicit, and this reinforces a power imbalance between novice (writer) and expert (tutor). This imbalance of power is an important aspect of social practices and exists not only between individuals (student and tutor) but also between individuals and institutions. This applies equally to universities and social work agencies. Lea and Street suggest that at an institutional level:

> The institutions within which tutors and students write defines the conventions and boundaries of their writing practices, through its procedures and regulations (definitions of plagiarism, requirements of modularity and assessment procedures and regulations), whatever individual tutors and students may believe themselves to be as writers and whatever autonomy and distinctiveness their disciplines may assert. (Lea and Street, 1998: 169)

Lea and Street here refer to 'writing practices'; this term has arisen from research into writing as a context-driven activity in which the writer is influenced by a range of factors when any single text is written. These practices operate broadly at two levels: first, ways of writing that become established as a result of social, cultural or institutional conventions. For example, when writing a formal letter there are culturally specific expectations of the formality of vocabulary used and also of the layout of the text on the page, and this will contrast with an email, even in an equally formal context, where the vocabulary, and certainly the layout, will differ. The second level is influenced by individual writers and the choices, conscious and unconscious, that they make when writing any particular text. One very explicit choice might be the physical method of writing (word processing, pencil, phone text, etc) but there are many multilayered and more subtle choices that are made, such as writing in silence compared with background noise and the use or otherwise of drafts. There are some practices which overlap with the individual and cultural/institutional levels, one example being the use or otherwise of images such as diagrams or emoticons. Some texts may require or exclude the use of images, but others may leave room for individual choices so that the use of them illustrates personal expression. The concept of writing practices is important and is referred to throughout this book. Lea and Street (2000) suggest that the study skills and socialisation models have limitations – the skills model because it disregards the diversity and complexity of writing across disciplines and genres, and the socialisation model because not only does it imply homogeneity within disciplines, which Lea and Street claim does not exist, but it excludes issues of personhood and identity of the writer. Lea and Street (1998, 2000) therefore challenge the traditional view of language as being a transparent code, which can be learned, applied and re-applied, in different contexts. Thus, academic literacies move literacy studies from a common-sense view of 'good writing' to recognising the significance of individual contextualised writing acts, where the importance of both writer and 'addressee' are acknowledged.

Within the UK, the academic literacies model was developed from 'new literacy studies', represented by the work of Street (1984), Barton (1984) and Barton and Hamilton (1998). This research examined community-based literacy practices, and was concerned with the social (as opposed to the cognitive) and cultural influences on reading and writing. Barton and Hamilton's work, therefore, illustrates an interest in literacy as a 'social practice', where literacy is conceived of as dependent on social context and relationships. These ideas have been applied to higher education, and in doing so challenge the skills and socialisation models with the 'academic literacies' model, which recognises the contested nature of academic and student writing and the diverse positions and identities that participants take up. The academic literacies approach moves away from problematising individual students or even student sub-groups, but instead focuses on institutional practices. One of the most important areas of institutional practice is that of disciplinarity through which individual disciplines contain both implicit and explicit rules governing writing, or writing conventions.

Disciplinarity in social work writing

This book is concerned with student writing in the specific context of the discipline of social work. Debates on disciplinarity are of particular relevance due to the broad theoretical base of social work which draws on sociology, psychology, social policy and evolving discourses of care (Lyons, 1999). Research drawing on a social practices approach to academic writing has included work specifically concerned with writing in practice-based higher education, both graduate and postgraduate. Three important features distinguish these particular disciplinary fields. First, they share a requirement for students to undertake assessed practice alongside academic learning. Second, they lead to a professional qualification with a licence to practice; and third, they involve heavily externally prescribed curricula often drawing on a range of disciplinary discourses. Such practice-based disciplines include teaching, nursing and social work. Writing undertaken on such programmes of study can pose particular challenges to students as it draws on both academic and practice-based learning, which not only involves the use of a range of discourses, but also positions the student in different identities, most obviously as 'student' and 'professional'. The implication of applying a social practices approach to social work writing is that students (and social workers) only form part of the picture; writing is also influenced by the institutional and social contexts that determine what 'good' or 'effective' writing looks like. Such institutions determine a whole range of factors which writers need to negotiate in their writing, including factors such as the tools that they write with, required content, structure or organisation of ideas, style and timescales. In other words, writing is an 'institutional practice', it is something that is carried out in institutions (such as universities or social work agencies) and governed by a wide range of expectations which, as identified by Lillis (1998), re-enforce and re-create habitual ways of interacting.

Social work students routinely encounter a range of expectations of their academic writing, particularly on programmes taught across faculties. Baynham (1995), focusing on nurse education, suggests that new or emergent disciplines in higher education, such as nurse education and social work, require students to navigate a greater range and diversity of disciplines through their writing than single discipline subjects:

> So pity the poor nursing student, who is required to write at times like a sociologist, at others like a philosopher, yet again like a scientist and finally as a reflective practitioner. (Baynham, 2000: 17)

He further suggests that the disciplinary differences have an impact not only on content, but also on the way in which knowledge is conceptualised in writing. Baynham proposes that in nursing, for example, there are potential conflicts between practical theoretical knowledge and practice-based versus professionalised learning; this potential tension is illustrated throughout this book, as the focus turns from essays and reflective writing to portfolios and finally, writing undertaken in practice.

Lea and Street (1998) identify 'course switching' as a common feature of study on courses drawing on different disciplines. They are here borrowing the term 'switching' from the concept of 'code switching'. Lea and Street (1998), drawing on the work of Bazerman, suggest that academic staff in their study were strongly influenced in their expectations of student writing by their own disciplinary backgrounds, and that dissonance arising from any divergence from these expectations was frequently expressed in criticism of 'surface features' of students' texts, such as spelling, grammar and punctuation, discussed above. Such dissonance, and consequent criticism, was more common on modular or multidisciplinary courses, particularly where the assessment strategy included students undertaking diverse writing tasks such as communicating with non-specialist audiences or writing tasks which related specifically to a professional task. The consequence of this disciplinary orientation was that:

> ... underlying, often disciplinary, assumptions about the nature of knowledge affected the meaning given to the terms "structure"

and "argument" … elements of successful student writing are in essence related to particular ways of constructing the world, and not a set of generic writing skills as the study skills model would suggest. (Lea and Street, 2000: 39)

This lack of clarity in relation to writing requirements resulted in students finding it very difficult to write across disciplines and writing tasks. Advice from tutors was conflictual and inconsistent, resulting in students attempting to stick closely to familiar disciplinary conventions or guessing at what they thought assessors required. Very similar findings were identified in social work education by Rai (2008), with students and tutors being challenged by the working across theoretical and practice-orientated modules, with particular difficulties identified in reflective writing assignments:

Unlike previous research which has identified considerable difficulties with the concept of the "essay", data from this study suggests that where the "essay" was explicitly taught using consistent and relatively prescriptive guidance, students and tutors were comparatively confident in both writing and assessing. Difficulties arose, however, on the practice-based course, where tutors expected a "house style" which differed significantly from the "essay" explicitly taught to students previously. (Rai, 2008: 352)

Reflective writing is discussed in some detail in Chapter Three. One of the particular challenges for students writing reflectively resulted from the expectation that they would write in a target style that implicitly breached several commonly accepted conventions of academic writing. This occurred as students were expected to write about personal and practice experience, an element of writing not commonly found in other forms of academic writing. Writing about experience was particularly challenging for students in Rai's study, where they also had to embed such discussions in theoretical essays that, in other ways, resembled more conventional essays (Rai, 2008).

Baynham (2000) also highlights the importance of using experience in vocational subjects, and suggests that students authorise (or provide authority to) their writing through the use of such practice-based experience in addition to the use of more traditional academic citations. Although both were important, students relying on practice-based experience alone were disadvantaged less than those who struggled to write about experience, but the highly successful students were those who could draw both together (Rai, 2008: 222-4).

Hoadley-Maidment (2000), focusing on students studying health and social care, identified the difficulty experienced by students in combining narratives of personal or practice experiences with academic discourses based on argumentation. Tutors in her study had expectations that students would demonstrate the ability not only to use argument and narrative, but also to combine them in one assignment. Based on her study, Hoadley-Maidment suggests that the skills required to achieve this synthesis involve the high-order cognitive skills of analysis and critical reflection (2000: 174). Hoadley-Maidment's work identifies the significant challenges faced by students in combining experience and academic argument in their written assessments. The skill for educators in social work, as in other practice-based education, is to weave a path between these contrasting disciplines to enable students to write as practitioners in their field, rather than as 'ethical scientists' or 'practical theorists'. In social work the differences in writing conventions between subjects may not be obvious to students but can include different valuing or expectations about the inclusion of personal or practice experience, acceptance or otherwise of the use of 'I' and differences in expectations around the organisation and structure of assignments. (Each of these issues is explored further in Chapter Three in relation to essays and reflective writing, and in Chapter Four in relation to writing evidence for portfolios.)

Recognising individual and institutional writing practices

Writing is a core task in social work. Social workers spend a significant amount of their time writing, and are required to produce a range of different texts that vary from setting to setting. Just as with academic writing, professional writing is frequently invisible within the workplace. During the review of social work education in England which took place in 2011, concerns were raised about the quality of social workers' writing (Munro, 2011), and these have been associated with reviewing entry-level literacy skills for social work training. This response is comparable with historical responses within higher education to problematic academic writing; the focus is on the individual student, and any problems that arise are frequently associated with the writer's skills in functional aspects of writing such as spelling, grammar or punctuation. As discussed above, research into student and academic writing in the UK and US has challenged this assumption and introduced a range of factors that can have an impact on the relative success of individual texts. This is not to imply that the functional aspects of writing are unimportant, but rather that it is an over-simplification to suggest that competence in writing relies solely on the writer's ability to construct a grammatically correct text.

Throughout this book writing is treated as a form of communication, the success or effectiveness of which relies as much on the writer's ability to adapt it for a particular use as it does on any de-contextualised notions of 'correctness'. Writing in social work, in common with professional communication, is challenging and requires workers to engage with a wider capability base than only literacy, including sensitivity to the individual needs of service users, colleagues and the specific purpose of each text. The effectiveness of any text, therefore, relies as much on the writer's understanding of and ability to respond to these contextual issues as it does on the correctness of the written language. Writing, or the way in which we write, can be invisible or taken for granted by the writers themselves. The complexity of professional writing arises in part, therefore, due to writing being both an individual and an institutional practice. By this I mean that the way in which we write is influenced by the capabilities and choices of the individual writer as well as by the institutional demands. It is important, therefore, for social workers to be able to adapt the way in which they write in order to meet such institutional demands, but in order to do so it can be helpful to be conscious of their own personal writing practices.

Individual writing practices

Digital communication is increasingly becoming the primary way in which literacy is experienced by many people, and offers an even greater degree of choice. The use of smart phones, tablets, e-readers and computers offers a range of text types from text that is designed to look like print through to texts that are rich in embedded multimedia elements, such as video, images and hyperlinks.

Just for a moment, readers should pause and think about the way in which they write, or their own 'writing practices'. Most writing practices are either governed by the context of the specific text type (such as the institutional demands outlined above) or by the author's 'choices', although such choices may be unconscious. To illustrate the significance of individual writing practice, readers should think back to the last time they wrote each of the following:

- SMS[1] 'text' message
- social media post
- diary or journal entry
- greetings card
- completion of a form or questionnaire
- shopping list, packing list or similar 'to do' list
- any kind of text created in the course of your work.

Keeping in mind a specific text written recently, readers should try and answer the following questions about each one:

1. What materials or tools did you use (paper, pen, phone, tablet etc)?
2. What physical context were you in (sitting at a desk, lying in bed, in the car etc)?
3. Did you review the text, and make any corrections and changes?
4. Was anyone else involved in creating the text?
5. Who is the intended reader?
6. What was your emotional state while you were writing?

The answers to each of these questions provide a small insight into the range of individual and text-related writing practices that lie behind the creation of any text. They also illustrate the ways in which some practices, possibly not within one's conscious control, have a huge impact on how social workers write. In the following section some of the key influences on writing practices are discussed, beginning with the tools of writing.

Tools of writing

Although most commonly sent and received using a mobile phone, SMS text messages can also be sent using landline handsets and, increasingly, from computers and mobile devices using social media websites. Greetings cards may be hard copy which are purchased off the shelf, handmade or personalised, but they can also be digital and personalised; forms and questionnaires can be paper or digital; and a shopping list may be written on anything from the back of a hand to a commercially devised shopping planner. The materials that are used to write (pens and paper through to spray paints on a wall or electronic software programmes) have an impact on the way we write, the choices available to us about what we communicate and how we do so. Digital communication is increasingly becoming the primary way in which literacy is experienced by many people, and offers an even greater degree of choice.

Language

One of the possibilities that different writing mediums offers is alternative 'languages' or modes of written communication including images and signs. For example, digital communication (including mobile phones and other mobile devices such as tablet computers) increasingly involves combinations of commonly accepted abbreviations and images such as 'smilies' or 'emoticons'. The proliferation of Twitter has also brought the 'hash tag' into common usage. This allows the writer to mark a communication that enables other people interested in the subject to find it and follow related conversations. Other variations offered by technology include dictation software that translates voice recordings or finger drawings into text. This kind of technology, which used to be uncommon and available primarily for people with disabilities, is increasingly an option on any smart phone, mobile device or computer. Such technological developments sit alongside the infinite options associated with the everyday choices made in written communication (as with all communication) that are associated with culture, context and individual creativity.

Multiple authorship and design

When thinking about examples of texts above, did any of them involve more than one person in creating them? If we think of a text in its widest sense, it is very common for more than one person's creativity and endeavour to be involved. A greetings card (hard copy or digital), although it might be handmade by the person who writes and sends it, often has multiple authors. For example, it might be designed and manufactured commercially, contain a message written by several people or even be designed and written with an online tool using a mixture of given and author-supplied text and images. The author of a greetings card, therefore, has extensive design choice over the final product, either through creating the entire text or selecting elements of the text from commercially available options. Questionnaires and forms, as used in professional writing, for example, are designed to give the person completing them limited choices about the final content or design. It is less clear in this example who the 'author' is, as the person completing the form has had little control over the design and limited control over the content. This is true of both paper and digital 'forms' where the author or designer of the template is able to build in restrictions on the content that is entered. Tweeting and blogging using social media offer new possibilities for multiple authors contributing to developing text over time. Thinking about academic and professional writing in social work, academic writing is generally expected to be the original work of one author, while professional writing frequently involves more than one person. Even academic writing, however, will draw on the research and ideas and theories of published writers (appropriately referenced). (The significance of such multiple contributors to a single text in practice writing is explored in Chapter Five.)

Intended reader

Question 5, 'Who is the intended reader?', is possibly the most important consideration in written communication. Adapting verbal (and non-verbal) communication for the needs of the service user is a basic element of social work communication. Adapting to the needs of the reader, or audience, in writing is equally significant. There is a wide range of choices an author can make depending on the needs of the reader, such as the level of formality, complexity of vocabulary, use of humour, need for translation or appropriate medium (email, text, letter etc). Such choices can become very complex when the intended reader is anonymous, such as in much academic or, as is frequently the case, with professional writing, where there are multiple readers with very different needs. The significance of having an awareness of the reader in practice writing and ways in which writers can adapt their writing more effectively is addressed more fully in Chapter Five, where writing is explored as a form of interpersonal communication in which the identity of the reader and writer is highly significant.

Emotional involvement

The final question, 'What was your emotional state while you were writing?', may have seemed a little odd, but research suggests that writing in social work can be an emotional experience (Rai, 2011). Writing in many contexts can be very emotive depending on what is being communicated. Readers should think for a moment about their own feelings writing and receiving feedback on assessed academic writing. This can be a very emotional process, not only because of the stress attached to work being judged as 'pass/fail', but because even in relatively objective academic writing we invest a lot of ourselves, our identities. The assessment of writing is also an assessment of the writer, particularly in social work education, where the writing is about highly emotive issues such as values, ethics and personal experiences. The emotive nature of professional writing in social work is unsurprising; what is more surprising is that social workers manage to write very de-personalised, un-emotive writing based on highly emotive content.

Purpose, audience and context

Reflecting on individual texts can provide an insight into the range of factors that unconsciously influence the ways in which we approach different writing tasks. Figure 2.1 illustrates just some of the possible range of factors that can have an impact on the texts that social workers write.

Figure 2.1: Contextual factors influencing writing practices

While it may be helpful for social workers reflecting on the writing process to become more aware of the spectrum of influencing factors, taking conscious account of all of them at the point of writing would make producing texts a very slow task. Becoming more aware of one's own writing practices is one way in which writers can take more control of their writing. These aspects of the context of writing are considered across this book as they become relevant. As professional writers, social workers can consider three particularly significant questions to help them to write more effectively for the context of a particular text:

- *Purpose:* what am I trying to achieve in this text?
- *Audience:* who am I writing for, and how can I communicate most effectively with them? This is particularly complex in professional writing where there may be multiple potential intended readers who are using the text for different purposes and who have different perspectives.
- *Context:* how does the context in which I am writing have an impact on the text?

As indicated in Figure 2.1, context is complex and can involve not only the immediate physical and social context of the writer, but also the wider institutional and political context surrounding the particular text. Experience and familiarity with writing specific kinds of texts will reduce the need to think consciously about these questions, but they provide a useful reference point when approaching writing where there is an unfamiliar audience, context or purpose to a text.

Purposeful writing

In order to write effective text it is essential that the writer is clear about its purpose. This may seem obvious, but while in academic writing the purpose is generally clear (assessment of learning and competence), it is common for professional writing for multiple texts to be produced which may potentially have slightly overlapping purposes or which may interconnect in some way. In professional writing it is common for a single text to have multiple purposes at different points in time or for different audiences as events unfold. For example, an entry in a case record may be a routine account of a contact when written, but may become a key piece of evidence in a safeguarding assessment or court report at some point in the future. It is also common for continuing work with service users to be handed over to new workers, so an account written by a worker familiar with the case will also need to be easily followed by someone picking up the threads of previous interventions.

The purpose of a specific text may not always be clear. Practice texts may be referred to institutionally in particular ways, such as by the name of the software programme or agency database name, but these may not necessarily clarify the purpose of the text. To an outsider of a specific team or agency, the names used to refer to specific documents may seem obscure, but within the institutional culture of the organisation they become familiar, even where they do not describe the purpose of the document. In youth justice, for example, the assessment tools with its associated documents are referred to as 'ASSET reports'. This system and terminology is used nationally in England and Wales within youth justice, but not in other children's services or in youth justice in Scotland. Some systems are shared in this way within one service across a country, but others are specific to one organisation. Since the departure from national guidance on software and recording systems in children's services across England and Wales, (ICS) agencies have had the freedom to commission their own software systems, which has led to even more variation across the country in the systems, documentation and terminology used. One of the first tasks for a social worker joining a new team, therefore, should be to familiarise themself with the specific purpose, or purposes, of each of the text types that they will be required to undertake in their role and how these are referred to within their agency. While the way in which a specific text type is referred to may give an indication of its purpose, commonly used names may be relatively obscure, as in the example of ASSET reports given above. Some of the common purposes of texts include:

- communication between agencies
- communication directly with service users
- assessments of need and/or risk
- reviews of assessments of need and/or risk
- recording events, decisions, professional judgements and recommended actions
- care plans
- funding requests or approvals
- paperwork required by the courts, including reports
- notes of supervision meetings
- therapeutic writing.

Determining the purpose of a text is crucial to enable the writer to include the appropriate content and also to use the appropriate language or 'style'. The concept of style is problematic when considering writing, as the particular styles cannot easily be precisely defined. Style is also a term used to refer to personal preferences in writing as well as loosely being connected with particular genres of writing. For example, 'academic style' refers to a range of aspects of writing which include content, organisation of ideas within a text, vocabulary, syntax and methods of acknowledging the work of others, to name a few. There is, however, no single 'academic style' as expectations of academic writing vary across disciplines (Lea and Stierer, 2000). The expectations of style for texts for practice writing are also variable. There are some common expectations of all practice writing, such as clarity, but there are also many differences arising from the specific purpose of a text. Taking account of the limitations of the concept of style, it is used here to refer to the following specific aspects of written language.

Use of colloquial/technical vocabulary

The use of informal language or local dialect may be appropriate when communicating with service users, particularly young people when building trust in a relationship. This contrasts with, for example, a court report in which it may be important to use technical language such as precise medical terms.

Formality/informality of vocabulary, spelling and syntax

The formality/informality of a text relies not only on the vocabulary used, but also the use of standard spelling and sentence construction. Social workers will commonly be expected to use spelling and sentence construction of Standard English, but there may be times when it assists communication to deviate from this, such as when communicating on a mobile phone or using writing for expressive, therapeutic purposes with a service user.

Use of multimodal texts

A multimodal text is a text that uses a variety of forms to communicate meaning, including combinations of writing, tables, diagrams and/or pictures. There are many texts that may need a multimodal style; one commonly used in social work would be the inclusion of diagrams of the body indicating injuries in safeguarding assessments. Multimodal texts may also be used for therapeutic purposes such as drawing genograms[2] or ecomaps,[3] but also, the development of the digital writing environment, such as social media, opens up much greater possibilities for multimodal texts through embedding images, videos, hyperlinks and comments. The following example illustrates the way in which even very short social media posts, such as those on Twitter, can be richly multimodal. The tweet is fairly typical:

#socialworkwriting #socialwork How hard is it to involve service users in recording? Some good advice here www.scie.org.uk/publications/nqswtool/information/

The tweet includes two hash tags that enable anyone searching for the subject in the tag to find this tweet, and also a hyperlink to a relevant webpage. The tweet also includes an image. The purpose of this tweet would be to generate debate and to attract interaction from anyone with a shared interest in the subject. If the tweet was a reply or was relevant to a specific person, it could also have the person's name in the tweet, for example, @ WestUniversity or @LRai.

Voice or position of the author

Social workers frequently write as a representative of the agency for whom they work, but they are also trained professionals who are expected to hold an informed view. While it would be uncommon for social workers to write from their own personal viewpoint, they are expected to both indicate their individual professional opinion and also at times to express the view of their employing agency, even if they may not fully agree with this position. One illustration of the way in which it is important for the writer to be aware of whether they are writing as a private individual or as a representative of an organisation is the use of social media. Where someone writes a post in their capacity as an employee of an organisation (academic or professional), they have a responsibility to ensure that the views they express are broadly consistent with those of the organisation. It is also possible, however, for both social work students and practitioners to set up and use accounts, for example, on Twitter or Facebook, as private individuals, and any communication using these accounts should in theory be independent of any organisational or professional responsibilities. Twitter accounts have a profile page in which the owner can make a statement about whether posts are made on their own behalf or as a representative of an organisation. The dividing line between private and organisational roles is, in fact, not so clearly defined, particularly for individuals with a recognised public profile who may be associated with an organisation or their professional role, even if publishing online using an independent account. Developing the ability to think carefully about oneself as a writer as well as about the intended audience is a challenging aspect of much social work writing, and one to which I return.

Professional discourse[4]

In simple terms, social workers write like social workers. This is not quite as tautological as it may appear. Social work writing is social work practice *in* writing, and it therefore reflects the values, ethics, ideas, vocabulary and theories commonly used by the profession. As a trained and experienced social worker, the discourse of social work may become increasingly invisible with greater familiarity, but will contain features that distinguish it from writing undertaken by, for example, lawyers, nurses or teachers.

Format

Format is used here to refer to the tools used to create a text; for example, digital texts may be created using particular software programmes on computer systems or mobile devices, and texts may also be handwritten or drawn. It is important to be aware of the variety and significance that digital software programmes have on the ways in which texts are written. Word processing software, such as Word, allows the writer substantial freedom over the content and presentation of ideas, and can be either printed out as a hard copy text or stored electronically. It is increasingly common, however, for social work texts to be written using software programmes which are stored on a central database, and to limit the freedom of the writer through the use of restrictions on the number of characters and the use of confirmation tick boxes. Social work agencies may also use pre-formatted word processed texts that allow the writer more flexibility than entering information on a database, but also create a structure for the required content and presentation. The significance of digital software is discussed further in Chapters Five and Six.

There is a strong connection between the purpose of a text and the helpfulness of the style of writing in terms of its effectiveness. Experienced professional writers may be able to adapt their style relatively intuitively, and even less experienced social work writers will have a rich resource of experience outside of their professional writing to draw on, both from writing other kinds of texts and communicating in many contexts. Equally, even very experienced social workers are likely to come across text types which are new or rarely encountered, and which need some thought to ensure that the style is appropriate for the purpose of the document. Part of determining the purpose of a text involves an awareness of the intended reader or audience.

Audience

Thinking about and adapting communication to meet the needs of the service user is a standard part of social work training. Social work practice writing requires the same consideration of the needs of the reader, be they a service user or colleague. As with style, some aspects of adapting writing for audiences will be intuitive to many writers developed through basic literacy teaching in school and life experience. Making writing accessible for a specific audience or reader involves thinking about the aspects of style outlined above, but there may also be a need to pay very specific or detailed attention to some aspects of writing style when writing for service users or professionals outside of social work. There is a particular challenge in social work, as some texts need to be accessible for a range of readers with different needs.

The development of the use of social media as part of the way in which we communicate with friends and the general public may be changing our experience of writing for a large and unspecified audience. Most social media sites allow the writer to select their audience which may be limited to one person, specific friends or public for anyone to read. This is a function that has rarely been available to most people outside of publishing, and presents both challenges and opportunities that can provide valuable learning for students and professional writers in social work. Writing for a vast and unpredictable audience presents real challenges for this writer, particularly when writing within a professional role. The challenge of clear communication is even greater when using very limited words (such as on Twitter) to convey meaning that is potentially complex. Although tweets are restricted to 40 characters, it is common for them to embed either links to more extensive writings (such as on other websites), hash tags linking to wider conversations or to include images. These devices, along with the ability to expand a conversation in order to see the tweets of those joining a conversation, make interaction on Twitter a rich, multimodal space for communication.

Two elements of context are explored in some detail in this book – the first relates to the institutional context in which writing takes place while the second focuses on the individual and interpersonal context arising from the identities of the writer and reader.

Institutional context

The institutional environment in which writing takes place has an important impact on the texts produced, whether they are academic or practice contexts. Much has been written about the impact of higher education on student writing (Lea, 1998, 2004; Lea and Stierer, 2000), and there is also a gradually emerging literature on professional writing and the context in which it takes place (Le Maistre et al, 2006; Paré and Le Maistre, 2006; Rai and Lillis, 2012, 2013). As discussed in Chapter One, social work institutions, just like universities, have policies, procedures and embedded cultures that have an impact on practice writing. Some of the most striking aspects of institutional context are discussed in more detail in Chapters Five, Six and Seven, but one example that has been particularly influential has been the development of the use of new technologies in social work writing. The significance of institutional context and the impact of new technologies on social work practice writing (and consequently on practice) is well illustrated by Hall et al:

> Social workers reported to the Task Force[5] that the new ICT systems were not supporting them in their work. The bureaucratic demands arising from the new systems had increased to such an extent that they were failing to support their professional judgement and were having the effect of removing them from direct contact with children and young people. The atomised and fragmented nature of the information required and the mechanisms for both inputting and accessing it were such that it had become very difficult to identify the key relational and social nature of the work. (Hall et al, 2010: 409)

The research on which this quote is based demonstrates that social work writing is governed both by the tools used (here the ICT systems) and also by the policy that drives the design of information systems. Hall et al suggest that the impact on practice has been unhelpful in that it has resulted in poorer professional decision making as information becomes so disjointed from its context that it loses its meaning. Individual social workers are also important players in the creation of texts, and although the control exerted on texts is significant (particularly where they are governed by new technologies), it is possible for the author of a specific text to adapt and subvert according to their own professional judgement.

Here White et al note the importance of professional knowledge (the discourses of social work), of the immediate strategic context of a text and also of the relevance of interpersonal factors. What they illustrate is that in the creation of any individual text, the author will make decisions that may be more or less conscious. Such decision making will vary depending on the individual, but is based on not only the author's professional judgement about the case they are writing about, but also strategic decisions arising from engaging with the organisation with which they work. Broadhurst et al (2010) refer to the use of 'workarounds' or ways in which social workers are creative in findings ways to work with problematic or constraining bureaucratic systems in their writing:

> Whether these short-cuts take the form of early categorizations based on incomplete information, or the fudging of details of a "home-visit", all are attempts to cope with a system that is replete with design faults. (Broadhurst et al, 2010: 365)

An example from the WiSWAP Project of such practices is given by a social worker in a long-term children's team. She describes the accepted use of a full stop when completing electronic forms to replace the required information. This may sound bizarre, but the practice arose as a result of electronic forms requiring information to be input in specific fields; failure to do so would result in it not being possible for the form to be signed off and processed. While on the surface this may seem reasonable, the required information sometimes did not exist, repeated information was detailed elsewhere or was not relevant, and failure to process the form was more significant than omitting information from one field. The system could not, however, make a judgement about the content of information, so entering a full stop enabled the form to be processed. In this example, what began as a 'workaround' eventually influenced agency policy. The software designers were asked to de-activate some fields that had initially been considered to be 'essential' so that the workaround was no longer necessary. This is an example of policy-driven writing practices (eventually) responding to the needs of the users of the system based on their experience and professional judgement. Hall et al (2009: 410) suggest that systems should be:

> Designed in such a way that they are attuned to the working environment of the users (practitioners, children and families), and not seen primarily as trying to re-engineer that environment.

The concept of writing as a social practice offers policy makers, managers, educators and social workers an alternative to focusing on the writing skills of individuals that, as a result, opens up new possibilities for understanding problems when they appear as well as identifying solutions. A social practices approach to writing in the context of professional writing has not been widely researched to date, but we can learn from the work that has been undertaken in the context of student academic writing in the form of academic literacies.

Interpersonal interaction

As identified above, writing is a form of communication, and as it takes place between people, it is an interaction. While the concept of writing as communication may be clear in the context of letters, emails and even reports, it may not seem so obvious for students working away on assignments which may be assessed by an unknown marker, but the reader is significant regardless of their immediate visibility to the writer. One way of thinking about writing as communication is through framing reading as a process of translation. Hall recognises identity as intrinsically relational and also as incorporating *difference* in an essential way. Hall's analysis of the relational nature of identity (Hall, 1996; Hall and Maharaj, 2001) provides a useful conceptual frame for thinking about individual interactions. Drawing on Bakhtin (1981), Lacan and Saussure, Hall (2001) suggests that all texts and conversations are both embedded in and dependent on cultural practices, and that individuals' experiences and interpretations of such cultural practices differ, resulting in 'cultural translation'. This means that, in the context of student texts, the reader and author are both involved in a 'cultural translation', and their translations will differ more the greater the cultural differences there are between individuals.

This can equally be applied to professional social work writing. Hall's use of the word 'cultural' is very broad, and suggests that the cultural (or social) context of each person is unique to that individual. This makes all dialogue (whether written or spoken) a form of translation which, as the receiver translates based on their own cultural perspective, is always imperfect. Texts and other forms of communication are the same in this respect; they are always interpretations. Hall's discussion of translation provides an important perspective on texts and identity. Inevitable cultural differences between reader and writer will result in differences in understanding of meaning. Hall is suggesting that meaning-making, and interpretation of that meaning-making, is *inevitably* a site for imperfect translation and for the enactment of power differences as represented in identity.

This perspective has particular relevance when considering Lillis' research with non-traditional students (Lillis, 2001) in which she is also concerned with writer identities. Lillis' research demonstrated the impact of identity positions deriving from the student role, gender, social class and ethnicity, all of which provided examples of relational powerlessness. Lillis (2001) suggests that 'essayist literacy', or institutional assumptions around how essays should be written, is one such practice to which students are expected to conform, even if conforming creates internal identity conflict. Lillis uses examples from her work with non-traditional student writers to illustrate how they are inclined to minimise or exclude aspects of 'themselves' that they perceive as being contrary to the social practice of essayist literacy in the university. The importance of the reader is heightened where there is an emotive or personal aspect to the content as this sensitises the writer/reader relationship and draws the identities of each into sharper focus. The reader/writer relationship is also commonly framed within an imbalance of power. Drawing on the example of reflective writing in social work education, the following case study of 'Bernie' is taken from research with social work students on their second year of training (Rai, 2008), and illustrates the connections between the student identity and the student–tutor relationship.

Bernie

In the context of our discussions about her writing, Bernie focuses on several identities that appear to be particularly salient for her: Bernie as a Black Jamaican, Bernie as a reflective, religious woman and Bernie as a person who values education. Each of these identities carries with them an association with particular discourses, but they also carry particular emotional significance for Bernie. Taking the example of religion, Bernie suggests that her 'religion and faith' is the source of her ability to reflect, and has been something she has done for a long time. For her, reflection is associated with a moral imperative:

> 'I always know that for a person you need to reflect on where you are coming from and what you are doing all the time and whether it is right or wrong, and I need to do that as part of religion and faith, I have to do that all the time and I am always reading self-help books. So when I picked up this course I said yes [with emphasis]! I really wanted ... but it never really helped me.' Bernie: Interview 2

When she encounters reflection as part of experiential writing on the practice learning course, therefore, she associates it not only with something familiar that she can do, but also with a central aspect of her identity that carries spiritual value. The close association between education and Bernie's identity as a black woman, based on her difficult childhood experiences, have unsurprisingly stayed with her and appear to be influential in the way in which she experiences her relationship with her tutors. Despite there being very little evidence of criticism of her writing from her practice learning tutor, she expresses concern that he is making unjust racialised judgements about her writing. This example illustrates the importance of discourse and emotion because it offers Bernie an interpretation of her tutor's behaviour. She depicts her tutor's behaviour as matching her prior experience of education that she associates with a particular discourse of racist educational practice. Bernie describes her experiences of racism at school as a child,

> and links this to her belief that white teachers (by implication, in higher education) focus disproportionately on black Caribbean students' writing when looking for and commenting on surface language errors.
>
> This identity and subject positioning was subtly reinforced by a gender position only hinted at by Bernie when she suggests that, whilst it would be very difficult for a white man to understand black people's experiences, a black woman's ability to understand would be "different". In suggesting someone who would be able to understand her experiences in a different way, she aligns not only the ethnicity but also the gender with her own. This suggests that Bernie's identity as a woman as well as a black person (in contrast to her white male tutor) was influencing their relationship.
>
> (Rai, 2008: 310-11)

In this case study the student's relationship with her tutor is influenced by a number of factors:

- her own personal and education history;
- the nature of the writing which was highly personal and reflective;
- the institutional context with an inherent imbalance of power;
- her own identity (both social and psychological);
- the identity of the tutor;
- the interactions with her tutor, through both written feedback and face-to-face contact.

These factors interact in a very complex way, but the case study illustrates that even in the relatively impersonal context of academic assessment there are high-stakes interactions that are potentially both emotionally charged and unhelpful.

Conclusion

Managing the complexities in an academic context is a shared responsibility between the student, the tutor and the university. In the context of professional writing there are similar issues of writer and reader identities, but these are far more complex as the readers may be multiple and not fully predictable. As in academic writing power imbalances exist, but they are not so clearly delineated. For example, the social work writer will generally be in a more powerful role than the service user audience, but in a less powerful role than the line manager who may also read and be responsible for approving a particular text. Discussion of the importance of an awareness of the reader/writer interaction in specific contexts is the focus of discussion throughout the chapters that follow.

Notes

[1] SMS, or 'short message service', is the system commonly used on mobile phones to exchange what are commonly referred to as 'texts'.

[2] A genogram is a diagram that depicts family structure and relationships.

[3] An ecomap is a pictorial representation that identifies an individual or families' social networks and relationships (both positive and negative).

[4] 'Professional discourse' is used here to refer to the type of language used in a particular context or subject.

[5] Social Work Task Force, that undertook a review of social work in 2009.

3

Essays and reflective writing in social work

Introduction

The focus of this chapter is on two of the most common forms of assessed writing that social work students undertake during their studies – essays and reflective writing. It also considers writing dissertations, which are commonly required on master's level courses. In order to understand these text types additional key concepts drawn from academic literacies (introduced in Chapter Two) are used to help students understand and make more informed decisions in their writing. These concepts include academic conventions, labelling of text types, disciplinary diversity, implicit and explicit assessment expectations and managing 'theory' and 'experience'.

Drawing on the exploration of the nature of academic writing in social work provided in Chapters One and Two, this chapter outlines the differences and challenges of each form of assignment, and offers students some strategies to write effectively. Examples of essay and reflective writing texts are used to explore the ways in which individual writers approach assessed writing. Examples from research also illustrate some of the complicating factors influencing effective academic writing including student–tutor identity issues and the 'use of self' in reflective writing.

Social work students are commonly assessed through a variety of written tasks which can require them to familiarise themselves with a diversity of writing requirements. This diversity arises in part, as discussed in Chapter Two, due to the inherent multidisciplinary nature of social work, which draws on sociology, social policy and psychology in addition to an increasingly well-established tradition and knowledge base of its own. The focus in this chapter is on essays and reflective writing, but these are only two of the many different types of written assessments that social work students may encounter. As discussed further below, it would also be misleading to suggest that all essays and all reflective writing tasks are the same – there are both explicit and implicit differences in expectations or requirements across universities, disciplines and (unfortunately) sometimes between individual assessors on a single programme. In common with the rest of this book, therefore, the aim of this chapter is to equip the reader with an understanding of how to approach any writing task based on being able to ask themselves informative questions in order to understand more clearly what is required of them. The first part of this chapter explores the essay as perhaps the most common or even default form of academic assessment.

Is it all about essays?

Social work students are assessed through a wide variety of written and non-written tasks, but essays form a significant part of this writing. The Quality Assurance Agency (QAA) benchmark statement for social work suggests that:

> Assessment methods normally include case-based assessments, presentations and analyses, practice-focused assignments, essays, project reports, role plays/simulations, e-assessment and examinations. (QAA, 2008a: 16)

The word 'essay' is commonly used in higher education to refer to what is assumed to be a well understood form of writing. Research from the field of academic literacies, however, has challenged this notion (Street, 1984; Lea and Street, 1998; Baynham, 2000; Lea and Stierer, 2000; Lillis, 2001), suggesting that the requirements of essays vary, in fact, and are based on discipline-specific conventions. These conventions, or assumptions about how an essay should be written, may be explicitly taught or explained in course guidance, but research suggests that this is not always the case. Assumptions are either made about the 'common-sense' nature of essay writing, or there is an expectation that students in higher education will have become sufficiently familiar with the requirements of essay writing from their previous studies so that they should be able to transfer these writing skills to higher education (Lillis, 1997). Lillis identifies particular difficulties with what she calls 'essayist literacy':

> Essayist literacy provides a way of talking about student writing which acknowledges the relationship between literacy practices and knowledge making practices whilst situating both within a specific socio-historical position. (Lillis, 2001: 40)

Here Lillis is suggesting that the conventions that surround the essay not only relate to the layout, style and organisation of writing, but also the ways in which knowledge is conveyed. Moreover, both literacy and knowledge-making practices are determined by the specific and current social and historical context. The term 'essay', therefore, is problematic, as while it is used loosely to refer to an institutionally labelled text type, it actually signals (often implicitly) very specific ways of constructing knowledge and texts. Lillis suggests that student writing frequently labelled as an 'essay' can disguise complex and implicit expectations of students' writing that may not be made clear to students:

> Unfortunately, explicit teaching and exploration of conventions is not common practice, one of the reasons being that within the institution, conventions continue to be viewed as appropriate and unproblematic, as "common sense". (Lillis, 1997: 186)

Assumptions about the common-sense nature of essay writing belie a diversity of expectations both within and across courses. Lea and Stierer (2000) highlight the ways in which different academic writing conventions are presented to students, not only between institutions and disciplines, but also within disciplines in one institution. Assumptions cannot be made, therefore, that students (or tutors) who move across disciplinary areas (as well as between institutions) will share a common understanding of particular terms such as 'essay' or the conventions that lie behind them (Rai, 2008). The disciplinary differences within social work can result in a diversity of writing conventions, not only within one course, but also between assignments, even where they are similarly labelled as 'essays'.

> The presumption of a generic set of academic writing conventions is problematic, even within one "discipline" and this is compounded where one course of study includes diverse disciplines. The foundation course, as a broad theoretical course providing the knowledge underpinning care, drew upon a range of social science disciplines, including sociology, psychology and social policy. (Rai, 2008: 236)

Curry and Lillis suggest that the label attached to the text type such as 'essay', 'reflective commentary' or even 'assignment' may all in fact refer to identical expectations, but could equally refer to very diverse text types (2003: 18). In a study of student social work writing Rai (2008) identified that terms such as 'essay' and 'assignment' were used interchangeably but did not communicate to students the differences in 'house style' required in particular texts. By house style Rai was referring to the expectations of writing on a specific course that were understood by tutors and experienced students but often a mystery to new students. Students faced different challenges arising from such unclear expectations, and developed writing practices to manage them:

The writing expected of students on the practice learning course was significantly different from that on the foundation course. This difference was masked by written guidance, which implied that academic writing conventions based on essayist practices were straightforward and transferable across both the foundation and practice learning courses. (Rai, 2008: 238)

In order to clarify expectations of students' writing, therefore, it is important for educators responsible for assessment guidance to be explicit about expectations about particular ways of writing, and to differentiate between specific kinds of written tasks. Once writing is labelled as distinctive from the generic concept of an 'essay', for example, as a reflective writing task, it becomes possible to identify specific expectations which distinguish it or define it. The 'house style' becomes public and can be questioned or used by students. Closely associated with the naming of expectations, however, is the assumption that students will understand and have the skills to translate guidance into their own writing. Based on research into essayist literacy (Lillis, 2001), it would seem probable that implicit assumptions could remain, even where expectations are made more explicit through written guidance. An alternative approach is to build in teaching specifically intended to enable the student to understand the expectations of their writing and to develop and practice relevant writing skills. For example, in Rai's study (2008), one assignment required students to write about their personal experience and values, to evaluate practice undertaken in the workplace and to critically apply theory to practice. In addition, tutors wanted students to integrate theoretical and experiential writing. To achieve this task a number of distinct literacy and cognitive skills were needed, including the ability to construct a narrative based on their own experiences (often involving 'moving' between moments in time), and to build an argument drawing up both examples from personal experience and authoritative sources. These are complex tasks for which students need the opportunity to practice and to build their skills incrementally, receiving feedback on their writing before major assessment points. It is not enough to just make these expectations explicit in assignment guidance, although this is an important first step. In the remainder of this chapter two common forms of written assignment are explored – the social work essay and reflective writing.

The self in academic social work writing

It is a common requirement on all social work programmes for students to be assessed through writing about their personal experiences, their values and beliefs, and on the ways in which their practice changes and develops, all in the context of theoretically grounded critical discussion. This requirement demands academic writing which is markedly different from the expectations of many disciplines, and the particular demands of reflection in social work can demand a form of writing that implicitly breaches several commonly accepted conventions of academic and practice writing. Social work as a discipline, therefore, places the self at the centre of much student learning, including academic writing, particularly through reflective writing. This valuing of the self has implications for academic writing in social work education. It also raises questions about the way in which academic writing in social work might be out of step with academic writing in other disciplines, and therefore presents significant difficulties for both students and tutors. Figure 3.1 illustrates a notional spectrum of expectations in relation to the explicit presence of the self in academic student writing.

Figure 3.1: Writing about self across a notional spectrum of academic disciplines

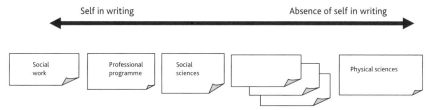

There are many ways in which the self may appear in a text; it is common in social work for the writer to be expected to include accounts of and reflections on both personal experience and experience derived from practice. In addition, students are required to explore their own personal values in relation to professional values laid down in the Code of Practice applicable to social workers (GSCC, 2002). The inclusion of personal information involving the self in texts has implications for students and tutors within the context of academic-assessed writing. The inclusion of such personal information in social work writing has some parallels with what is referred to as 'personal' or 'expressionist' writing in the US higher education context that developed in the 1960s and involved students writing assessed academic memoirs.

Although not undertaken in the context of professional education, 'personal writing' or 'expressionist writing' shares with reflective writing the importance of the writers drawing on their own personal or professional experience. The purpose of each form of writing is a little different, the personal writing being undertaken in order to develop the writer's skills in conveying their ideas in writing, while reflective writing is generally employed to develop the writer's reflective skills. Berman (2001) draws on the practice of composition students in the US undertaking this kind of writing, and evaluates the benefits, risks and practices surrounding what he depicts as 'risky writing'. Berman suggests that great care is needed in responding to personal writing in, for example, highly sensitive experiences such as abuse. This is particularly pertinent for the kinds of reflective writing undertaken by social work students, in which they may not only be exploring experiences of working with emotive topics such as abuse or discrimination, but may also write about their own personal experiences.

Students also need to be aware of the potential emotional impact of writing about such emotive experiences, and the possible impact that being sensitised in the writing process can have on responding to feedback. The work of researchers such as Berman (2001), Waller (2000) and Boud (1999), although not all concerned specifically with the writing of student social workers, all identify the importance of student/tutor dialogue where writing involves the student sharing personal information. By this they mean that there needs to be two-way communication about writing which goes beyond traditional grading and feedback on written work. Talking about the emotional impact of writing has not traditionally been a feature of study support in higher education, but within the helping professions, where sharing personal information is common-place, there is more recognition of the emotional aspect of communication. For example, in supervision and therapy such sharing of personal experience is sometimes referred to as self-disclosure. The concept of self-disclosure has its roots in sociological perspectives on human interaction, the existence or degree of self-disclosure being based on normative behaviour relating to the level of intimacy between individuals. Goffman (1963) was one of the first researchers to explore self-disclosure, and suggested that conditions for the relative appropriateness of self-disclosure depended on both the social context and the nature of the social relationship. Chelune (1979) proposed the following definition:

> The term self-disclosure has been loosely used to describe the degree to which persons reveal information about themselves to another, including their thoughts, feelings, and experiences…. Self-disclosure includes any information exchange that refers to the self, including personal states, dispositions, events in the past, and plans for the future. (Chelune, 1979: 152)

Chelune's exploration of the functions of self-disclosure concluded that it is a potentially powerful tool, the impact of which depends on the context and relationships within which it is used. Chelune (1979) refers to three important aspects of self-disclosure that have an impact on its function.

First, the 'normative' nature of the context in which self-disclosure takes place, or in other words, how socially acceptable or common-place self-disclosure is. For example, it may be more socially acceptable to share intimate or personal information with a GP than with a shop assistant. The second factor is the 'expressive value' of the self-disclosure, how honest, detailed and significant to the teller the information is. The same piece of information may have a very different meaning or significance depending on who discloses it and who receives it. For example, a disclosure of a bereavement may be relatively insignificant if the death was a long time ago, concerned a person to whom the teller was not emotionally close, or even if, although the death was significant, the information is given in such a way as to protect the teller through humour or other defences. The third feature is 'voluntariness'. This relates to the power balance between the teller and listener, and whether the self-disclosure arises from independent volition (maybe arising from trust or some other motivation which benefits the teller) or from a degree of compulsion. Members of less powerful groups may disclose more intimate information than they receive, thereby increasing their vulnerability to influence (Chelune, 1979: 164):

> … it should be noted that social norms may inhibit self-disclosure and isolate individuals from one another. For instance, males may be expected to avoid self-disclosure, particularly in areas that emphasise personal concerns, weakness, and emotional difficulties.

Within the therapeutic context, and that of mental health in particular (Rogers, 1962; Jourard, 1971), self-disclosure is a foundational concept which originally referred only to information flowing to the helper from the service user. Self-disclosure is used in psychoanalysis to refer to the sharing of personal information, particularly in the context of an analyst sharing information with an analysand.[1] In this context such personal information is shared with great caution, but in the belief that such exchanges can potentially build trust within a confidential, therapeutic relationship (Sticker and Fisher, 1990).

The discussion in this section is particularly significant as social work students are required to engage in such disclosure in the context of assessment, which is neither confidential nor necessarily trusting. Not all academic writing in social work education requires the kind of disclosure of personal or emotive experience discussed above. We return to reflection on personal experience below, in a discussion on reflective writing, but first, it is important to understand the role of more traditional academic writing such as the essay that also plays a significant role in student learning, and forms the foundation of much academic and professional writing.

Social work essays

It is perhaps unhelpful given the discussion above to offer the 'social work essay' as a predictable text type at all given that it is very difficult to generalise the expectations that might be applied to it on any particular course. There are, however, some useful commonalities about the nature of essays in social work that are likely to be relevant to most courses, but importantly, this section offers questions for students to clarify specific requirements on their own course before beginning to write. An increasing number of social work students are following master's level qualifications and have therefore already studied a degree, perhaps in an unrelated discipline. It is important to understand, therefore, that just because assignments share the label of 'essay', this does not mean that a social work tutor and a tutor in history or psychology will share the same expectations of their students' writing. Creme and Lea (2008: 32) identify the following as elements that are common features of university essays:

- developing an argument
- linking theory and evidence
- drawing a conclusion
- analysing
- being critical
- developing a central idea
- processing information
- incorporating facts
- correct terminology
- logical order
- use of evidence to support an argument
- use of primary texts
- use of quotations
- drawing on personal experience
- expressing own opinions
- using personal interpretation.

Creme and Lea emphasise that not all essays will require all of these elements, and students need to consider each essay question and guidance to identify which are relevant. This will not only depend on the subject of the essay, but also on the level of study. There is an expectation in higher education that assessment tasks build greater complexity and therefore require greater cognitive and literacy skills throughout the course. Table 3.1 illustrates some of the ways in which the expectations of complexity can build.

Table 3.1 is illustrative of the kinds of ways in which expectations of student writing develop at different levels of study – they will vary from

Table 3.1: Expectations of how complexity can build in academic writing

Demonstrates knowledge and understanding of key concepts	→	Additionally offers original or insightful critical interpretations and comment
Substantially descriptive	→	Substantially analytical or questioning
Simple argument drawing on a limited number of theories or ideas	→	Complex argument which critically interrogates a wide range of theories and ideas and presents original comment or conclusions
Evidence from recommended reading lists only	→	Independently researched reading and journal articles
Written language and organisation of ideas is clear	→	Use of complex and discipline-specific language; sophisticated organisation of ideas

university to university, but are broadly based on the QAA benchmark statement on honours degree skills (QAA, 2008b). As indicated above, the nature of essays differs from course to course, but as can be seen from Table 3.1, there are some broad common components that students are expected to develop as they progress through their studies.

Demonstrating knowledge

One of the basic principles of assessment is that it should test students' knowledge based on the teaching provided; put simply, that they have learned what was taught. In reality, higher education is more complex than just acquiring knowledge, and in a vocational subject such as social work, there is also an expectation that such knowledge is applied. Demonstrating the acquisition of relevant knowledge remains an important starting point in all assessments. The key word here is *relevant*. A student may demonstrate a great deal of knowledge but will not do well in their assessments if this knowledge is not relevant to the intended learning of the course, usually outlined in learning outcomes. The starting point for planning an essay, therefore, should involve identifying what knowledge is required through examining the title and assessment criteria for the essay and the learning outcomes of the course or module. Sometimes it will be fairly clear that an essay is assessing a specific block of study that may narrow down the required knowledge to be demonstrated. More advanced essays will involve students drawing on and integrating knowledge from across a range of modules, and may require them to undertake significant independent research rather than relying on knowledge delivered directly through teaching. The following essay title provides an example of the way in which knowledge can be drawn on:

> What relevance does attachment theory have in the assessment of children in need or at risk, and how can it inform decision making?

This essay question specifically indicates within the title an area of theoretical knowledge that is required: attachment theory. The teaching and reading list on the specific course should direct the student to particular sources, and these normally include seminal work (such as that by John Bowlby and Michael Rutter in this example), but also recent publications. At graduate level the expectation would be that students would refer to more than one theorist or writer, and demonstrate the ability to compare and evaluate different sources. The question not only asks for a critical evaluation of attachment theory. In common with many social work essays, there is also the expectation that the student applies this theory to a practice context. For this essay this would require the writer to include the demonstration of knowledge of relevant policy and current practice relating to the assessment and decision making for children in need or at risk. It is common for some guidance to be provided which should help identify any essential knowledge or sources that should be included.

Moving from description to analysis

Knowledge can be demonstrated in many ways other than through an essay, such as multiple-choice short questions, reports or reflective journals. An essay requires that knowledge is presented in a particular way, but these requirements will vary depending on the subject, question and level of study. One of the ways in which the complexity of essays is defined is through the move from description to analysis. The concept of analysis is not straightforward, in part because it is used to mean very different things by different tutors (Creme and Lea, 2008: 79). One way of understanding the difference between description and analysis is that description involves presenting information or ideas without questioning or unpicking them, while analysis requires the writer to think a little more deeply. Creme and Lea (2008: 79) suggest that this can involve asking questions such as:

- What does this mean?
- Why is this important?

- How does this work?
- How is this put together?
- Can you explain this?

In social work, the following questions might also be relevant:
- How does this relate to practice?
- How can social work values and ethics be applied?

Analysis therefore broadly involves adopting an inquiring approach to presenting information and ideas, and this is commonly achieved through developing an academic argument.

Constructing an argument

An argument, in the context of academic writing, involves presenting or discussing ideas or theories arising from different sources or perspectives, and then drawing some kind of evaluative conclusion. The concept of an academic argument, as with analysis, is used to mean different things depending on the context of writing. Curry and Hewings suggest that some of the ways in which students are commonly asked to develop an argument in an essay include being asked to take up a position, to put forward points for and against a particular position and to link theory and evidence (Curry and Hewings, 2003: 26). The ability to consider, present and make judgements on a range of different, often conflicting, theories is one of the defining features of academic practice, and also has considerable relevance for social work practice. A sophisticated essay will not only present ideas from more than one theory clearly, but will also identify areas of difference and offer comments on the relative value, relevance and merits of each. The early stages of developing skills in constructing an argument may only involve two perspectives, building to more complex discussion of several competing, overlapping or even complementary angles on a discussion. Argument and analysis are both needed for an effective academic essay as analysis is needed in order to construct an argument. In the example essay question above, for example, Bowlby's work on attachment theory could be outlined as a seminal work, but this would then need to be critiqued by drawing on other writers. Michael Rutter provided a significant critique of Bowlby's work, but his publications, although important, are also somewhat dated now, and so while still valid, it would normally be expected that recent publications would also be used which critically appraise and apply theory to the current practice context.

Providing evidence and drawing on reading

Another cornerstone of academic practice is the rigorous use of evidence to support argument and analysis. Evidence here refers to the original, published sources that are used to support the ideas or claims made in an essay. The most common source is a published book, but it can also include journal articles, newspapers, electronic sources such as webpages and audio visual materials. The key word here is *published*. There is an expectation in all academic writing that sources used should be 'authoritative' or, in other words, that they have been through a process of scrutiny or quality control. The highest standard of scrutiny is generally considered to be 'peer review' which is applied to academic journal articles, and involves drafts being reviewed anonymously by experienced colleagues with a specialist interest in the subject of the article. Compare this with, for example, an online blog written by an individual, which is published directly on the internet without any process for reviewing the quality or accuracy of content. The latter will have no checks for accuracy, objectivity or quality of content, and could be either misleading or strongly biased. Where published sources are used in an essay, they must always be referenced, or in other words, the original source and author must be acknowledged clearly. Failure to do so is referred to as plagiarism and is considered to be a serious act of academic misconduct. Where plagiarism is repeatedly or extensively evident, it is treated as cheating and attracts serious penalties, and on professional programmes such as social work, academic misconduct can be treated as evidence of professional unsuitability. This means that failure to both understand and to employ good academic practice can result in students' fitness to continue training being reviewed by the awarding university, with the possible consequence that they will be unable to complete their professional qualification. Full guidance on requirements and methods of referencing are available to students, so it is crucial that these are fully understood and applied.

Language and organisation

The importance of analysis, argument and using evidence in academic writing is generally well understood in higher education teaching, and students should be provided with guidance on them in either course or university-wide guidance. Expectations of the use of language and organisation can be considerably less well explained to students, remaining implicit in the expectations of students' essay writing. One aspect of becoming familiar with a discipline involves learning the specific vocabulary associated with academic writing generally (Hyland, 2006), and more specifically, in discipline or professional contexts (Bhatia, 2004: 157), such as social work. The appropriate vocabulary is unlikely to be directly taught, but rather students are expected to become familiar with it as they study. The use of discipline-specific vocabulary signals that a student is becoming an 'insider' to a particular 'discourse community' or collection of people who share a common understanding and language with which they debate a particular topic. The successful use of language and ideas associated with a discourse may result in better grades for written work, as this signals a deeper understanding and application of specific knowledge. The expected organisation of ideas can also remain weakly defined, particularly where this diverges from the 'traditional' essay structure of an introduction and conclusion top and tailing paragraphs of main content. Creme and Lea (2008: 36) suggest that students are familiar with the traditional essay structure, which might look like:

- Introduction: What is the essay going to be about?
- Main body: What are the themes that I am developing to support my argument?
- Conclusion: What are the consequences of what I have written?

They also suggest that this model is not necessarily straightforward to put into practice, and that it does not neatly fit within the requirements of all assignment types (2008: 36). This is certainly the case in some social work assignment types such as reflective pieces, simulated reports and case studies. It can be unhelpful, therefore, for students to learn models of writing which are presented as universal where they will subsequently encounter exceptions to the rule, as illustrated in the experience of 'Bernie' a student from Rai's research introduced in Chapter 2):

> 'That's why I was annoyed that he [tutor on her practice course tutor] put down that my structure wasn't clear because I aim to make my structure clear. I'm not trying to be big headed but I struggled with that and once I get something I never sway from it. And I got that from doing the foundation course.'

Bernie had found the support on developing an effective structure on her foundation course very helpful. This was the first course that she studied on her social work programme, and it was modelled on a traditional essay. She moved on to her first practice-orientated course with confidence that she understood how to write an essay, and was not surprisingly frustrated when she encountered criticism of the organisation of her writing which arose from implicit differences in her tutor's expectations on a more reflective, practice-orientated assignment (Rai, 2008: 234). This raises a genuine dilemma about whether it is more helpful to teach inexperienced students one simple approach to writing an essay to build their confidence, or whether students need to learn early on about the complexity and differences in writing in different contexts. In social work education students are likely to encounter relatively traditional essays, but perhaps more commonly than in many disciplines they will also be required to undertake a wide range of other forms of writing that differ significantly in important ways. It is for this reason that this book approaches writing through asking the right questions rather than providing set templates of correct ways of writing. In relation to language and organisation, therefore, the questions involve exploring an appropriate way of organising ideas for the specific task, and finding words that reflect the specialist language discipline.

Reflective writing

Writing in the context of practice, which often requires some form of reflective writing, can pose significant challenges for students and tutors. Reflective writing commonly involves two dimensions – 'experiential' and 'theoretical' writing. While the 'theoretical writing' dimension has something in common with what could loosely be termed an 'essay', the emphasis is less on marshalling knowledge to build an academic argument and more on using knowledge (including, for example, legislation and policy as well as theories of practice) to undertake a critical evaluation of the author's own practice. 'Experiential writing' encompasses writing in which the author outlines and reflects on experience based on either their practice or personal experiences, including values. There are some important implications arising from the fact that in reflective writing the author is central to the text. Any discussion or theory or knowledge revolves around the author's own experiences and values. This brings into contention the nature of objectivity, a stated objective of 'academic writing'. The following example from Rai (2008) of the experiences of a recently qualified social worker illustrates the potential tension between expectations of essays and reflective writing:

> When she [Patricia] wrote the first assignment for the practice course, she did not appreciate that anything different was required of her writing.... Patricia was consequently surprised by grades and feedback on her first two pieces of assessed writing. She spoke of the frustration that she felt; she thought that the particular "style" expected on the practice course should have been made explicit. (Rai, 2008: 229)

This quote is from a very able second year social work student who encountered unexpected differences between writing more traditional essays to reflective, practice-based assignments. There is no problem with expectations of writing to differ across assignments and modules; what is problematic is when these differences are not made explicit to the student, as illustrated here.

Social work education requires students to draw together academic and practice learning; this involves integrating real-life experiences and theoretical learning through reflection. Reflective learning has an established place within social work education, and there is abundant literature aimed at both social work educators and students on the subject. Despite this extensive interest in reflective practice (Boud et al, 1985; Boud and Solomon, 2001; Watson, 2002; Bolton, 2003), the assessment of reflection is contentious, and Boud (1999) in particular warns of the complexities involved in assessing reflective learning. He suggests that professions favour the teaching of reflective skills as they support the concept of professional self-regulation, but that there are dangers in associating *assessment* and reflection. Boud suggests that conflating assessment and reflection is unhelpful as there are inherent contradictions in the nature of reflection and the nature of assessment:

> Assessment involves putting forward one's best work…. Reflection, on the other hand, is about exploration, understanding, questioning, probing discrepancies and so on. There is always a danger that assessment will obliterate the very practices of reflection with courses aim to promote. (Boud, 1999: 127)

According to Boud, therefore, assessment which incorporates a judgement on students' developing ability to reflect on their practice should both avoid penalising students for exposing practice which is not 'their best', while providing clear guidance as to what is expected in terms of '*exploration, understanding, questioning, probing discrepancies*'. Boud also emphasises the importance of taking account of the learning context when setting up reflection tasks, and identifies some specific barriers to effective reflection which include intellectualising reflection, allowing or failing to protect students from making inappropriate disclosures and most significantly, placing reflection in the context of writing an essay.

The place of reflection in social work was originally established as a core aspect of assessment in social work education through the Central Council for Education and Training in Social Work (CCETSW) requirement that students '*demonstrate that they have … reflected upon and critically analysed their practice*' (CCETSW, 1995). The national occupational standards for the social work degree, set by the QAA in Higher Education, reflect the CCETSW requirement. While being less prescriptive about the method of assessment, the QAA subject benchmark includes 'reflection on performance' as a key element of learning, defined as:

> … a process in which a student reflects on past experience, recent performance, and feedback, and applies this information to the process of integrating awareness (including awareness of the impact of self on others) and new understanding, leading to improved performance. (QAA, 2008a; p 14)

The importance of reflection became firmly established in social work pedagogy through the influence of authors such as Eraut (1994), Kolb (1970) and Schön (1989), but self-reflection has much deeper roots in the profession. Reflective practice, in all but name, has been a feature of social work education since its early psychoanalytic roots. It can be traced back to the psychoanalytic origins of social work in the UK, which have had enduring influences on the discourses that surround practice and also the pedagogies of social work. This close connection arose through the understanding and use of the concept of 'self' which is integral to practice learning. Ruch (2002) suggests that the degree of interest in reflective practice is indicative of the profession's reclaiming of the relevance of the self in practice in the context of the increasing complexity of the professional task, and moves towards competency methods of assessment and managerialism:

> The pivotal characteristic of reflective practice is its recognition of the breadth of knowledge accessible to an individual and in particular the attention it pays to the non-rational as well as the rational responses to experiences. (Ruch, 2002: 203)

By 'non-rational' Ruch is specifically referring to the sometimes unconscious types of knowing and experience, including emotion, which is the concern of psychoanalytic theory. This non-rational aspect of reflective practice is a form of knowledge not commonly addressed in academic learning. Social work in the UK, as elsewhere, inevitably operates in a highly politicised environment, and practice is influenced and guided by organisational change. Despite the growing managerialism in social work, shadows of its psychoanalytic foundations remain and are interwoven implicitly through its pedagogy. Up to the early 1980s, psychoanalytic perspectives in social work education were not only important as influences on casework, but also influenced the nature of social work education:

> Self-knowledge has been stressed as a desirable objective in social work education for several decades…. In psychoanalysis the self-

knowledge of the analyst, acquired through his own analysis, is essential. A weaker version of this was adopted for social work. (Timms, 1977: 4)

This 'weaker version' could be seen on qualifying courses in the form of modules such as 'Use of self' (University of Bristol, 1986-87), which encouraged students to develop self-awareness, and an 'internal supervisor' in post-qualification practice. Although the curriculum no longer prescribes such modules, the development of skills in self-awareness and reflection continue to be required.

Moon (2004) advises careful planning and setting of learning objectives where such reflective writing is assessed. For example, in the context of reflective journals, Moon advises educators to be clear about whether they are being used as a learning tool, in which case the *process* is central, or as an outcome, when the *product* is the main focus. Moon has also produced a pictorial conception of the reflective writing process and an illustration differentiating between descriptive and reflective writing. The implication from Moon's work is that, although reflective writing is different from the academic essay, assessment of it should not prove any more challenging as long as academics are thoughtful about the purpose of particular pieces of writing and guide students clearly. Creme (2005) provides an insight into both the restrictive influence of academic genres, such as the essay, and of the outcome of writing being for assessment rather than for self-reflection and learning. Where reflective journals are assessed, Creme (2005) suggests that the need to create a final product (as opposed to using them as a reflective tool) can be unhelpful for some students:

> Student writers can invest what they feel is a good deal of "themselves" in their writing and can feel wounded when it is not well received. It is a long and arduous process, rarely completed, to become detached from what we produce, and not to feel criticized as a person for it. (Creme, 2005: 292)

This comment has great resonance for social work students who are required to invest so much of themselves in their writing that the 'product' that is assessed can indeed become very emotionally charged. Feedback from tutors, which could be interpreted as relating only to the mechanics or organisation of students' writing, can be construed as deeply personal criticism where the content of reflective writing is emotive and personal. The following quotation from Creme conveys well the challenge posed by assessing personal writing, such as learning journals, and the reflective writing undertaken by social work students:

> In the case of learning journals, the sense of a relationship between writer and text seems particularly close, as the student quote expresses, "She felt that her record of study in some way exposed herself, and that with this kind of vulnerability a formal assessment would be an insult." Only if it were not "judged" could she feel able to be "honest". (Creme, 2005: 293)

Although reflective writing is routinely used with undergraduate social workers, much of the research relating to reflective writing and journaling has been based on postgraduate studies, suggesting that it is a writing skill associated with higher order cognitive skills. Hoadley-Maidment (2000) and Jasper (2005) endorse this view, suggesting that the skills developed in reflective writing are just those required in research, such as creativity, transferability of learning, critical thinking and analysis. The academic rigour of reflective writing, together with the potential pitfalls in assessing it, call into question why and how reflective writing is used in undergraduate social work studies.

Research in social work student writing (Rai, 2008) highlights a dichotomy between the need for 'academic' and 'reflective' content. Tutors suggested that both were needed in order to write a good assignment for the practice course in the study, but that these two features were very difficult for students to combine in one text, as required in reflective assignments:

> Swaying too far towards the academic drew tutor criticism of being "defensively academic" whilst at the other extreme students risked the criticism of being anecdotal. Tutors' expectations, although imprecise, implied the need for an integration of writing based on experience and writing which drew on theory and "authoritative knowledge", or in other words published sources. Despite this expectation, tutors acknowledged that such integration was extremely complex and difficult. (Rai, 2008: 340)

By 'academic' writing tutors were referring to writing containing the features of 'objective' writing typically expected in essays. 'Reflective' writing encompassed writing that demonstrated the ability to share personal experience. The challenge of integrating these facets of writing is exemplified by the following comment from one of the tutors in the study:

> 'I tend to find that students who write a very academic and technical piece have great difficulty in getting into the kind of introspective, reflective approach. And some students can be very anecdotal and be quite reflective but don't make the links between professional practice, course materials and underpinning concepts. You have

the two extremes and you are looking for something in the middle.'
(quoted in Rai, 2008: 220)

This comment suggests that students, in this tutor's experience, tend to be good at one or other aspect of writing, but that most find it challenging to integrate them both. Reflective writing, therefore, frequently needs to be simultaneously academically objective and openly personal. This research suggests, therefore, that there is a writing 'style' demanded by reflective writing that is particularly complex and challenging to achieve due to the range of targets that need to be hit. Integration involves students moving between several key dimensions:

- a narrative position, in which the author recounts a practice (or indeed personal) experience;
- a reflective position, in which the author critically comments on the experience; and finally
- an analytical position, in which the author supports this critical comment through argumentation using authoritative sources (the theoretical element).

Rai (2008) suggests that students in her study partitioned experiential from theoretical writing. This enabled them to regulate the emotive impact of reflective writing as well as separating out cognitively two potentially different ways of writing.

The experiences of students in Rai's research supports Hoadley-Maidment's argument that an integration of such skills is demanded of students in their first year of study, and that many students found such integration difficult (Hoadley-Maidment, 2000). Subsequent research undertaken by Rai and Lillis with qualified social workers reflecting on their qualifying studies resulted in similar findings:

> Writing in a reflective way was really difficult I felt ... difficult in terms of what I'd done in previous learning. I never kind of wrote about myself and that's sort of the key aspect of ... at first it was really difficult just to kind of get the balance between writing about yourself and bringing in sort of the theory. (Rai and Lillis, 2013: 7)

Despite its challenges, social workers perceived reflective writing as making an important contribution to supporting student social workers in developing capabilities in reflective practice and an important aspect of social work education:

'I suppose the reflective writing sort of helps you understand what reflective practice was … I did see the value of it … I think it was and definitely gets you into the mind set of understanding what reflective practice is and kind of get comfortable I suppose at analyzing your work and being able to say I didn't do that very well or you know I learnt from these so yes it's definitely valid and worthwhile.' (quoted in Rai and Lillis, 2012: 8)

Requirements of reflective writing vary considerably from course to course and assignment to assignment; the label 'reflective' really only signals that the writer should be including an element of critical commentary on their own experience. This means that it is difficult to provide an example of reflective writing which is meaningful in its application to any reflective assignment. The following extract is from a practice-based reflective essay from Rai (2007):

> I have worked in partnership with Ann to gain her trust and to advocate on her behalf as she has tried to assimilate so much distressing information and navigate her way through the unfathomable depths of loss – loss of independence, of dignity, of credibility and ultimately of life itself. I reflect that the strength of my support for Ann is largely a result of the empathy I feel for her as she attempts to protect her values from being compromised. The positive identity, with which Ann was admitted to hospital, is being systematically undermined by the inference that she is unreasonable, unrealistic and difficult, basically because she has refused to conform. Individuals who are perceived as "difficult" appear to find it hard to take advantage of the opportunities for choice (K100 Block 3 p 43). In this instance Ann is both being labelled, and being discourage from making an informed choice about where she feels her future care needs should be met.

This example is not offered as a model illustration of how to write a reflective account as this would be misleading, as discussed above. It does, however, illustrate some of the features of reflective writing in social work. Firstly the writer uses the first person (I have worked, I reflect, I feel for her) and makes direct reference to specific examples of experience, in this case practice experience. Secondly, the extract illustrates to combination of reflections on experience and references to theoretical knowledge. There is only one direct citation here, but the writer signals an awareness of relevant key concepts through the use of terms such as loss, identity, dignity and labelling. In doing so this student is demonstrating her ability to apply knowledge through reflection on practice experience.

Social work dissertations

Dissertations have become more common in social work education due to the expansion of postgraduate-level qualifying courses, although they are sometimes also required in undergraduate courses which award a degree with honours. Writing a dissertation has much in common with an essay, although they are longer pieces of writing which therefore require more planning and careful organisation. The exact length varies from course to course, but is usually around 10,000-15,000 words. The length of a dissertation can be daunting for many writers, so it can help to break the text down into chapters and approach planning and writing at this more manageable level. Although requirements vary, most dissertations will include an 'abstract', which is a short section of between 200-500 words providing a précis of the dissertation. It is also usual to include an introductory chapter and some form of either discussion or concluding chapter at the end. The focus of the chapters making up the rest of the dissertation depends on the topic as well as course guidance. Drafting and re-reading also takes on a greater significance with a longer piece of academic work, in part to edit out minor textual errors, but also to check for repetition and inconsistencies across a larger body of work. For those who are very daunted by writing a longer piece of academic writing, drafting can be helpful as a first draft enables the writer to get some ideas down on paper with the reassurance that they need not be read by anyone other than the author. A first draft is a starting point, a thinking space where the writing can formulate thoughts that can later be crafted into a text for the intended reader. Worrying about the final text can be very inhibiting, particularly when writing a longer piece, so it is important to allow some time to write initial, imperfect drafts that can then be developed.

The use of the first person, discussed above, is an issue for some careful consideration in a dissertation. Carey, for example, suggests that the first person should not be used in the context of a formal piece of academic writing, such as a dissertation (Carey, 2013: 195), while other sources suggest that it is acceptable to use 'I' in some chapters, such as a methodology chapter which is largely descriptive (Smith et al, 2009: 134). Individual courses generally provide guidance on the required style of writing, including the use of the first person, but where a dissertation involves the student reflecting and commenting on their own practice, it is clumsy to avoid referring to the author's own work and reflections in the first person.

One key difference between an essay and a dissertation is that while an essay is based on a given question, a dissertation requires the student to construct their own question or topic to write about. Courses generally provide guidance and support to help students identify a suitable area of investigation and the question or questions to interrogate it. Undertaking a dissertation demands a range of scholarly skills in addition to the ability to write well, and these skills will depend in part on the kind of dissertation required. Dissertations broadly fall into two categories: literature reviews and research-based dissertations. In social work it is common for 'research'-based topics to be based on an examination of an area of practice. A research dissertation, whether based on practice or other empirical research, requires the student to design a methodology and to understand all of the processes involved in undertaking a research project. A literature review does not require original data to be collected, but involves a detailed search and analysis of published work relating to a specific area of investigation. Both literature reviews and research dissertations involve the ability to select, interpret and critically analyse information from a range of sources and then martial this into a cohesive discussion. The writing is necessarily integral to these broader scholarly skills, as indicated by Carey:

> Ideally the writing of a social work dissertation should not only start early but also proceed in tandem with a more holistic and interrelated research process.... Such an iterative journey back and forth occurs due to the impact of new findings, further reading or personal reflection, all of which may lead to a reform or extension of earlier arguments. (Carey, 2013: 194)

This iterative process of writing will be new for many writers, particularly those who have previously undertaken all of their preparatory reading and planning before beginning to write. Writing in this way makes it an integral part of the analysis process, and for many writers, writing becomes a tool for thinking rather than a final product.

Working with your tutor

Tutors within the university and supervisors in practice are important resources for helping students to develop both academic and practice writing skills. University tutors can make a difference at four key points in learning:

1. Designing the curriculum
2. Designing the assessment strategy, including assessment outcomes, and associated clear guidance on writing
3. Providing study skills and writing support
4. Providing feedback

Practice-based supervisors and assessors additionally have an important role in offering support and feedback that enables students to contextualise learning and writing skills developed in the university to the practice context. Each of these areas is addressed in Chapter Eight from the perspective of designing and developing writing support on social work programmes. The focus here, however, is on what students can do to make the most of support that is offered on social work programmes.

Understanding assignment guidance

While the amount and nature of information on how to write an assignment will vary between programmes and even modules, there should always be some guidance available for students. It is vital to be familiar with such guidance on each assignment as there can be important differences in what is expected and valued when marks are given. As discussed above, social work programmes frequently draw on modules from a variety of disciplines, and as a result, tutors may be looking for different things when marking written assignments. Sometimes programmes offer a large amount of guidance that can become confusing or overwhelming. Occasionally guidance can appear conflicting, for example, between university-level general rules, programme-wide rules and assignment-specific guidance. Ideally module tutors will ensure that there is consistency and clarity, but if students are confused, it is better to clarify expectations and requirements with the relevant tutor before beginning to write.

One of the common areas for confusion on social work programmes is around the use of the first person pronoun 'I' in assignments. Academic writing traditionally uses what is called the 'passive voice' in which 'I' is not used. For example, the following would be a commonly accepted way of writing in many social science disciplines:

In this essay three theoretical frameworks will be critically examined to explore poverty in modern society.

Compared with the following written in the first person:

In this essay I will critically examine the three theoretical frameworks to explore poverty in modern society.

In this example both forms work equally well, but some programmes (or individual modules) might penalise students who use the second example. In writing that requires students to draw on experience, it can become difficult to construct a discussion in the passive voice, and switching between the two forms can be challenging; it can also be very confusing moving between modules with different expectations, as illustrated by the experience of one student in Rai's research:

> 'It's the style that is so different because [my practice tutor] wants "I want, I think, I feel I felt" where as the [theory tutor] is looking at writing in the third person.' ('Patricia', quoted in Rai, 2008: 169)

Here, Patricia personalised the requirements (the tutor wants), whereas the difference between the modules may arise from common discipline-wide differences or agreed expectations outlined in each module. Where these expectations are not explicit it can be very unhelpful for students negotiating moving between modules. Writing in the first person, although in some ways more familiar to many writers than more formal impersonal writing, can also pose a challenge to students who have become familiar with academic writing, as indicated by this tutor reflecting on working with social work students:

> 'I have students in workshops [who] find it very difficult indeed to write essays from the first person perspective, some of them having gone through academic courses, although a lot of them haven't, where they have been asked to write typical undergraduate essays which is about other people's work and not their own.' (quoted in Rai, 2008: 195)

What many students find very difficult is blending writing about experience in the first person and making links with theory:

> 'I tend to find that students who write a very academic and technical piece have great difficulty in getting into the reflective approach. And some students can be very anecdotal and be quite reflective but don't make the links between professional practice, course materials and underpinning concepts. You have the two extremes and you are looking for something in the middle.' (quoted in Rai, 2008: 220)

This tutor recognises the tricky balance students need to achieve in many reflective assignments where their writing should express honest, personal reflections alongside cogent arguments supported by theory. There is a risk that writing can appear too impersonal if the first person is avoided in practice-orientated modules where reflective writing is required. Failing to convey a sufficient level of person engagement can result in students' writing failing to convincingly engage in the level of reflection expected in practice courses such as social work:

> The student writes almost as an intelligent observer rather than someone who will have to go in to work tomorrow and make decisions based on values, amongst other things. (Rai, 2008: 222)

While students are occasionally penalised for writing only in the passive voice, the fact that this is the more accepted academic form means that it is more common for students to be caught out and penalised for using the first person in a context when it is not accepted. In order to avoid being penalised in this way it is important to clarify module requirements, particularly when writing practice-orientated or reflective assignments, where it would be cumbersome to avoid using the first person.

Making the most of assignment feedback

Developing assignment writing skills involves a circular process through which students submit an assignment, receive feedback, reflect on and apply learning from feedback and write again. This process is only effective, however, if there is some consistency of expectations of writing across assignments, and if students are both provided with and use feedback effectively. Difficulties arising from inconsistent expectations are addressed in Chapter Eight, so the focus here is on making good use of this circular process based on well-planned assessment strategies and guidance.

Students' individual writing practices (discussed in Chapter Two) can be thought of as operating across three stages: pre-text, in-text and post-text (see Figure 3.2). The pre-text stage represents thinking (including reflecting on prior feedback and experiences) and drafting. The in-text stage represents that which is made available for the intended reader, and the post-text stage is when the author reflects on the text and receives feedback from the reader. The pre- and post-text stages share the feature of what I refer to as 'shadows' that influence practices taking place in them. These shadows represent the factors that influence the writer and involve three features:

- autobiographical shadows (arising from the writer's past experiences)
- interpersonal shadows (arising from the consequences of specific interaction with others which leave a mark on the writing practices)
- discoursal shadows (arising from the writer's relationship with the discourses of social work).

These three aspects may overlap. At the in-text stage these shadows become 'representations'; in other words, they become preserved within a text and are available for interpretation by the reader rather than transient experiences that influence the writing and review stages of the process.

Figure 3.2: The drafting process

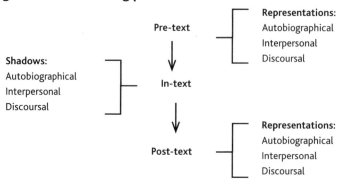

An understanding of the influence of shadows and representations can help student writers to reflect on their own individual writing practices and, where necessary, make changes in order to develop their writing more effectively. The following case study continues an exploration of the experiences of Bernie, a second year social work student, who was introduced in Chapter 2:

Bernie

Bernie undertook her social work training as a student sponsored by her employer. Through talking about her academic writing she identified a number of experiences that influenced her writing in important ways.

Autobiographical shadows

Autobiographical shadows include personal, cultural and educational experiences. Bernie described herself as a black woman of Jamaican origin and her family, social and educational historical experiences carry significant emotional meaning for her. Bernie provided a detailed account of her prior educational experiences and her identity as a British-born woman with Jamaican parents. She described herself as a child who was academically able, but she did not feel that this was recognised by her teachers at school. Bernie also said that she was hindered in her learning by the attitudes of her teachers, her cultural heritage and a lack of proactive support from her parents. Although Bernie was born in England, she lived in Jamaica for just under two years prior to returning to the UK, and joining a British primary school at the age of seven. As a young child she experienced both Jamaican and British culture and language, both through an extended visit to Jamaica and through her parents, whom she described as speaking Jamaican English, or Patwa, at home. In reflecting on her childhood educational experiences, Bernie identified some particular memories that she felt had an impact on her education. Some of these memories stemmed from the attitudes and actions of influential adults in her life, and others from the cultural and linguistic context of her family. The first issue related to Bernie's memory of her own academic aspirations and the failure of her teachers to support and encourage her. Her recollections are mixed in relation to her teachers. Although she speaks of being mis-placed in remedial classes, for example, she also talks of this being quickly rectified, and of particular teachers who recognised her abilities and encouraged her. She also reported direct discrimination in school, for example, being pushed towards sports rather than more academic subjects:

'Oh they were unfair in that they did not push you in the areas that you wanted to ... they picked up that all black people were good at running, so therefore get out there on the field – I mean I missed out on classes because ...whenever there was a field race or sports day ... they want me to go because they think just in case I change my mind – so I just sit there not doing anything.' (quoted in Rai, 2008: 305)

At home Bernie felt that although her parents expected her to achieve in school, they did not actively support her, and she felt that growing up with English spoken as a mother tongue and her parents' lack of experience of the English school system made it difficult for her to be well supported at home. For example, Bernie recognised that the British education system assumed that children would have culturally based knowledge such as nursery rhymes, fairy tales and proverbs. As a child raised in a family where Jamaican English was spoken alongside British English, and with parents who did not move to the UK until they were adults, Bernie believed that she did not have sufficient familiarity with such culturally based knowledge to enable her to perform well in school. While there is no way of determining the facts of the discrimination described by Bernie or the extent of her parents' lack of support, particularly compared with other children, the important issue here is that Bernie experienced the actions and attitudes of her teachers and parents as being negative and unsupportive.

The impact of Bernie's experiences were sufficiently strong to remain in her mind as an adult reflecting on her educational history and her current experience of academic writing. The specific ways in which they influence her as a writer generally or as author of a specific text are difficult to determine, and are influenced by more recent experiences as well as these historical ones. There was evidence, however, that these autobiographical shadows affected Bernie's writing in important ways. First, as an mature adult learner Bernie remained determined and passionate about her learning, but also very sensitive to any potential injustice from her tutors, and very aware of her identity as a Black woman. The above examples illustrate that Bernie's identity as a black English-born Jamaican was central to her very difficult prior educational experiences. These experiences involve emotive memories, but also her familiarity with particular discourses such as those relating to racism and education. These discourses and emotions remain with her as an adult, and shadows of them can be seen in her discussion of her relationship with her practice learning tutor and her 'interpersonal shadows'.

Interpersonal shadows

The key (but not only) source for interpersonal shadows arises from students' relationships with their tutors. Interpersonal shadows can be closely related to historical autobiographical experiences, although this is not necessarily the case. Bernie had significant issues with her second year tutor that appeared to have arisen in part from her prior educational experiences. In one example Bernie felt that this tutor was scrutinising her written language more closely than her peers because she was Black. There was very little evidence of such criticism in the written feedback on her writing from her tutor, so this example illustrates how powerful previous experience can be as she depicts her tutor's behaviour as matching her prior experience of education, which she experienced as unhelpful and unhappy due to racist stereotyping. Bernie's response to her tutors also illustrates the importance to her of receiving feedback on her writing practice that she trusted in a contrasting relationship with a first year tutor. Bernie talks about being reluctant to read and respond to feedback on her writing when she began her social work programme, and said that this was due to negative experiences on a previous course. As a result of very positive support from her female first year tutor on the social work programme, her confidence built significantly:

'I have come a long way, because at university [this was her previous course of study] I would never read the teacher's comments because they would put me down and I didn't like it. Not put me down, I mean you think any comment is going to put you down ... and it was not until I started the foundation course [of the social work programme] I took everything to the book, I went through all the classes ... all the ideas that they gave you I took on-board and when someone advises you to read the comments because it will help I did it to the letter, I did it.'

Bernie's difficulties at school and on her first degree seemed to have made it difficult for her to trust the advice given to her. Her hesitancy in trusting tutors and when she had a positive experience in year one followed by what seemed to be contradictory advice in year two made it hard for her to accept criticism or to follow advice from her year two tutor. The differences in advice most likely arose from changes in expectations from year one to two and also between a theoretical foundation module in year one and a more applied practice module in year two, but Bernie did not appear to have understood that expectations of her writing would change across years and modules, and so attributed differences to her tutors:

'I could not connect with this teacher [year two tutor] at all so I didn't want to, it was a waste of time trying because I was never going to get there. I felt a sense that I was never going to get there, I was wasting my time so I gave up trying.'

Here Bernie is clear that there was something about her tutor on the second year module that led her to the conclusion that she was 'wasting her time'. For Bernie the interaction of autobiographical and interpersonal shadows created real difficulties for her in developing her writing as she progressed through her studies.

Discoursal shadows
Discoursal shadows arise from connections between the writer's own experiences or identity and the subject that they are studying. Bowl (2000, 2003) illustrates this well in her research with non-traditional students, one of whom says:

'They talk about people like me in Social Policy – with disadvantage. I feel as if I'm living Social Policy rather than just reading it in text books, which other students are.' ('Salma', quoted in Bowl, 2000: 96)

Students will vary in their experiential connections with particular discourses, but Bernie shared a similarly close identification with aspects of her studies to those of 'Salma'. When talking about challenging racism in the workplace, for example, Bernie drew on her own experiences, and these inevitably influenced her engagement with the academic and practice-related debates in her writing. In one example she wrote about a Black colleague on placement who had challenged a racist incident that took place within her team. Reflecting on the feedback that she received, Bernie commented that:

'I think he was taken aback when he read it. I felt it made him think. Because I think anybody would stop and see another perspective on how Black people think and that we don't all think that you're all prejudiced, but we do think that you are sometimes … if it was a woman that was black. They would have looked at it in a different way.' (quoted in Rai, 2008: 315)

The significance here is that Bernie saw herself as having a different insight into discourses of racism than she believed that her tutor would have, on the basis of her own identity and experience. Her writing about this discourse was influenced by her acquisition of knowledge and familiarity with the discoursal debates gained through her studies and practice learning, and also from her own personal experience. Discoursal shadows do not necessarily relate to such personal identification with the subject as spoken of by Bernie and Salma; they may reflect only a particular understanding or engagement in a discourse arising from previous academic study or possibly individual values or beliefs. What is significant is that students bring something individual to their engagement with a discourse, and this is reflected in how they write about it.

Making use of an understanding of representations and shadows

Representations differ from shadows only in that they can actually be seen in the text written, as opposed to having an influence on the thinking processes that are involved in preparing or responding to feedback. An awareness of shadows can help students to reflect on otherwise unconscious influences on their writing that, although sometimes helpful, can also create misunderstandings or unhelpful blocks. Greater self-awareness offers the possibility of making better use of tutor support generally, and of feedback more specifically, and in assignments that permit or encourage reflection, an awareness of shadows could be used to strengthen the quality of reflective writing. Tutors can also usefully draw on the concepts of shadows and representations, and this is discussed further in Chapter Eight. If readers reflect on their educational history, this is a very good starting point for thinking about their own shadows, and for many students this should also include their own language history.

Undertaking a language and education history

The language that we use reflects who we are – our experiences as we grow up play an important part in determining the language we speak. When we are very young the language of our parents and immediate family is the most important influence, but as our social world expands, we are increasingly influenced by friends, school and work colleagues. If readers reflect on their own language history, this can help in understanding how their own use of language developed, and how this has had an impact on their educational experiences, including learning to write in different contexts. This is relevant whether or not English is the first language, but there may be particular significance for speakers of English as a second language and for people who speak a dialect of English. Variation in spoken English comes from dialect and from accent, which varies according to where we were born, where we live or which social group we come from. Accent and dialect are a very important part of who we are, and many of us will hang on to them in certain circumstances, such as with family and friends, but adopt a different style of language in more formal situations and in academic writing. This switching between varieties of language is useful, but we need to know which 'voice' is appropriate for different situations. Readers should think for a moment about the questions below:

From birth to school age:

- Which language(s), or dialect(s), do you remember hearing and using?
- Which one did you learn to speak first?
- Where there different languages or dialects that you used in different contexts?

Through school:

- Thinking about school (including primary and secondary education), which language did you learn to read and write in?
- Did you use a different language in school from home?
- What memories do you have of your experiences of learning to read and write both in school and elsewhere?

Work and study since school:

- What language(s)/forms of writing have your studies and/or jobs since school required of you?
- Has your studies/employment required you to learn new ways of writing and talking and if so how has this affected you?

Current studies and/or employment:

■ How do you think that your experience could help you be an effective student and social worker? For example, you might understand more about the nature of language itself, or know that some languages are seen as being of a higher status than others.
■ Which language skills do you think you need to develop now, if you are to become an even better student?

Undertaking a language history of this kind and sharing reflections with a tutor can be a very helpful way of developing greater self-awareness in writing (and studies generally) and also to make better use of support when writing assessments and in developing written skills in the workplace. This process enables writers to think about themselves in their writing, and the impact that past and current experiences and relationships have on writing. This is particularly significant in social work due to the centrality of issues of 'self' in both reflective academic writing and in practice, as discussed above.

Conclusion: seeking and using writing support

This chapter has focused on essays and reflective writing in social work education, but there is a huge variety of different kinds of writing that students can be asked to undertake – essays and reflective writing are just two of the more common forms. Even within these two forms there can be significant differences in expectations from programme to programme and module to module. Even for the experienced student, therefore, the key to successful writing is to fully understand the requirements of each individual piece of assessed writing. Much of this guidance should be laid out in written guidance at module or university level, but it is sometimes necessary to clarify specific points directly with the person who will be marking the assignment. For less experienced writers it can be helpful to seek support with writing skills early on, either from a subject tutor or from someone able to offer more specialist writing support, either through the library, study skills resource or, in some universities, a specialist writing centre. Working on and improving writing skills is an integral part of academic study for students at all levels of education as there is a constant need to develop and adapt to new writing tasks in new contexts. Students seeking help does not mean that they are 'poor writers', but that they recognise the importance of adapting writing to each context and task, and are able to reflect and develop their skills. A good example of this is the practice learning element of social work training in which students are frequently required to undertake assessed academic writing, portfolios and 'real-life' practice writing. The academic writing skills acquired through school and previous higher education may help, but these new forms of writing will inevitably present some new challenges for all students.

Note
[1] www.oxforddictionaries.com/definition/english/analysand

4
Developing writing during practice learning opportunities

Introduction

So far social work writing has been discussed in terms of the academic writing students complete as part of their studies. This only forms part of academic assessment, however, and although much of the focus during practice learning placements is on direct work with service users, a significant element of assessment in this work is conducted through writing. This chapter focuses specifically on writing undertaken during practice learning opportunities, and offers strategies for transferring student learning from academic writing to practice writing contexts. So attention here is on assessed writing undertaken in the course of practice learning often compiled within portfolios of evidence. Issues discussed include how and where students can be supported in learning to write, the ways in which learning can be transferred from academic writing to practice writing and also the importance of understanding the context of writing in practice. The word 'academic' is used here to indicate any writing that primarily has an academic function. For students this includes all assessed writing set and assessed within a university context.

Social work students are also assessed through writing that could be argued to be only partially academic as it relates primarily or solely to practice and not academic pursuits. Academic writing has been discussed in some depth in earlier chapters, and practice writing is considered in Chapters Five, Six and Seven. Chapter Five provides a broad introduction to writing as a social work professional and the challenges of writing diverse texts for diverse audiences. Chapters Six and Seven focus on two of the most important kinds of writing in social work practice – case recording and assessment reports. Practice writing here refers to all writing undertaken in the course of professional practice, including practice placements. Social work students are also assessed through a third form of writing that sits between academic and practice writing. The focus in this chapter is on writing undertaken during practice placements, particularly writing that primarily has an assessment function, such as portfolios, discussed below.

This chapter also explores the demands involved in writing under pressure and juggling the time demands of practice contexts, making effective use of supervision and developing effective use of electronic and manual writing tools. The concepts of 'audience' and 'purpose', developed in Chapters One and Two, are used to illustrate how students can write better assessed work and develop an awareness of best practice in professional writing. This chapter also explores the roles of tutors and practice assessors in supporting students to develop competence in professional writing. Finally, the challenge of involving service users effectively in practice writing is introduced.

Practice placements normally involve students undertaking two broad forms of writing: 'portfolios' and 'practice writing'. The purpose and format of portfolios varies from course to course, but they are commonly intended to assess students' competence against prescribed practice outcomes and can therefore include a wide range of texts including examples of practice documents, reflective pieces and also texts written by supervisors, colleagues and service users. Practice writing encompasses all the writing undertaken by students during the course of their everyday social work practice while they are on placements. It is assessed either directly, where it forms part of a portfolio, but can also be indirectly assessed as an element of the student's practice. While support is generally offered to students to help them develop the academic writing skills needed to complete academic assessments, less attention is given to the writing undertaken during practice placements.

Portfolios can be challenging, due to the range of text types included in them. They also require students to develop skills in selectivity, good indexing and organisation in order to present information clearly. Some universities are also moving over to electronic portfolios, which demand an additional set of skills. Practice writing is discussed in depth in Chapters Five and Six, but the demanding context of writing in practice is introduced here, alongside the ways in which students learn to write in practice.

Learning to write in practice

The portfolio (discussed in more detail below) is the main overt text through which many social work students are assessed in practice, but they will also be engaged in many other forms of practice writing that will contribute to their assessment as practitioners. Writing in practice can come as a shock to some students as it presents very different challenges from academic writing. For many students there is very little preparation prior to beginning a placement and being expected to start writing as a trainee social worker, which can be a daunting experience. The focus of most courses is on academic writing, and although most universities provide advice and support in developing assignment writing skills, it is not common for similar support to be available for practice writing. O'Rourke suggests that, based on her research, the majority of social workers in adult services were offered little or no training in recording, either as part of their qualifying course or as in-house training (O'Rourke, 2010: 81). She suggests that while the justification given for this is that courses could not prepare students for the diversity of recording systems that students are likely to encounter, this argument focuses on the mechanics at the cost of recognising the common professional issues involved, such as what should be recorded and how (O'Rourke, 2010: 166). One of her participants (a manager) commented:

> 'So recording isn't a straightforward task; you really have to think and, you know, when you're here at sort of 5 o'clock on a Friday afternoon, and you've got three hours' worth of visits to record, and they're all high-risk situations, and you're tired, it's pants. So there would be a plea from me (which I'm sure – I hope – my colleagues would agree with) to give us some concrete training.' (quoted in O'Rourke, 2010: 91)

Some social work courses may ask students to undertake an assignment that simulates a practice document, such as a report, but this can have limited value as the requirements of such documents vary so much from setting to setting, and students are writing them outside of a genuine practice context. While the process of undertaking an assessment is commonly included in the curriculum, students rarely gain experience of writing an assessment. Assessment reports in their various forms are a central aspect of social work practice that requires social workers to draw on a range of skills. (See Chapter Seven for a full discussion of writing assessment reports.)

The following two case studies illustrate some of the common experiences of students moving from the academic to the practice environment.

Duncan

My first placement was in a mental health team. I had never worked in an adult setting before but I am a sponsored student and have been working for eight years in a looked after children (LAC) team as an unqualified social worker. I wasn't too worried about the writing in practice as this was not new to me and I had been getting good grades in most of my assignments. I realised that there would be some differences between adults and children, but didn't really think about what these might be until I began my placement. I had a two-week induction with another student, and this included being given the agency recording policy that mainly covered things like confidentiality, service user access to files and procedures for setting passwords etc. There was also some general guidance on writing concisely and separating fact and opinion. I also had an opportunity during my induction to read other social workers' case recording for the cases that I was picking up. I was surprised at how much difference in style there was ... some people seemed to keep their recording very short and factual while others did include more professional opinion or evaluation. This was something that I brought up to discuss in my supervision, which was very helpful. I was also surprised that I did not seem to be expected to get my reports signed off or approved by my line manager, as I had done in the LAC team. The only form I did need approval for was the funding/resource release form, but in the LAC team there were a few reports like assessments and reviews that needed to be signed off on the system. The online assessment forms were very different too and seemed a bit repetitive to me, but I was told by other people in the team that they did a lot of cutting and pasting. I also found some of the assessment forms a bit odd as I was told to write them from the perspective of the service user, and this did muddle me up a bit as I wasn't sure whether to write 'I/me' or 'he/him'! I found it easiest to print off the forms and take them out to service users' homes where we could complete them long hand, and I then typed them up onto the system in the office. This was not something I had ever done in the LAC team, but I wondered if it might be useful in that context too.

Hayley

I was excited but really nervous about my first placement as it was my first real experience of working in a social work office. Before this I had worked as a volunteer in a homeless shelter and also observed for a week in a local authority nursery, but this was very different. My placement was in a short-term/duty children's team, so it was pretty full on! I was given lots of support though, and had a really excellent practice assessor who had supervised lots of students before me. She was very busy though, and although I had excellent supervision, it was pretty hard to talk to her between our meetings, so I got a fair bit of advice from other social workers in the team and also a third year student who was also on placement. I don't remember being given anything in writing about recording policy or anything like that as we were really expected to just get on with it a bit, which was a bit daunting. I found I took much too long writing up my contacts, but people in the team talked about getting very behind with recording and I didn't want that as it would have made me anxious. The forms and paperwork that were on the main server were OK to use, we just accessed them from the system and completed them in Word. Some of these were more like a checklist for guidance anyway, and we could write them up more how we thought appropriate. The recording and statutory assessment/review forms were all on the integrated system though, and we had to complete those online. Everyone said the system was a nightmare as it always crashed and you couldn't access it from home and some of the forms weren't very user-friendly. I did have the system crash on me a couple of times and had to start again, which was pretty annoying. I found the recording the hardest bit as the other forms were pretty clear about what information went where, but I was never sure how much detail to put into my recording and was worried about putting my own opinions down in case I made a mistake. My supervisor said recording was not only about getting the facts down though, and I should be using my professional judgement to record an evaluation and recommendations, but she did say she would help me with this.

Duncan and Hayley's experiences are different, but they illustrate some of the issues that students encounter when developing practice writing skills during practice placements, and these are discussed further in this chapter. These issues include where support for writing development comes from during placements, finding a way around the ICT systems and how these differ from agency to agency, and the challenge of finding time to record practice effectively when there are competing demands. Each student's experiences will be different, but the aim of this chapter is to outline some of the common features and challenges of writing during placement to enable students to prepare for writing effectively. Throughout this chapter it is helpful to keep in mind the discussion in Chapters One and Two of the audience, context and purpose of texts. Duncan discovered that moving between contexts challenged his assumptions about how to write, but also that gaining experience in a new context enabled him to reflect on his writing practice and to take this learning back to another context. Hayley was challenged by the need to include her own professional view in her recording, a requirement arising from the purpose of case recording being more than just documenting facts – they are also tools for reflection and planning.

Environment and conditions of writing

Writing in a social work context is very different from writing academic assignments at home, and so can be unexpected experience. Many social wok students will find themselves working in large open plan offices, perhaps hot desking with their colleagues. They will not have control of their environment as they would studying at home, and will need to write with telephone conversations going on around them and frequent interruptions in the form of colleagues asking for or sharing information, emails or incoming calls. The nature of much social work practice is that it is very difficult to preserve any uninterrupted periods of time for writing, and documents often have to be written in snatched moments between visits and meetings. In addition, social workers write a huge variety of documents which will all vary in their requirements, so switching between writing tasks may necessitate changes in writing style and, perhaps more significantly, changes between paper-based and different forms of electronic formats. One student in Rai and Lillis' study (2013) suggested:

> 'I don't think there is any preparation, the chaotic nature of our writing. I don't think you can prepare for that.' (quoted in Rai and Lillis, 2013: 8)

While another commented that:

> 'It could be a shock for someone newly in the field for the first time to experience … how much multi-tasking is involved in terms of your recording, the types of recording you're involved in … you are expected to record in so many different ways – how to write, and so many different styles. It takes time really to experience, you know for it to improve over a period of time.' (quoted in Rai and Lillis, 2013: 7)

Both of these students concluded that it would be very difficult for courses to prepare students for writing in practice; the reality was that they needed to learn through the experience of writing in real social work practice contexts. It is important, however, for students to be aware that writing will be a significant part of their role as social workers, that they will encounter different kinds of writing and that their writing will often be undertaken in challenging contexts. It is also the responsibility of university courses to ensure that there is support available to students in developing this essential skill, and that students know where this support should come from.

Paré and Le Maistre (2006) undertook research with student social workers writing during their practice learning placements in Canada. They suggest that students learn to write through observing and receiving guidance from more experienced social workers through which they learn the discourses and accepted ways of writing within a particular agency. Through this process of observation and informal feedback students became sufficiently familiar with accepted ways of writing, and so were gradually able to undertake independent writing. Paré and Le Maistre describe this process of learning as an 'apprenticeship' method in which guidance from more experienced colleagues was more significant than any more formal input from academic teaching. UK students in Rai and Lillis' study (2012, 2013) also reported little formal teaching of practice writing, with support being offered on an ad hoc basis by more experienced colleagues in practice.

Learning through 'doing' therefore seems to be a common approach to practice writing, although the benefits of making it a more explicit taught skill is addressed in Chapter Eight. One of the particular challenges for many students is that writing differs significantly from agency to agency as well as from document to document. It is not a safe assumption, therefore, that an approach to writing in practice can be fully transferred from one setting to another. Being aware of this alone can be helpful as students will be prepared to ask questions and seek support and guidance when they encounter new documents or move to a new setting. The following student from Rai and Lillis' study moved from a children's services team to a mental health team, and encountered significant differences in how she was expected to write:

> 'I never said to her [the student's practice assessor] how do you expect me to write up my case notes, I just automatically did them the way I do in children's services ... and then spoke to someone who's from the field who then explained, no this is what that means and this is what you should be looking at.' (quoted in Rai and Lillis, 2013: 7)

Rai and Lillis (2013) also argued that social workers received little direct support with their practice writing. Those students who were supported received help not from academic tutors but from experienced social workers, either on their practice placements or subsequently in professional practice. Such support included colleagues commenting on each other's writing and feedback from line managers but notably not from practice assessors. One student in this study commented that:

> 'There's nowhere on the degree programme or practice learning that covers the actual work that we do ... producing the report using the information we get from the children and families and writing the statutory report is required of us and it's nowhere in the degree or placement where they look at those reports.' (quoted in Rai and Lillis, 2013: 10)

Using supervision to develop skills

It is not uncommon for the development of writing skills to remain an implicit expectation during practice placements. Students can be expected to have developed writing skills as part of their academic study and to be able to transfer these to the practice setting. Certainly competence and confidence in academic writing skills provides an excellent grounding for developing practice writing skills, but support and guidance are still needed. The practice assessor may not be the only person on the placement who is able to provide this support, but as the person responsible for the overall learning experience and assessment during the placement, they have an important role to play. It is important for students to be clear about how they will be supported in developing their writing skills in a new agency, even if they have had a previous placement or worked in a social work agency. One approach for students moving into a new or indeed first practice setting is to have a clear plan to prepare themselves for adapting their writing skills based on the following questions that they can use with their practice assessor:

- Who in my agency will support me with my practice writing, and where will this be discussed?
- Is there an agency guidance or policy document on recording/report writing?
- Is there any agency-based training on recording/writing in practice that I can participate in?
- How will I be inducted to the use of the agency database and/or software systems?
- How will I be inducted to the use of agency pro formas and forms, such as those used for assessments and review reports?
- What, if any, administrative support is available to support me with my recording and archiving of recording?
- What is the agency policy on paper-based documents, and if the agency is paperless, how should paper documents that are received be archived?
- What are the agency procedures for involving service users in recording and access to files?

This is far from a definitive list, but these questions should enable students to begin a conversation about support for developing their writing skills in an agency with their practice assessor. Paré and Le Maistre (2006) suggest that it is the student's role not only to learn how writing is done in their agency, but also to learn how to challenge established ways of writing in order to enable organisations to respond and develop:

In order to keep current and dynamic, organizations depend on the careful induction of new members. In social work, as in many professions, that task is generally given to experienced practitioners who supervise and manage the gradual transformation of novices into effective professionals. The process is critical for both organizations and newcomers: the former require new practitioners who are capable of respecting and emulating current practice, but also able and willing to challenge and revise the way things are done; the latter require a quick, deep immersion in organizational life if they are to participate in and influence practice. (Paré and Le Maistre, 2006: 363)

This can be a big ask for inexperienced students, particularly where they lack confidence in their written skills. For some students, or newly qualified social workers, however, offering an insight from a different agency or as a newcomer to an agency can result in very positive debates about best practice in writing. (See Chapters Five, Six and Seven for more detailed discussion of writing in practice.)

Relationship between academic writing and practice writing

A common experience that students bring to their placements is the academic writing that they have undertaken. Although there are differences between academic and practice writing, there are also some important aspects of academic writing that are relevant. One of the purposes of academic writing is to train the writer to present their ideas clearly and succinctly, and this is equally important in practice. Readers need to be able to access information in social work recording and reports quickly and without risk of misunderstanding. Academic writing also schools the writer in developing a cogent argument supported with high quality, clearly referenced evidence, another important skill in practice writing, although the nature of both 'argument' and 'evidence' will differ. Practice writing does have a greater emphasis on 'factual' content, but it is also very important for recording and reports to include the professional view of the social worker, which must be substantiated by evidence. Social workers in Rai and Lillis' study (2013) identified a number of ways in which their academic writing supported the development of their practice writing. For example, writing essays enabled them to develop a more selective and concise writing style, while reflective assignments had direct parallels when writing case notes or reports. They also suggested that encountering different kinds of academic writing prepared them well for the range of texts that they would be expected to write in practice:

> 'Adaption is key… if there's something I've taken from [my social work programme], it is having that variety of writing skills and being able to use that in practice.' (quoted in Rai and Lillis, 2013: 9)

This study also identified that students were able to transfer learning from the academic to the practice context through developing the ability to focus on a particular point, from essay writing to report writing:

> 'I'm really sure that having to sit down and agonise over those essays has helped me but I can't identify or pinpoint exactly where. But it has to have helped me because I do all sorts of reports for work and although it's nowhere near like writing an essay I think the fact that you have to focus on a certain point and draw out the significance of it helps you somewhere.' (quoted in Rai and Lillis, 2013: 9)

Academic writing can also support non-writing practice skills. Social worker graduates in Rai and Lillis' study (2013) recognised the value of reflective writing as they were able to make links relatively easily between reflective writing and reflective practice:

> 'I suppose the reflective writing sort of helps you understand what reflective practice.… I think it was definitely valid and definitely gets you into the mind set of understanding what reflective practice is and kind of get comfortable I suppose at analysing your work and being able to say I didn't do that very well or, you know, I learned from these so yes it's definitely valid and worthwhile.' (quoted in Rai and Lillis, 2013: 6)

Graduate and employability skills

The QAA requires that all students gain graduate and employability skills during their programme of study. Graduate skills are those that are expected of all graduates, and include numeracy, literacy and ICT skills, but each subject also has more specific skills identified. The following extract is from the QAA benchmark statement for social work:

> As an applied subject at honours degree level, social work necessarily involves the development of skills that may be of value in many situations (for example, analytical thinking, building relationships,

working as a member of an organisation, intervention, evaluation and reflection). Some of these skills are specific to social work but many are also widely transferable. What helps to define the specific nature of these skills in a social work context are:

- the context in which they are applied and assessed (eg communication skills in practice with people with sensory impairments or assessment skills in an inter-professional setting)
- the relative weighting given to such skills within social work practice (eg, the central importance of problem-solving skills within complex human situations)
- the specific purpose of skill development (eg, the acquisition of research skills in order to build a repertoire of research-based practice)
- a requirement to integrate a range of skills (ie, not simply to demonstrate these in an isolated and incremental manner). (QAA, 2008a: 10)

Writing is closely aligned to a number of other skills such as communication, analytical thinking, reflection and evaluation, so it is helpful to think of the interrelated nature of skills and ways in which they can complement each other. Importantly, the benchmark statement emphasises the significance of *context* and *purpose*, a theme returned to throughout this book. As discussed above, there are frequently implicit expectations about how a particular document should be written, and these can vary considerably across contexts even when they are labelled as the same kind of text, such as an 'essay' or 'report'. As indicated by the QAA, an important element of graduate skills is the ability to think critically about how to adapt skills to the specific requirements, and this involves reading guidance, asking questions and seeking support until the writer is familiar with the task.

In addition to general graduate skills there has been an increasing requirement that universities are able to show that they are able to provide 'added value and employability' for graduates through the acquisition of skills valued by employers (QAA, 2013). Vocational qualifications such as social work have always emphasised skills that are relevant to the professional role, and these encompass communication, including academic and practice writing. One of the skills that has become increasingly significant in the workplace and is closely associated with practice writing is computer literacy.

Developing computer literacy skills for practice writing

Social work students in England, Scotland and Wales are required to acquire computing skills commensurate to the European Computer Driving Licence (ECDL), an internationally recognised standard of competence. This requirement was introduced due to the increasing importance of using technology in social work for recording and sharing information. Completion of the ECDL would enable social work students to competently use word processing programmes, store and organise files and use digital communication such as email. These are essential skills for social workers today, with the majority of practice writing being completed not only on computers but also often using agency databases and software systems designed to facilitate information sharing. There has been considerable controversy about the impact of moving towards electronic recording in social work, particularly with regards to the use of ICS that was introduced in 2007. According to Ince, reporting on behalf of the Social Work Task Force in 2010:

> A major part of the work of British social workers in children's departments is interacting with one of a number of initiations of an IT system known as the Integrated Children's System (ICS) that implements both record keeping and reporting functions. After a relatively short time in operation, the implementation of the system is now regarded as deficient and, disturbingly, there is a body of evidence to suggest that the impact of the implementation has all too often been antithetical to core social work values and ambitions. (Ince, 2010: 1)

ICS was largely discredited due to being based on a software system that was not fit for purpose, but although there have been considerable developments in the systems used, there has been no U-turn on the dominance of such data management systems in social work. The nature and impact of ICT systems on recording is explored in more detail in Chapter Six, but for the purposes of discussion here, it is sufficient to recognise that the acquisition of ICT skills is now an essential aspect of social work education and is integral to practice writing.

Many students on placement will encounter the use of digital technology in professional writing for the first time. Spending time talking to colleagues in the placement agency, as well as to practice assessors and supervisors, will be invaluable to understand the systems and their glitches. In most social work agencies the software systems remain imperfect and in development, in part due to resource constraints, so it is helpful to be forewarned of any problems or limitations in the systems used. Research undertaken by Shaw et al (2009: 621) reported that:

> There were serious problems over IT. Our users reported problems over complex logging-on procedures, entering data, finding data located on different screens, reading screens that flickered or were too small, crashing systems and remote access. Users maintained parallel paper files, could not scan in letters and reports and were unable to sign off documents or transfer data securely by electronic means.

There has been a move towards making these systems more user-friendly, for example, by reducing the emphasis on the over-use of restrictive fields in documents that focus on 'data capture' (Shaw et al, 2009: 624) rather than a developed narrative and analysis. The over-use of such inflexible fields was found to result in poor quality, often repetitive, information that did not focus well on the reality of service users' needs or experiences. It is important, however, that key factual information is collected and recorded carefully so the use of data fields has its place where there is the facility for professional discretion and the overall system is geared towards collecting information that supports high quality professional practice. As indicated above, the skills needed for working with digital technologies are not easily separated from the writing skills needed in order to work effectively with such systems (see Table 4.1).

Table 4.1: Using ICT and writing skills when using databases

ICT skill	Writing skill
Understand what a database is and how it is organised and operated	Collate and select appropriate information
Access the database using relevant security protocols	Write concisely and with clarity
View the database content in various modes	Write with an appropriate reader(s) in mind
Search and retrieve specific information from a database	Write both factual and evaluative content as appropriate
Enter, modify and delete records using specific fields	Support writing where required with evidence and cross-references

This division between 'ICT' and 'writing' skills is in reality an artificial one, and the range of skills needed to work effectively with databases would also include all the other professional social work skills such as analysis, reflection and use of values and knowledge. It is important, therefore, for students to acquire and apply their learning about ICT skills in the context of their practice and to continue to develop these skills within the specific context of their agency. One of the key supports for students during their induction and throughout their placement will be their practice assessor.

Practice portfolios

Portfolios can be used in different ways on specific courses, but one of the common uses within social work is to provide evidence of competence in practice based on an assessed practice placement. Such practice portfolios are generally comprised of a collection of documents, some of which are written by the student, but all of which are *compiled* by the student. This section considers compiling a specific form of practice portfolio, the style of writing required and also how portfolios are assessed. Whether assessing practice or a different aspect of the course, students will need to refer to the specific guidance on their own course.

Compiling a practice portfolio

> The portfolio ... offers students an opportunity to organize and present the work that they have completed in a comprehensive manner. In the process of doing this, they further develop and demonstrate core competencies, including skills in problem analysis, report preparation, and information dissemination; critical consciousness as applied to the formative and summative evaluation of their practice; and the formulation of their individual framework for professional social work practice, as well as its implications for their subsequent professional development. (Rosegrant Alvarez and Moxley, 2008: 93)

In its most basic form, a portfolio is simply a collection of documents, sometimes accompanied by a commentary. A commentary might just explain the purpose of the collection and the reason for including particular items including linking them to required assessment outcomes, but in some cases it also requires the author to provide some analytic or reflective discussion. The particular items to be included in the portfolio may be specifically designated within the assessment guidance, or selected by students; many portfolios are a combination of teacher-selected and student-selected work. The purpose of a social work practice portfolio is to demonstrate competence in practice through written evidence. As such, the writing itself could be argued not to be the focus for assessment, but as the conduit for evidence of competence, and in the context of an academic programme, the quality of the writing does form part of the overall assessment, even if implicitly. The quality of writing can also be considered to be an indication of the professional competence of the student as a prospective social worker.

Some documents within a portfolio may not be written by the student, and most will not be written in the form of an academic assignment. A typical social work portfolio will include:

- index or table linking contents to elements being assessed
- case summaries
- reflective commentary on practice and/or values
- practice assessor's report
- practice learning agreement
- copies of practice meetings (mid-way and final)
- service user feedback
- feedback on direct practice observation written by supervisor
- examples of practice writing
- testimony from colleagues.

Not every social work programme will require students to complete a practice portfolio, but where there is an alternative method of assessing practice, at least some of the above elements are likely to be required in some form or another. As this list illustrates, a portfolio is a complex document, and it requires as many skills in planning and coordination as it does in writing. Each element may require very different writing skills – some students may be given a pro forma or even a tick box table to complete while others will require an academic style very similar to an essay or reflective assignment. The diversity of requirements from programme to programme means that students will need to familiarise themselves with the regulations and guidance for their own programme, but there are some common questions that will help determine what each element should be like.

Confidentiality

All practice-related writing requires all information that might identify a service user to be removed or anonymised. This should normally go further than just changing or deleting the names of service users, family members and carers and should include, for example, anonymising the names of professionals and places such as hospitals or care homes. Attention to detail here is essential as careless failures to adequately address confidentiality will usually be treated as a breach of professional conduct, and work will not be passed without revisions being made. Very serious breaches may be considered to be evidence of such poor professional ethics that a student might not be given the opportunity to resubmit. Within digital documents anonymisation can be as easy as using 'find and replace', but more challenges are posed when photocopies or scans of original documents are used. Liquid paper and felt pens provide an imperfect solution as the original wording can usually be seen through the back of the paper, so if this method is used, then the papers need to be re-photocopied. Although apparently an administrative task, getting anonymisation right is vital, and demonstrates that the student social worker understands and appreciates the significance of service users' rights.

Referencing

Documents in portfolios may not need to include references to published texts. Documents that are examples of practice writing such as reports and emails, for example, will generally not include references. Very occasionally a formal report may make use of theory and include a reference or two, but this is not the norm for practice documents. Similarly, documents contributed by a third party (such as colleagues and service users) will not generally include any discussion or mention of theory. It is possible that practice assessors might refer to a theory, policy document or legislation, but as this is not written by the student, it is the assessor's responsibility to ensure that this is done correctly. The main area for careful attention to regulations will therefore be in reflective commentaries or similar texts that are written by the student and may or may not be required to include discussion of theory, policy or legislation and therefore need to be referenced. It is not uncommon for such a text to be included in portfolios as a method of assessing the student's ability to apply theoretical learning to examples of their practice. As in all academic writing, any texts that include mention of published sources must attribute these correctly with whichever referencing style is required by the specific university. This is normally, but not always, the Harvard method of referencing as used in this book.

Balancing description and analysis

Most documents written by students to be included in a portfolio will discuss specific examples of practice, with the exception of actual practice texts. This usually necessitates a degree of description to enable the reader to understand enough about the practice example in order to follow the related discussion. There is a risk that such descriptions become overly long and detailed, using up valuable words where there is a limit, and making it more difficult for the assessor to focus on the important 'discussion' element. Assessors generally have a significant amount of reading to do in a short period of time, and so it is important to make it as easy as possible for them to find relevant material to help them reach a judgement. It is important to remember that the assessor will not necessarily read all the elements of the portfolio. The evidence is included to support and substantiate the discussion, so although the assessor may read it to reassure them that it provides the evidence claimed by the student, they may also take this on trust. This means that the discussion or commentary is particularly important, as this is the only section that the assessor will definitely read fully.

When writing a portfolio a limited collection of carefully selected items is of much more value than a large number of items that are poorly organised and unfocused. Writing selectively and with clarity is an important skill that can be applied to many practice documents post-qualification, so this is a good opportunity to develop skills in this area. While it is important to get the descriptive element right, the analysis (where this is required) is where students' ability and learning will be assessed, so this is where most attention should be paid. Analysis here refers to providing an explanation drawing on evidence; critical analysis also involves providing discussion of different perspectives and evaluating their relative merits, again drawing on evidence. Analysis in social work education frequently also involves an element of reflection as the focus for analysis usually involves the student's own practice or practice that the student has observed. The following extract from a portfolio commentary illustrates the way in which description, reflection and analysis can be combined:

> [*Description*] Working with Mr B involved undertaking a full assessment of need and risk in partnership with both the service user and her daughter who was her main carer. I undertook this assessment over two visits as on the first occasion I was only able to meet with the service user as his daughter was not able to join us. [*Reflection*] On reflection I am aware that I should have planned my first visit more thoroughly as I was not aware until I arrived that it would be so important to have Mr B's daughter at the assessment meeting and the service user became quite confused and agitated during my visit. He was more relaxed on the second occasion when his daughter was present to help him understand the reason for my visit. [*Analysis*] Careful planning and consideration is a vital aspect of all social work practice and one of the key tasks in effective assessment is ensuring the involvement of key individuals such as family and carers. Social work assessments frequently take

place at a time of crisis in people's lives and it is important not to underestimate the way in which a visit which is routine for the social worker may be confusing and anxiety provoking for the service user. (NICE, 2012: 177)

This short extract illustrates the way in which a short description of an intervention can be used to illustrate the writer's ability to reflect on both strengths and areas of development in their practice, and to link this to analysis arising from reading of theory. Many portfolios will require a summary of work undertaken in practice that can be referred back to in reflective commentaries, which reduces the need for extensive description and repetition.

Reflection

Refection is the process of learning from experience, and it plays a significant role in social workers' learning and ongoing practice. Practitioners are expected to continually think critically about their practice and how it can be developed or improved. Reflection contained in portfolios generally focuses on learning from the practice that the student has been involved in and includes discussion of values, ethics and the theory underpinning practice. Most portfolios will require reflection in some form, either in a commentary section reflecting on learning and development, or elsewhere in the portfolio documents. Reflective writing is discussed above in Chapter Three, and reflective writing in portfolios is similar to reflective writing in assessed academic writing. The following questions are good starting points when reflecting on practice:

- Why did you act as you did?
- What informed your decision making?
- How did legislation/policy/theory inform your decision making?
- What is the relevance and significance of values and ethics to your decision making and action?
- What you have learned, and how has your practice developed or will it develop in the future?
- What are the service users'/carers' perspectives and wishes?

It is common for assessors to value students' ability to recognise where practice could be improved as part of the reflective process. It may seem odd in the context of an assessment to point out perceived weaknesses in one's own practice, but all practice should provide room for development, or at least undertaking it in a slightly different way next time with improved outcomes.

Paper versus digital portfolios

For paper portfolios, using colour coding, dividers and a well-organised index at the front of the portfolio can all be helpful, assuming they are permitted within the regulations of the specific programme. It is increasingly common, however, for programmes to require portfolios to be submitted digitally. Whether paper or digital, portfolios should be carefully planned to ensure that it is as clear as possible for the reader. E-portfolios are becoming increasingly common, and tools are now available online for structuring these documents. One example is PebblePad (see www.pebblelearning.co.uk/), which has been successfully used on social work programmes (Howe and Collins, 2010). E-portfolios have advantages over paper versions that can be bulky and therefore cumbersome and expensive to distribute to assessors. Digital documents are also easier to store and edit, but they do present some limitations for social work portfolios that need to include paper documents that would need to be scanned.

Making links with assessment criteria

As with academic assignments it is important to be very clear about the criteria against which writing is being assessed. Portfolios are no different, and may require the student compiling them to explicitly demonstrate how each item of evidence meets specific areas of the assessment criteria, such as the National Occupational Standards and, in England and Wales, the Professional Capability Framework (PCF).[1] Individual programmes may ask students to explicitly identify criteria that they are meeting, but these may also be embedded within more general assessment criteria of the programme. Either way, there should be clear guidance for the student about the criteria that are being used to assess the portfolio, and the requirements for cross-referencing these against items in the portfolio.

Less is more....

When compiling a portfolio, as with any piece of writing, it is important to think about the reader. Social work portfolios are sometimes assessed by both practitioners and academics, so there might be more than one reader, each with a slightly different focus. Both should be checking that the portfolio meets the assessment criteria, and will therefore want the layout to be logical and straightforward to follow. It can be very unhelpful for portfolios to be unnecessarily long, so guidance should be followed carefully on the number of pieces of evidence that are required. The contents of a portfolio should be guided by the inclusion of required numbers of items (such as direct observation reports), and then checking that all the assessment criteria have been met. It is unhelpful to add additional documents that duplicate these requirements as this makes the job of the reader/assessor more difficult. The inclusion of unnecessary duplicates of evidence can result in more important documents being hidden. The art of a good portfolio, therefore, is in careful planning to ensure that only the best and most relevant documents are included and then clearly signposted for the reader through a good indexing system.

Planning and organising a portfolio

It can be helpful to begin to collect items for a portfolio long before it is time to pull the final document together, and even at this early stage it is worth thinking about how to organise the portfolio. This is as true for a digital as a paper-based portfolio. At the beginning of a practice learning placement, for example, set up either hard copy or electronic folders, depending on how the portfolio needs to be submitted. Even for hard copy portfolios it is likely that many documents will be created digitally and can be stored as digital files. These folders can be used from day one to store items that might be useful for the final portfolio. Setting up folders and sub-folders is one way to become familiar with the portfolio requirements, but the purpose of this exercise is to create a dumping space where any items that might be needed later can be stored (see Figure 4.1). Making decisions about which items will make it to the final version comes much later.

Creating folders in which potentially useful documents can be deposited as they are written or received saves the chore of hunting for material closer to the deadline for submission. It also enables texts to be anonymised as they are collected, and for a coherent indexing system to be set up and used consistently. There is no single method for indexing, but it should be easy for both the person compiling the portfolio to use and for the reader to follow. The folders in Figure 4.2 have been labelled A, B and C; a simple indexing system could list items within each folder as A1, A2, A3; B1, B2, B3; C1, C2, C3 etc. Each document will need a heading containing the label, and then to be listed in a table of contents at the beginning of the portfolio or (during the process of collating document) in a separate file.

Although it is helpful to collect more documents than will be finally needed in the completed portfolio, it would also be unhelpful to anonymise

Figure 4.1: Organising a portfolio

Folder A:

Letters, emails and other communication

Folder B:

Direct observation reports and reflections

Folder C:

Service user and colleague testimonies

and save copies of every document written during a placement. Some selectivity is needed, particularly on placements where a large number of documents are created. When selecting which documents to save, think about whether they offer a good example of practice and whether they provide evidence of meeting one or more of the assessment criteria. Ideally each document will evidence more than one assessment criteria. When beginning to finalise the portfolio this method of organising and indexing documents can be used as the basis of a document in which all assessment criteria can be cross-referenced. Individual programmes may provide a template for such cross-referencing, and where this should always be used where available, but as an illustration, a cross-referencing document might look something like Table 4.2.

Figure 4.2: Organising documents in portfolio files

Folder A:

Letters, emails and other communication

Contents of Folder A:

A1, A2, A3

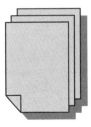

Document A2:

Letter to Housing Association about P family

Assessment criteria met:

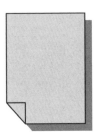

Folder A: Letters, emails and other communication

A1: Email to GP re J family

A2: Letter to Housing Association about P family

A3: Email to line manager re-funding request for P family

Table 4.2: Itemising evidence in a portfolio

Assessment criteria/PCF for end of first placement	Evidence	Reflective commentary
With guidance use a range of verbal, non-verbal and written methods of communication relevant to the placement	A2 A3 C2	
With guidance communicate information, advice, instruction and opinion so as to advocate, influence and persuade	A2 C3	

Writing style in portfolios

Chapter Three explored the ways in which writing requirements may vary across different kinds of assignments, such as essays and reflective tasks. This variation is even more pronounced in portfolios as by their nature they are compiled from documents written for different purposes and intended for different readers. Some documents will be written specifically for the purpose of assessment and will therefore be directed at the assessors of the portfolio, but not all of these will have been written by the student. Other documents will have been written independently of the portfolio but included as evidence. Such documents may have been written for a variety of readers including other social workers, professionals working in related agencies or service users. The style of writing will therefore differ significantly, but all documents should be written with the primary reader in mind, which may not be the assessors of the portfolio.

Descriptive or context-setting documents

Some programmes will require sections in the portfolio to be primarily descriptive in order to set the scene for the rest of the portfolio. This information is written by the student (or occasionally the supervisor), and should generally be succinct and clear without unnecessary detail. It has a very instrumental purpose in providing sufficient context for the reader to make sense of the other documents in the portfolio, but essentially it is about providing information only. Examples would be a description of the agency in which the placement took place or brief case summaries. There can be some overlap between such descriptive sections and reflective commentaries, discussed below, so it is important to be clear about the assessors' expectations.

Example

> My placement took place at Rooks Assessment Centre, an independent
> sector resource for children and young people in North Town. Rooks
> is located in an area of social deprivation and services the whole city,
> taking referrals from social services, education and health services. The
> centre is staffed by four social workers, one teacher, a psychologist and a
> play worker. Services offered include individual and family assessments,
> counselling, family work and group work.

Reflective commentary

Reflective commentaries are written by the student and have a more
instrumental role in assessment. The purpose of a reflective commentary is
to demonstrate understanding, insight and the ability to relate experience
to theoretical learning. It is frequently the reflective commentary that pulls
the portfolio together, making links between the learning that has been
achieved and the evidence presented. Description should be very limited
here, and the focus should be on the student's own thoughts and ideas, but
these should be clearly linked to either evidence in the portfolio, theory in
the form of references reading, or both. Individual programmes will vary in
their requirements for reflective commentaries, so it is important to be clear
about the guidance and requirements. For example, some programmes may
require a single, extended piece of reflective commentary, while others may
ask for several shorter pieces pertaining to specific items in the portfolio.
E-portfolios also encourage students to undertake reflection over a period
of time rather than at a single point towards the end of the placement
(Rosegrant Alvarez and Moxley, 2008: 89). Reflective commentaries have
much in common with reflective academic writing. They are both generally
written in the first person and can include very personal and potentially
emotive content.

Example

> While working with the G family I became aware of the importance of
> understanding the impact of social exclusion when supporting young
> people. Shepard discusses the role of social workers as advocates in
> encouraging service users to participate and develop more of a sense
> of citizenship (2006: 34). This reflects the role that I was able to play
> with Mr and Mrs G in supporting them to contact J's school and discuss

their concerns about bullying. In part as a result of this intervention Mrs J was able to join a local anti-bullying parents group that has developed her confidence and social support network.

Evaluative comment

The difference between an evaluative comment and a reflective commentary is that it is not written by the student. The most common form would be the report written by the assessor, but portfolios commonly also include testimony from other professionals able to comment on the student's practice and service users. This comment may be in the form of a report or a questionnaire. It can be helpful for students writing their reflective commentary to cross-reference to the evaluative comment so that it is easier for the reader/assessor to see where the evidence correlates. The primary source of evaluative comment is from the practice assessor who will be responsible for writing some form of report, and often also comments on direct observations of students' practice.

It is also common, however, for courses to require evidence in the form of comments on student practice from service users and other professionals the student has worked with. Gaining feedback from service users can be particularly sensitive and therefore requires some careful thought and planning. The first challenge is identifying a suitable service user to ask for feedback – the welfare of the service user must be a primary consideration that may exclude more vulnerable service users. Involvement with some service users may also be too conflictual at the time when comment is needed to enable them to provide a fair evaluation of the student's performance, so ideal subjects will be those with whom the student has been able to establish a cooperative, participatory relationship. Even when such a service user can be identified, they may need considerable support from either the student or a colleague to enable them to express and record their feedback, taking account of levels of literacy, understanding and the potential emotional impact of providing their views. Particular care is required not only because of the potential vulnerability of service users, but also due to the significance of honest service user feedback within the portfolio. A tokenistic or superficial approach to gaining feedback from service users is of little value, and the process of seeking it will often provide an important learning experience in itself.

Practice documents

These documents are included in a portfolio as evidence, but the primary purpose when they were written was as a tool for professional practice, not as a student assessment tool. They are real-life artefacts of practice, and the assessment purpose to which they are put in the portfolio should not have had any impact on how they were used. The student collating a portfolio should only turn to thinking about how they can be used to evidence their skills at the point of collation. While it is helpful to begin collecting potentially useful documents at the start of a placement (as discussed above), it is at the collation stage that careful decisions need to be made. Assessors do not want to be weighed down with huge portfolios containing duplicate examples of evidence, so it is important to follow the guidance on the individual programme. Where no such guidance is given, aim for no more than two items of evidence to support each learning outcome; it is usual for each item to evidence several learning outcomes. There is extensive discussion of writing practice documents in the chapters that follow.

Assessment of portfolios

It is normal for portfolios to be assessed jointly by academic tutors and practice assessors/supervisors, and on some programmes service users will also be involved in the judgement. This means that at least two people are likely to read each portfolio, and that a final decision will be reached or confirmed at a panel involving representatives of all of these groups. Undertaking a practice placement is a huge investment of time and resources for all involved, and it is therefore important that students are made aware of any concerns as early as possible so that they have an opportunity, with the support of their tutors and practice assessors, to address such concerns. Although the portfolio is more than a formality, it should not contain any surprises for anyone involved, and is primarily about documenting the evidence to confirm competence. The most significant item of evidence is likely to be the recommendation of the practice assessor, which is not written by the student, but the student does have a vital role in selecting and organising the documentary evidence to justify the recommendation of the assessor. In rare cases a panel may decide not to accept the recommendation of a practice assessor if the evidence provided does not support, or indeed contradicts, it.

Portfolios differ from most academic assignments therefore in that there is usually a 'pass/fail' result rather than a grade. This is because the purpose of a portfolio is generally to ascertain whether a student has achieved a sufficient level of competence as measured against specific practice-related criteria. Some programmes will provide qualitative feedback that will inform the student how well they have met each criterion, even though a grade is not given. Where not all of the required criteria have been met, students can be required to make corrections or to provide additional evidence prior to a final judgement being made; this is usually where the assessors are reasonably confident that the student has performed to the required standard in their placement, but the portfolio does not provide sufficient evidence or has not met all of the requirements.

Shortfalls can include the portfolios not being fully anonymised, word length or inclusion of all required elements. Where a portfolio is given an outright fail, this is likely to be either because the practice assessor has not been able to recommend that the placement is passed or, less frequently, the portfolio does not include the required elements, has very seriously breached confidentiality or in some other way, indicates to the assessors that the student does not meet the professional standards. This decision is not taken lightly, and it is rare that a student would fail a portfolio with no opportunity to make corrections if they had not already been made aware that there were concerns about the standard of their practice.

Conclusion

Students' first experience of writing in practice can be daunting, and this chapter has attempted to set the scene and offer some preparatory guidance. Every placement is different, however, as is the experience and skills that each student brings with them. It can sometimes be harder for students with considerable experience of working in a social work role to adapt to very different expectations than for those coming to practice for the first time, as it is easy to assume that there is more commonality of writing practices than exists in reality. For all students, therefore, it is important to make sure that support and guidance for writing is clearly on the agenda for supervision with practice assessors, and that time is allowed to become familiar with expectations and to develop skills. Writing is an integral and essential aspect of social work practice, and although it can seem like it takes time away from face-to-face work with service users, it also provides vital space for reflecting on and planning interventions as well as creating an audit trail and tool for inter-agency communication. Chapters Five, Six and Seven further develop discussion on writing in practice.

Note
[1] This was introduced in 2012, and identifies the capabilities against which social workers are assessed as they progress through their training and on through their careers.

5

Purposeful writing in professional practice

Introduction

This chapter builds on the discussion of social work practice, introduced in Chapter Four. Some of the challenges of writing in practice are explored alongside ways in which social workers can ensure that their writing is purposeful, or in other words, how the writing that they do can support and enhance best practice for service users. The chapter outlines the current issues and debates around sharing information, and the consequent complexity and diversity of written tasks required of social workers in practice, and how these vary between teams and services. The three concepts of audience, context and purpose, introduced in Chapters One and Two, are applied to writing in practice. In addition, the concept of 'voice' is introduced which can at times represent the individual worker's professional opinion, but at other times can represent the corporate view of the employer. The concept of audience is particularly challenging in professional writing, with some texts being written for multiple audiences including the courts, carers, children and colleagues. Using quotations and examples of texts, this chapter foregrounds the differences between practices in diverse professional settings in order to illustrate the significance of effective writing to the concepts of audience, context and purpose.

Writing here is not treated as merely creating accounts or records of social workers' interventions with service users, but as an intrinsic part of social work practice. In a recent study of the writing of social workers in children's services (Rai and Lillis, 2013), social workers were asked to identify how many different kinds of texts they were involved in writing over a five-week period. Participants identified a total of 22 different text types out of a total of 146 texts collected for analysis, including the following:

- case recording
- core assessment
- review of child protection conference
- placement information
- finance form
- record of observation

- email
- supervision plan letter/draft letter
- court statement
- text message
- core group meeting notes
- placement with parent agreement
- referral
- placement review
- transport request.

This list is not intended to be comprehensive, but illustrates the range of documents that social workers encounter and are required to either write or contribute to. Some of the variation identified here arises from the range of text types required within one agency, but it is also accounted for by the significant differences across services. For example, the requirements around case recording or assessment reports are very different in youth justice from long-term childcare teams in the study. Two of the most common (and perhaps challenging) document types are, broadly, 'case recording' and 'reports', and these are addressed in some detail in Chapters Six and Seven. In this chapter the focus is on some general principles of written communication in social work, and some of the less obvious forms that this takes, such as mobile phone texting, emails and writing for therapeutic purposes.

What is social work writing?

As discussed in Chapter Four, writing in social work practice can be a daunting experience for both students and newly qualified social workers. Whether beginning a practice placement or entering a new team as a qualified worker, there will almost certainly be new writing tasks or ways of undertaking familiar writing tasks. As Hayley and Duncan suggest in the case examples, there may be new software systems, new recording practices and also different expectations around support for and monitoring of recording and assessment reports. The nature and challenges of professional writing in social work practice have received very little attention from researchers to date, although there has been some investigation into professional writing in other fields. Work that does exist includes that of Rai and Lillis (2012, 2013) and White and her colleagues (2009; see also Broadhurst et al, 2010; Pithouse et al, 2011; Wastell and White, 2013). Rai and Lillis have explored case recording in adult services and professional writing in children's services while White's work has included research into risk and assessment, and also an analysis of the impact that new technologies have had on case recording.

Hall, Slembrouk and Sarangi (2006) also focus on social work in the UK, and provide an analysis of social work language, including writing – this work explores a range of examples of social work communication, and is primarily concerned with the way in which language used by social workers conveys and reflects their practice and interventions. Research has also been undertaken in Canada by Paré (Dias and Paré, 2000; Le Maistre and Paré, 2004; Le Maistre et al, 2006; Paré and Le Maistre, 2006; Morris and Featherstone, 2010) and in the US by Leon and Pepé (2010), which is relevant to practice in the UK. Both Leon and Pepé and Paré focus on the interface between academic and professional writing in social work and the ways in which students are prepared for writing in practice. They conclude that professional writing is not generally directly taught on social work programmes, and that most learning takes place once students are in practice. Leon and Pepé's work explores an initiative to introduce direct teaching of professional writing, and provides some interesting insights for social work educators (and is discussed further in Chapter Eight). Dias and Paré's research explores the ways in which students and newly qualified social workers learn how to write in the professional context. Drawing on Lavé and Wenger's concept of 'legitimate peripheral participation' (1991), Dias and Paré develop the concept of an 'apprenticeship' model of learning to write in the workplace (2000: 148). Legitimate peripheral participation is a process through which students or inexperienced practitioners begin to learn through experience by participating at the edges of the full social work role. As they become more experienced and competent, they participate increasingly fully through taking on more complex and central tasks, in this context, writing tasks. Dias and Paré therefore suggest that learning takes place during students' field placements through an informal and implicit apprenticeship where students are not directly or explicitly taught how to write, but as professional newcomers they develop a familiarity with accepted ways of writing. This process of apprenticeship enables students to learn how to write as social workers through reading texts written by experienced social workers, and then gradually writing more complex texts independently, with feedback from experienced colleagues (Le Maistre and Paré, 2004: 85). Both Leon and Pepé and Pare's studies suggest that writing has a very important role to play in the quality of social work as a core element of practice rather than merely as a tool to convey information:

'In producing professional documents, social workers do more than record: they select, arrange, interpret, imply, hypothesize, infer, catagorize, simplify, and on and on. They do not merely relay information, they create re-presentations. (Le Maistre and Paré, 2004: 83)

The concept of 're-presentations' implies that social work texts involve the writer undertaking social work practice *through* writing rather than the text being merely a representation of practice. In order to write even an apparently straightforward descriptive entry to a case record, the social worker needs to draw on a range of scholarly and professional skills. For example, the social worker will need to select appropriate content using their professional judgement of what information future readers will need. They will also need to present this information clearly and succinctly, making it clear what the source is of both factual information and views expressed. It could be argued that all texts therefore require social workers to use their knowledge and understanding of the professional task, and that texts become part of this practice rather than a record of it. Throughout the following three chapters, which focus on the professional context, writing is treated as an integral element of social work practice rather than as a *record* of practice. Social workers practice through writing as much, if not more, than they do through other forms of communication. Written communication is broader than case recording, as can be seen from the list of text types identified by Rai and Lillis (2013) above, and includes mobile phone texts, emails, handwritten notes and diagrams/drawings. What connects all of these written forms is the need for social workers to be purposeful and to use their professional judgement and skill in using them. The following sections explore the purposes of writing in social work.

Purposes of writing in social work practice

Writing takes many forms in social work practice and has numerous purposes, many of which apply to a single text. This section outlines some of the most important purposes, but it is not an exhaustive list. One of the skills that social workers will develop as they become more experienced is the ability to adapt their writing to new writing tasks.

Writing for communication

It could be argued that all social work writing has the purpose of communicating information, but the nature of this communication varies. Direct communication is a clear primary purpose of emails, letters and SMS texts between social workers and colleagues or service users. Such communications might be relatively short and factual, such as arranging a date to meet, or they might be for the purpose of sending another document, either as an attachment or as hard copy. Emails in particular may also be intended for more than one reader. Software programmes, such as ICS, were introduced principally to facilitate inter-agency communication as they were intended to allow core information to be accessible by professionals across social services, health and education. Reports and case recording also have a communication function in that they are tools to share information. They are written for a range of potentially unknown forthcoming (as well as current) recipients or readers, and may be used by future practitioners as a way to look back on accounts of previous interventions. The communication function of case recording is vital where cases are transferred to new workers or teams, opened as new cases but with a past history, or covered by another worker during periods of leave or sickness. Effective case notes should provide a clear account of previous interventions and risks to enable colleagues to pick up the key threads of a case quickly.

Just as in verbal communication, it is important to think about the reader's needs when communicating information, and this becomes much more complex when the readers are multiple, diverse and potentially unknown. It is possible, however, for the writer to think about the communicative function of a document and the likely groups of potential readers, such as court officials, professionals from the same and other organisations and other servicer users and carers. There can be important differences in the ways in which different kinds of texts are written and received by readers. One example of this is the difference between a letter and an email. Emails have become a more common form of communication than letters or telephone calls, but the speed at which an email can be written and sent can give rise to problems if care is not taken in thinking about the tone and style of writing needed for the specific task and audience. Care is also needed when forwarding or using the 'reply all' function that may inadvertently result in private or confidential information being shared with people for whom it was not intended. Outside of the informal communication contained in emails, there are very few documents that service users or their representatives do not have the right to read, or indeed an interest in. Where it is not possible to write in such a way as to be accessible for the service user concerned while also meeting the broader purpose of the document, thought is needed on the best way to assist service users in understanding documents written about them.

Writing for accountability

Accountability has traditionally been seen as one of the key purposes of case recording, although as this section illustrates, there are many purposes. Nonetheless, social workers are expected to be accountable for their decisions, actions and resources, and one way in which this is kept account of is through case recording. The accountability function of case recording and documentation on agency software systems became particularly prominent when new technology enabled agencies to keep track of performance indicators (PIs) through social work documentation. The measurement of PIs, such as the time in which assessments were completed, became a significant driver for the design and use of documentation, and was recognised to have become too dominant over effective outcomes in the final report of the Social Work Task Force (see Social Work Reform Board, 2010: 10). This audit function differs slightly from accountability in that it uses documentation to manage the performance of social workers, whereas the accountability function of recording provides evidence that social workers, as public servants, have acted ethically and in line with their legal responsibilities. Accountability and performance management will always play a role in recording in social work due to its openness and vulnerability to public scrutiny. As recognised by the Social Work Task Force, it is important however that this function of social work writing does not overshadow or hinder the provision of effective services.

Writing to support planning, assessment and decision making

One of the most important ways in which effective services are delivered through writing is through planning, assessment and decision making. Planning and decision making frequently take place through the process of written documents which pull together the evidence and views provided by the service user, their family and carers, colleagues and professionals from other agencies. The social worker often has the task of pulling together information from all of these sources into a single document, such as an assessment report. Based on information and recommendations from all of these sources, it is the responsibility of the social worker (with the support of senior colleagues) to make a recommendation. In some circumstances, decisions are finally made in meetings with the representation of key individuals, but the report written by the social worker is a key document in guiding the professional group towards their decision. Ultimately the purpose of an assessment report is to guide the decision-making process and the skill of the social worker in crafting the evidence, and the recommendation is central to the effectiveness of the report. Assessment and decision making not only applies to formal assessments – social workers should be using and expressing their professional opinion, where appropriate, in practice writing. This is particularly relevant in case recording, which should not only provide an account of what has happened, but also offer a judgement of the current situation and recommended next steps.

Writing for reflection

Social work education places a significant emphasis on teaching students to reflect on their practice, and this should continue into their professional lives. Writing can be a helpful tool to aid reflection, either privately in a journal, through the supervision process or where appropriate, in agency documentation. Reflection can be an unconscious outcome of the writing process, and this still has value, but consciously using writing to aid reflection can be a very useful skill. The professional judgements referred to above are a form of reflection and certainly call on the same skills, which include the ability to think critically about evidence, theory and the social workers' own actions in order to reach a conclusion.

Writing as therapy

Writing, or indeed drawing, for the purpose of therapy has played an important role in therapeutic practice with both children and adults for many years. Current statutory social work allows little time for therapeutic work, but there is still a place for using writing to help service users explore and express their feelings and wishes. This can be done in many ways, with individuals or groups. Some examples are:

- Life story work: scrapbooks compiled with children to help them understand their past.
- Genograms: diagrammatic representations of family relationships.
- Ecomaps: diagrammatic representations of an individual's interpersonal support network, showing positive, negative, weak and strong relationships.
- Life snakes/road: pictorial representation of a child's life journey based on a snake/road.
- Poems and stories.

As with reflective writing undertaken by social workers, these forms of writing can be useful in the context of a relationship to support service users of all ages to express themselves.

A conducive environment for writing

Social workers increasingly work in open plan offices where the use of hot desking means that they are working on shared computers. A typical working day will involve undertaking visits, attending meetings both on and off site and desk work. Time in the office does not afford uninterrupted periods for writing, as there will be interruptions from telephone calls, unplanned office visits and impromptu discussions with colleagues. Open plan offices are rarely peaceful places – colleagues will be talking both on the phone and to each other, there will be movement around the office and also the not uncommon distraction of crises that can draw a number of people into urgent action. Even when a day is set aside for writing, it is very difficult for social workers to create a space conducive to concentrating on complex writing tasks. Writers vary in the environment in which they would choose to settle to complex writing, but few would chose the relatively chaotic environment of an open plan social work office.

Distractions can also come in the form of emails and texts that can be difficult to ignore. It can be helpful for both management and individual social workers to recognise the need for at least some protected writing time to focus on complex tasks, and to create a space where interruptions can be avoided. This may be achieved by protecting both time and space for 'quiet writing', which involves identifying periods of the working week where a social worker has no visits or meetings and is provided with support to cover urgent phone calls. A protected 'space' should be one that each individual finds conducive to concentrating on writing; this might be at home or in an office space where there are fewer distractions. This might still be communal, as long as there are ground rules for this space to ensure that writers are not distracted by colleagues or the demands of competing tasks.

The challenge of protecting time and space to record is not straightforward, and is only likely to be effective with the support of direct and senior management as well as team members. O'Rourke (2010) undertook research on case recording with adult services social workers which identified that, although management claimed that the timely completion of recording was important, they did not support social workers in prioritising writing as an activity:

> Even when they [social workers] had arranged uninterrupted time to get on with a piece of work, they may then be seen by their manager as the most available person to deal with the unexpected emergency. This underlines the dilemma for many workers. While they tried to value recording as an activity and give it priority, they did not experience it as a priority as far as management was concerned. There was a sense of workers trying to protect precious recording time from all too frequent management incursions. (O'Rourke, 2010: 94)

This contradictory attitude to recording reflects the more general failure to recognise social work writing as a core professional task rather than an account of the 'real' work. This is not to suggest that face-to-face work with service users and other professionals is unimportant, but that writing can become hidden within the broad competency of 'communication' in social work training. Practice writing can also be minimised as an administrative task in social work practice. Where writing is subsumed into the classification of 'administration', there is a risk that the thinking, analysis, judgement forming and communication functions of writing are not acknowledged as essential elements of effective practice. Creating an environment conducive for social workers writing complex documents effectively, therefore, is a shared organisational as well as an individual responsibility.

Training and support

As discussed in Chapter Four, training and support for professional writing is at best patchy in social work, with a heavy reliance on the individual responsibility of students to transfer and apply the academic writing skills they have learned to practice writing. This is a demanding expectation, in part due to the differences between academic and practice writing, but also due to the diversity of texts that social workers need to write. Chapter Eight addresses teaching practice writing on qualifying programmes, but managers and training departments within social work agencies also have a very important role to play in supporting the continuing development of social workers' writing, and by association, practice skills. This support should begin during students' practice placements and continue on through their early career. Where writing skills are taught on qualifying programmes, the transition of learning from academic to practice settings is not straightforward, and support needs to continue through practice placements and on into early career development:

> Research indicates that students usually struggle making the transition from academic to workplace writing (Anson & Forsberg, 1990; Freedman & Adam, 1996; Winsor, 1996).... Scholars argue that individuals must be immersed in a discourse community to truly learn the epistemological, social, and generic characteristics of that community (Anson & Forsberg, 1990; Doheny-Farina, 1992; Freedman & Adam, 1996; Freedman et al, 1994; Winsor, 1996). According to Anson and Forsberg, "writing ... cannot be seen apart from its functions in various social, administrative, and managerial processes" (1990, p 203). (Shaver, 2011: 220)

Experienced workers will also need regular line management support with their writing and also periodic training when, for example, they change role or there are system or policy developments. O'Rourke's research indicates that more experienced writers become more critically reflective, recognising the complexities of writing for different readers and inconsistent writing styles, some using extended narratives while others used brief bullet points. What was lacking was consistent guidance from line managers who tended to model advice on their own writing style rather than any systematic approach to effective writing in the agency. Where feedback was given by managers, it focused on checking tick boxes were completed for the purposes of auditing PIs, or it was at the level of commenting on spelling and grammatical mistakes (O'Rourke, 2010: 84–7). Although these presentation issues are important (poor spelling or punctuation can change or confuse the meaning of texts), it is an easy target for managers to focus on and will not on its own support social workers in writing more effective practice texts. A focus on grammar and punctuation is also common by academics, and can be unhelpful in this context, as noted by Creme and Lea:

> In our experience academic staff focus too much on these particular concepts [grammar and punctuation] when they are talking about problems with writing, and students themselves often panic about their own feelings of insecurity in this area and lack of confidence writing in formal written English styles. (Creme and Lea, 2008: 157)

Support and training for practice writing needs to be multifaceted, starting with social workers beginning in their academic learning, but following through their practice learning and into professional practice. This means that practice assessors as well as line managers need to be clear about what constitutes effective practice writing, including the contradictions and challenges involved, and to have the resources and ability to provide the support and guidance that social workers need. At the time of writing, social work is again in a period of change, but one that might facilitate a shift from the recent preoccupation with PIs to more of a focus on autonomous, localised professional practice (Munro, 2011). This may shift the managerial focus away from measuring performance against targets, but will not necessarily assist managers in being any clearer about how to support staff with the challenges of writing more effectively. This will only come when practice writing is recognised as an integral part of social work practice that involves skills in communication, analysis and the application of ethical and value principles alongside literacy and IT skills.

There is further discussion of ways in which social work students can be best supported in developing their writing in Chapter Eight. Support for social workers once qualified becomes the responsibility of the employing agency, and should involve both training and ongoing line management support. In-house training, where received at all, has generally been procedural or focused on the mechanics of the systems used in recording. While familiarity with procedures and operating the systems is important, it will not on its own improve the effectiveness of practice writing, and therefore the quality of practice with service users. O'Rourke (2010) recommends that training on recording be included in qualifying social work programmes, but also offered to care managers in adult services who may not have a social work qualification. She recommends that training should help recording to be viewed as:

> Something that is inextricably entwined with professional practice, not simply an administrative task that relies solely on competent writing skills or familiarity with a particular IT system of set of forms. (O'Rourke, 2010: 170)

O'Rourke's research focused on adult services, but her comment is equally applicable to all areas of social work, White et al (2009), in their research into assessment of the use of the Common Assessment Framework (CAF) in children's services (discussed in Chapter Seven), comment that:

> Professionals are not "moral dopes", and their form-completion activity is affected by their own domain-specific knowledge, or lack thereof, and also by contingent strategic, interpersonal and situational factors. (White et al, 2009: 1214)

Social work practice is complex and social work writing reflects this; it requires the writer to draw on all of their professional knowledge and skills in crafting texts that provide a narrative through events, clear evaluations of risk and need and professional judgements. This involves the ability to write texts that are not only clear and accessible to a range of readers, but also persuasive and well argued. As noted by White et al, the writing undertaken by social workers is also written within an *interpersonal* and *situational* context.

Professional development needs will vary depending not only on the experience of the worker, but also on the context of each agency, but there are some areas that will be of relevance to most, and these include:

- policies and procedures
- confidentiality
- service user access to information/data protection
- multi-agency working/communication
- accountability and measurement of performance
- systems and mechanics
- induction to the use of electronic/paper records

- induction to specific software/forms used
- induction to line management 'sign off' procedures
- best practice guidance
- use of language
- awareness of audience
- coordinating many sources into one
- persuasive writing
- selecting, synthesising and using evidence
- expressing a professional opinion
- chronologies, story-telling and narrative
- recognition and use of power in writing.

The areas listed under *policies and procedures* and also *systems and mechanics* are generally the areas where training or guidance is currently available; finally and possibly more important area of best practice, could be overlooked. Managers and social workers need clear guidance on practice writing which engages with the intrinsic complexities and challenges involved, and the following discussion outlines some of the issues relating to best practice.

Best practice guidance

This section outlines eight areas of guidance that should support social workers in developing best practice through their writing.

Use of language

Social workers have a poor unhelpful reputation for their over-use of jargon (Seymour and Seymour, 2011: 122-3), and this might have developed for a number of reasons. Social work is a relatively new profession which has struggled to establish its status alongside older professions with more clearly defined theoretical foundations, such as medicine and law (Pierson, 2011: 60). Shared language is one way in which members identify themselves as part of a professional community, but it can also be used to claim status:

> The professional displays competence in using professional words and formulations in their speech and writing to justify their actions and assessments, to counter actual or potential criticism and display authority. (Hall et al, 2006: 17)

A common language, therefore, can be used to claim specialist knowledge and authority, but also to reinforce status and cohesion within a professional group. The less positive aspect of this 'insider' use of language is that it can exclude 'outsiders' including service users and sometimes other professionals. Language can also be used unhelpfully to mask meaning, either unintentionally or intentionally. O'Rourke identified in her research in adult services examples of social workers using 'implied messages':

> These implied messages involved the use of what was variously described as the "careful", "restrained" or "veiled" use of language, which suggests a dependence on shared codes. It raises the question as to whether these codes are peculiar to the profession, a particular authority or a specific team … "sometimes the facts are not comfortable to read, and knowing that it is going to be read by the service user … it can make it very difficult, you then have to try and work it differently, but another professional … they would understand what you're saying" (interviewee 2). (O'Rourke, 2010: 140)

This use of veiled language is not only ethically questionable, but also potentially very risky; as O'Rourke recognises, it is not clear how widely understood such coded language is, even within an agency. The chance of misinterpretation when other professionals and social workers from other teams and agencies need to read such documents seems, therefore, to be high. This strategic use of language is a good example of the way in which writing and practice are inextricably linked. The social workers in O'Rourke's study claim to use coded language not because they believe it to be good practice, but because they find it uncomfortable to put difficult, distressing or contentious information in writing that they know will be read by the service user. This suggests that either they are being less than honest with service users, or that they believe that they can communicate difficult information more effectively verbally, when in a face-to-face meeting, than in writing. Either way, this is an area of professional training and development that needs to be addressed. Social workers have a duty, for example, to share assessments with service users, and the knowledge of this will have an impact on how they write. O'Rouke's research suggested that social workers responded to anxieties about writing information that would upset or anger service users or by masking meaning in professional jargon:

> "People hide behind jargon to disguise what they're writing, I suppose when they're assessing, people who put down things in jargon, so that the client is not going to be able to understand" (interviewee 19). (O'Rourke, 2010: 141)

O'Rourke's research also suggested that sensitive information relevant to assessments was 'hidden' in case records rather than the main assessment document that had to be shared with service users, so they were less likely to read it. These strategies rely on the assumption that other professionals will be able to decode the jargon or search through extensive recoding to find essential information. While both strategies are ethically poor practice, 'hiding' information is potentially dangerous, as key risk factors may also lie hidden from colleagues, making future assessments unsafe. This example illustrates the ways in which both the language used and devious recording strategies can subvert good practice; neither would be addressed by training which only focused on spelling, grammar or the mechanisms of the recording system. These examples also illustrate the way in which writing and practice are deeply entwined; it is unhelpful to separate writing from practice as a discrete skill as one relies on the other. Practitioners elaborate strategies to avoid sharing sensitive information openly with service users, suggesting that there can be deeper concerns about their practice that relate to values and ethics, personal safety and essential principles about how to engage effectively in contexts of risk and conflict.

Careful use of language is also crucial when working across professional groups. Cleaver et al (2008) suggest that while some terms have a common meaning across professional groups (such as gender or date of birth), other seemingly obvious words can be understood very differently. They suggest that confusion may arise from the imprecise use of a word such as 'home' that might be variously interpreted as the birth parents' address or a current substitute care placement. Other misinterpretations can arise from profession-specific words, such as 'health surveillance', which has a very particular meaning for those with a medical background (Cleaver et al, 2008: 102).

Awareness of audience

The use of language, as discussed above, should be influenced by an awareness of the audience or reader. This is a familiar concept for social workers learning communication skills, particularly in relation to service users with additional needs and inter-agency working, but is less commonly addressed in relation to practice writing. All writers need to have some awareness of their audience, although how this happens varies depending on the purpose of the writing. A novelist, for example, may only need a fairly general, abstract idea about the potential group of readers they hope will read their book (Hunt and Sampson, 2006: 75), while a personal letter, text or email to a specific individual will be personalised for a particular person. The way in which a writer can personalise, whether for a general group or specific individual, includes the content, the words used and the style based on the level of formality. For many writers this adaptation for the reader is subconscious, but as professional writers, social workers need to take their audience seriously.

In social work the reader for many texts is not easy to visualise; for example, case records may have multiple potential audiences, each of whom may use the text for different purposes (Rai and Lillis, 2012). Other documents, such as court reports, have a clearer intended audience, but this can still be made up of multiple readers, some of whom will be primary and some secondary audiences. Taking a court report as an example, the primary reader for this document is 'the court'. The court is not an individual known to the writer, but as an audience the court has a clear purpose in reading the report, and the writer should have a sound understanding of the way in which they should write for this audience (there is further discussion of writing court reports in Chapter Seven). There are several 'secondary' readers of court reports, and these might include:

- the service user
- the service user's family
- solicitors representing both the agency and the service user
- independent advocates/guardian ad litem
- professionals from other agencies involved in working with the service user
- managers and colleagues from within the same agency.

It can be a risky strategy to make assumptions about the needs of the reader in abstract, but in broad terms this list could broadly be divided into 'lay' and 'professional' readers. Professional readers should have some familiarity with the language and issues involved in social work reports, and it should be possible to assume an adequate level of literacy. There are still risks involved in assuming too much familiarity with social work language or concepts (discussed above in relation to language use), so, even for an internal professional audience, it is good practice to avoid jargon and coded meanings. Similarly, although some service users will be more than familiar with many social work terms, having spent considerable amounts of time in the company of social workers, this cannot be taken for granted, and some terms may need to be explained, either within the documents or verbally, in a face-to-face interview.

Social workers also need to be very cautious about including information known to other professionals but that the service user or their family were not already aware of in reports – it is not good practice for a service user to discover new information for the first time in writing. Social workers should also be aware of the impact for a service user of reading a text that has been written for a specific purpose, for example, to gain access to a service or resources, and that therefore may emphasise risks or needs in a way that can be upsetting for the person concerned. Written documents should not mask or distort the truth, but all written information is partial and, as discussed below, is generally written to argue a particular case. This is not a problem as long as any potentially vulnerable readers are supported and prepared for reading sensitive information or judgements about themselves.

Multiple voices in writing

Social work writing is generally considered to be an individual activity, but many social work documents are the product of collaboration and the synthesis of contributions from many sources. Some may actually contain writing from more than one author (such as case records), but others are written by the social worker based on information (written or verbal) provided by other professionals or the service user and his or her family. Reports also frequently draw on documents written by the author, but for different purposes, such as previous assessments, case records or reviews. One of the skills of practice writing, therefore, is the ability to weave all of these sources of information together into a seamless document through using direct quotes from other written sources, paraphrasing or synthesising several texts into one.

This relates to the concept of 'voice', or the way in which the writer conveys their identity through writing; see, for example, Ivanič (1998: 96-7) and Lillis (2001: 45-6). In simple terms, 'voices' could refer to multiple writers contributing to one text, so in an assessment report the social worker may represent not only their own voice but also that of the child, the child's parents, the family GP and the child's teacher. It is also possible for one author to shift between several voices or elements of one voice, so the writer may in places draw on the following voices:

- *Personal voice:* this represents their identity as, for example, a Black, British, educated middle-class woman and mother. This is a complex and multifaceted identity with elements that may not be completely congruent with each other.
- *Professional voice:* this is the voice of the qualified, experienced social worker, drawing on the values and theoretical knowledge of their training.
- *Agency voice:* this may have many similarities with the professional voice, but there may be conflicts where the policies and practices of the agency are not completely congruent with the values or theoretical foundations of the social worker's professional training.

Shifting between voices is in many cases unconscious, but it can be helpful for writers to be more aware of when they are drawing on different voices. There are techniques that can be learned to effectively manage the voices of third parties, and experience in academic writing should offer some preparation. The two clearest examples of how this can be done are through either direct citations (direct speech) or reported/indirect speech. Making a shift from direct to indirect speech may make the text flow more effectively, but it does require the reader to think about changes needed to the pronouns, tenses, tense verbs (from first to third person singular), and place and time expressions. The following example illustrates some of the grammatical differences, underlined where there are changes:

- *Direct speech:* During the visit to Mrs Drake she said: "Toby is <u>my</u> mate, I like him and <u>I let</u> him mind the kids and they <u>are</u> fine. What <u>are you</u> worried about?"
- *Reported speech:* Mrs Drake informed me during the interview that Toby <u>was her</u> mate, she liked him and that <u>she lets</u> him mind the kids and they were fine. She asked me <u>what I</u> was worried about.

While it is common to change direct to indirect speech, it is not normally appropriate in a professional document to use the personal voice. The professional and agency voice may be used within one text, but this should be clearly indicated. Seymour and Seymour illustrate the frustration of a family court judge where the voices in a report are confused:

> 'I sometimes pick up a tension between the social worker and the line manager, who may well have a party line to follow. I wish that the actual social worker was able t state their own view even if they then go on to say that the party line is different.' (quoted in Seymour and Seymour, 2011: 104)

This is not an easy path to tread, but it is one that needs to be addressed directly through in-house training and supervision so that such tensions do not appear in court reports. Where taught and supported, skilful use of voices can be used to support the persuasive power of the texts.

Persuasive writing

Much of the writing that social workers do is rhetorical, or in other words, its purpose is to present an argument or to persuade its reader of a particular viewpoint. The need for rhetorical writing is clearer in reports than in case recording, but recording is also rhetorical in as far as the social workers select and present information based on their understanding of what is relevant and important at the time of writing. There are relatively few social work texts that contain only factual information, as the purpose of most documents is to provide a professional opinion based on evidence and expert knowledge. Even documents that appear to be factual are frequently rhetorical in as far as the writer has selected and presented information with the aim of persuading the reader. The following example is taken from a review assessment undertaken for a looked-after child. The two extracts are based on identical factual information, but each is presented to persuade the reader of a slightly different message:

> Emily had started to find her birth family contact more distressing but was able to manage the goodbye contact in a really positive way. She is aware that in saying goodbye she would not see her birth parents or siblings again, but she will need continued support around this as she matures and her understanding deepens. Other than this, her social development remains unchanged, she interacts very well with her peers and also adults, although can still be overly familiar with unknown adults, but this has reduced somewhat.

> Emily did not show any distress when she said goodbye to her birth family and it is unclear at her age how much she understands that she will not see her parents or siblings again. She has been informed that she would not see them again and said that she understood. Her social development is a concern and has not improved and her overly familiar behaviour with unknown adults continues and could place her at risk.

Slight re-wording of the second extract places more emphasis on the concerns about Emily's emotional development and uncertainty about her understanding of her situation. It illustrates the way, often unconsciously, that the writer embeds an argument for a particular perspective on factual information.

O'Rourke's study provides an example of adult care workers writing up assessments of need in such a way as to maximise the chances of gaining funding or services for a service user:

> Many workers described the experience of being under pressure to compete for scarce resources for their service users, and in those circumstances it was essential to make the strongest possible case. It was believed that any positive descriptions of what a service user was still able to do would only weaken the argument for funding. Eligibility is established by confirming someone's identity as a needy service user. Any information that might contradict that

designation would undermine the categorisation of the individual eligible. (O'Rourke, 2010: 129)

The reason for rhetorical writing might therefore be for making a case to secure funding or to persuade a court to make a protective order for a child based on the social worker's best judgement of risk, but both require the skills of persuasion. Such rhetorical or persuasive writing has much in common with writing academic essays in as far as both are based on making a case that includes:

- selection of information/evidence
- synthesis of information/evidence
- structuring information/evidence for building an argument
- critical analysis
- use of theory/knowledge to reach a conclusion/recommendation.

Skills around building a case or argument in an essay can be developed to practice writing, but this transfer is not straightforward and needs to involve developing a deeper understanding of the institutional context of writing (Shaver, 2011: 220), but recently qualified social workers in Rai and Lillis' research identified some links between their essay writing at university and report writing in practice:

> 'I'm really sure that having to sit down and agonise over those essays has helped me but I can't identify or pinpoint exactly where. But it has to have helped me because I do all sorts of reports for work and although it's nowhere near like writing an essay I think the fact that you have to focus on a certain point and draw out the significance of it helps you somewhere.' (quoted in Rai and Lillis, 2013: 9)

There is a training need, therefore, within the practice context (both during practice placement and on into qualified practice) to apply the skills learned in essay writing to rhetorical practice writing. There should be discussions with line managers about the purpose of writing, what the key messages are and the most effective way of convincing the reader through building a persuasive argument. This raises the need for training for line managers, who may also not be familiar with these techniques and lack confidence in supporting their staff. The two key elements that will make reports more persuasive are effective use of evidence and clearly expressing a professional opinion.

Selecting, synthesising and using evidence, and expressing a professional opinion

Much of what social workers write is based on a synthesis of information gathered from a wide variety of sources, including face-to-face meetings and written documents received from other sources. Whether writing a case record, assessment or report, the writing tasks involve selecting and ordering relevant material so that it meets the needs of the purpose of the document and the audience for whom it is written. The starting point for this process of selection and synthesis is the writer's professional opinion, as the evidence should be martialled in order to support the writer's analysis of the situation and consequent recommendation(s). So whatever the writing, the process looks something like Figure 5.1.

Figure 5.1: Using social work skills when preparing to write

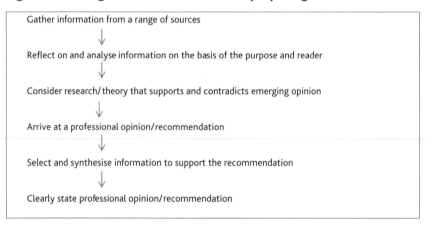

Gather information from a range of sources

↓

Reflect on and analyse information on the basis of the purpose and reader

↓

Consider research/theory that supports and contradicts emerging opinion

↓

Arrive at a professional opinion/recommendation

↓

Select and synthesise information to support the recommendation

↓

Clearly state professional opinion/recommendation

In reality this process is generally unconscious, an integral part of daily practice, but for more complex documents it can be helpful to step back and work through this process more consciously. In particular it can be helpful to be aware of the opinion/recommendation throughout drafting rather than at the end. This should help the writer to avoid including unnecessary information, and also to make sure that there is evidence to support the recommendation being made.

Such supporting evidence is primarily drawn from discussions or written documents from service users, their families and other professionals. Occasionally it will be appropriate to include evidence from research, particularly in court reports, but this should be done with caution and advice from the representing solicitor. Where research evidence is used it should be correctly referenced, and it is advisable to include a copy of the relevant article to the report along with any published materials that may not support the writer's view, and also to explain within the report the justification for the writer's opinion (Seymour and Seymour, 2011: 110). Careless use of research evidence can be unhelpful in court if the author of the report is not able to discuss it confidently in relation to recommendations made when cross-examined. Research evidence is not commonly used beyond court reports, but Rai and Lillis' study (2013) suggested that evidence based on theory should be used more extensively:

> 'I think the level of analysis is, is not there in our practice writing and very, very, very rarely do we, do I ever have the opportunity to use any kind of theory or evidence to illustrate my argument. I might write something about my suspected observations about why a child might be behaving in a particular way. You know, maybe kind of alluding to something like an attachment style. Very rarely within reports is it common for us to use, to kind of reference that in a way we might do with essays. Although that surprises me in some ways because I actually think we ought to be doing that.' (quoted in Rai and Lillis, 2013: 9-10)

Extending the use of theory in writing beyond court reports is an issue that can only be addressed locally within each sector and agency. There are pitfalls involved, but it could be a way to strengthen the reputation and quality of documents written by social workers.

Chronologies, story-telling and narrative

The term 'chronology' has both a specific and more general meaning in social work writing. Public law applications require a 'chronology' that is a list of key events which contains no analysis or opinion (Seymour and Seymour, 2011: 108). The purpose of this type of chronology is to brief the court, but this differs from chronologies used for the purpose of analysing case histories in, for example, assessments of risk. The benefit of completing chronologies as part of the assessment process is that it enables the social worker to see patterns of events over time that may have significance in relation to, for example, the assessment of risk, which is not evident from individual episodes. Wastell and White's research investigates the experience of social workers using an electronic recording system that incorporated a chronology tool. They suggest that this tool was ineffective as its rigid format did not enable social workers to use a chronology as a thinking and analytic tool:

The primary requirement of the social workers was the need to "make sense" of the case files. In particular, they need to produce summaries called "chronologies".…. The need for human judgement in producing these synopses is illustrated in the following dialogue:

> Facilitator: 'How about a question at the end of the DR1,[1] should this go into the chronology?'

> Social worker: 'It's not that simple – you build a chronology in terms of what you think is important about the case. If it's a drug use case, missing visits would be important. It's not a technical task, it requires a professional view. The automated chronologies are completely useless, I've seen them.' (Wastell and White, 2013: 4)

Wastell and White argue that the IT systems developed in children's services failed, partly due to the fact that they did not recognise the significance of story-telling or narratives in social work as part of the 'sense-making' process (Wastell and White, 2013: 6). A significant aspect of writing in social work, therefore, is constructing narratives of the lives of service users, not only to record events but also as an analytic tool that assists in interpreting complex chains of events in order to identify significant patterns of behaviour. This does not mean that social work writing should be long-winded or overly descriptive, but recording and documentation systems should not be driven by tick boxes and drop down menus which constrain the writer's freedom to construct a story based on their professional knowledge and understanding of events (Hall et al, 2010: 405-6).

Recognition and use of power in writing

The importance of teaching students about professional power is well recognised in social work education (see, for example, Scottish Executive, 2003: 31; HCPC, 2012: 8), but this learning should also be applied to writing. Writing has a particular power arising from its status in society and its ability to influence others:

> Because writing in general, but certain kinds of public writing in particular, is highly valued in our society, it confers status on (certain) writers. Because these writers have status they also have the power to influence other people, to get things done, and the more successful they become, the greater their status and the greater their power. (Clark and Ivanič, 1997: 36)

The social worker's role gives them enormous power, and this power is often enacted through written documents such as reports and assessments; the written recommendations of social workers can result in the provision or withholding of services, separation of children from their families and removal of freedoms. Social workers do not make such decisions alone, but they do play a key role in writing the documents that make recommendations to the court or within the agency to secure funding. Part of social work training involves teaching the skills of partnership and empowerment, but although these are enshrined in legislation as well as in the ethics of the profession, they are balanced against what is ultimately a powerful statutory role. In her research into assessment in children's services, Holland (2004) describes the way in which written agreements (or contracts) in child protection illustrate the tension between partnership working and power:

> Whilst clients, in theory, were invited to contribute to the making of the contact of agreement, the sameness of the contracts suggests that the social work agencies were the main driving force behind the content and form of the agreements…. Although such plans also contained the requirement that social work agencies should provide services, the clear message of such agreements is that the power remains with the social services department. (Holland, 2004: 124)

This example is based on a specific example from research, but is representative of the challenges of involving service users in written documents about them in an empowering way. Social workers are also subject to the authority of their employers and the courts, so there are times when they will also experience potential disempowerment. Holland suggests that child protection social workers can feel pressure to exercise power over service users, as they are ultimately answerable to the court for enacting plans (2004: 124). There are practical barriers created by documents being primarily electronic documents, which makes it more difficult to draft texts in service users' homes, but there are also the issues referred to above about social workers' discomfort in openly writing about sensitive issues when they will be shared with services users, and either 'hiding' them in documents that they are less likely to read, or masking meaning in coded language (O'Rourke, 2010: 139). Sensitive messages can have a greater impact when read in print than when conveyed in a conversation – there is no opportunity to mediate or justify or to use meta-communication to soften the message (meta-communication refers to the combination of non verbal communication that, often implicitly, support speech). This is another example of the very close relationship between writing skills and practice skills; managing professional power when writing is not only about finding the right wording, style or format, it is also about the broader communication skills and processes involved.

Information sharing

The failure to communicate effectively between agencies has been repeatedly identified as a contributory factor in several inquiries into child deaths (Gast and Patmore, 2012: 70). Much of this communication is in writing of some form, including shared electronic recording systems, emails (including attachment of other forms of document) and other documents shared electronically or with hard copy. Information is also shared through telephone messages that are then shared as written notes, and in some instances, by SMS texts. This plethora of written communication plays a vital role in social work practice, but is also a potential source of problems. The potential pitfalls of profession-specific language have been discussed above, as has the practice of writing in veiled meanings, both of which are unhelpful when communicating across agencies. There were efforts in the early 2000s to develop a 'common language' for professionals working with children in the hope of addressing some of the concerns raised in Lord Laming's report (2003). A common language project was set up by the Dartington Social Research Unit, which developed tools intended to improve interprofessional communication through research-based training (http://commonlanguage. org.uk/). White et al (2009) explored the potential benefits of a common language, and concluded that its contribution was limited. In some of the sites in their study a common language tool was no more than a 'bank of cant phrases' (White et al, 2009: 1214), which, they argued, was more problematic than negotiating the inevitable interpretation of language when used across professional groups.

Hall and Maharaj (2001) suggest that all texts are both embedded in and dependent on cultural practices, and so involve 'cultural translation'. By cultural translation, they are referring to the interpretation that the reader makes when reading a text based on their own experience and knowledge. Their use of the word 'cultural' is very broad, and suggests that the cultural (or social) context of each person is unique to that individual. Translations will differ more the greater the cultural differences there are between the individuals, whether these arise from differences in professional training or other aspects of identity such as gender, social class or cultural heritage. This makes all reading and writing of texts a form of translation which, as the reader translates based on their own cultural perspective, is always imperfect. The implication of this is that it is not only professional differences that can lead to imperfect communication of ideas, but also that communication is influenced by many other aspects of who the reader is. White et al suggest, in the context of the (now abandoned) CAF, that interprofessional communication *should* be interpretive and involve professional judgement as the alternative is a system through which '"knowledge" is increasingly transformed into "information" to enable electronic manipulation, transfer and storage' (White et al, 2009: 1213). Written communication, just as with spoken communication, remains a complex process that requires considerable professional skill, and this is true for communication with professionals and service users. Care is always needed in considering the perspective of the reader and the language that will be most effective for the purpose of a particular document, but there will also be times when it is necessary to talk about a document to make sure that, through dialogue, the meaning is effectively conveyed.

Conclusion

The aim of this chapter was to explore the nature of social work writing, the context in which it takes place and some of the challenges involved in writing effectively. While each individual document is written for a purpose and in a specific context, social work writing more broadly also takes place in the changing context of social work. Although still often implicit, in recent years writing has increasingly been foregrounded as an essential, if not always popular, aspect of effective practice. Discussion of writing has often been immersed within debates about the development of new technologies (Hall et al, 2010; Ince, 2010; Wastell and White, 2013), inter-agency communication (Laming, 2003; Cleaver et al, 2008; White et al, 2009), management scrutiny and concerns about the amount of direct contact time with service users (Broadhurst et al, 2010; Pithouse et al, 2011), but 'writing' has been within each of these debates.

Effective writing, whatever the current political or theoretical framing of the debate, relies on the writer having a good understanding of purpose, audience and context. Effective writers also need the time and support to develop and adapt their writing to the current tasks; being an effective academic writer provides many relevant skills, but it does not enable the writer new to a team to understand the nuances involved in institutional-specific writing practices. It also does not enable social workers to write complex documents intended for multiple readers and purposes, to compose them in chaotic and distracting environments. Writing in social work has increasingly involved large elements of information management, but this is not at the core of social work writing. Practice writing in social work is not a discrete, technical skill, but rather one element of social work practice; it sits alongside and relies on other key elements such as other forms of communication, analysis and the use of ethics.

There has been considerable focus here on training and professional development. Learning to write effectively in practice certainly begins with the practice-orientated academic writing undertaken by students during qualifying courses. It is unhelpful, however, to leave the responsibility for transferring this learning to the complex professional environment of the student on placement, or the newly qualified social worker. As discussed above, there are many areas involved in learning to write effectively, and each of these intersects with other areas of professional practice.

In-house training needs to go beyond inducting social workers to policies and systems, and should also include explicit discussion of writing in supervision and team meetings. Although writing in statutory social work will always contain an element of accountability, it is unhelpful for writing to be seen as primarily a tool for management scrutiny. Effective writing supports and contributes to effective practice; for example, a good report should aid good assessment and decision making. Wherever possible, service users of all ages should be actively involved in creating records about their lives and, where disagreement exists, this should be openly acknowledged rather than hidden from those who might object or challenge.

Writing is a very concrete form of communication compared with verbal communication that often only exists in the memories of those present until it is captured in writing through the perspective of the writer. All writing inevitably presents an incomplete and partial reflection of real events, but it is more helpful to acknowledge this than to present it as complete and unbiased. Bias here is used to suggest that the writer has a view; where this view is a professional one, it should be based on the theoretical understanding and ethical principles of social work training. In crude terms, a parent may fully believe that it is in their child's best interest to remain in their care while a social worker, based on their experience and knowledge, believes otherwise. Committing either view to paper does not make it 'right', but it does lend the view significant authority. One of the ethical responsibilities of social workers, therefore, it to recognise the power of writing and to ensure that, even when views differ, each is presented fairly. Ultimately it is the responsibility of social workers to use their skills of communication, analysis and judgement to craft texts that are ethical and that contribute to effective practice, but this responsibility does not sit alone with frontline social workers. Although writing is often an individual activity, it takes place in an institutional context, and so line managers, training departments, senior management and academic staff on qualifying programmes also have a responsibility for ensuring that social workers are well supported and trained. (The role of educators is returned to in Chapter Eight.')

Note
[1] DR1 is a short form recording details of a home visit.

Effective case recording

6

Lucy Rai, Theresa Lillis, Amanda Harrison and Guillermo Garcia-Maza

Recording is a key social work task and its centrality to the protection of children cannot be over-estimated. (Munro, 2011: 111)

Introduction

Case recording refers to the records that social workers keep of all contacts with service users. In this chapter an individual entry in a case record is referred to as a 'case note', and all other texts are referred to as 'documents' (these include a wide range of texts). The name given to such records varies from service to service, for example, care record, case note, case diary. Although the focus in this chapter is on case recording, in reality case records sit within a sequence or network of such documents. This network of related documents may be in many formats, both digital and paper-based, and can include:

- emails
- letters
- reports written by other agencies
- referrals
- assessments
- reviews
- funding applications
- court reports
- conference and meeting reports and minutes.

This is not a comprehensive list – the range and nature of documents depends on the service and agency; for example, they can be integrated into the main recording system, stored on a separate digital file or stored as hard copy in a paper file. Some key documents stored in digital files, such as assessments and reviews, are completed using pro formas or guidance designed or adopted by the agency. These might be standard nationally, such as paperwork used by the Youth Offending Service in England, or designed by independent agencies, such as the assessment documentation developed by the British Association for Adoption and Fostering (BAAF), the use of which has been implemented in many children's services in England and Wales. Whatever the system used, it is important to be aware of the close relationship between running case notes and key documents, which are generally completed periodically, such as assessments and reviews. Failure to recognise the connections between these documents could result in unnecessary repetition or, more seriously, the omission of key information or records of analysis and decision making. Any individual case note might draw on a range of such documents, but may also refer to specific documents. Some content may be duplicated, even copied between case notes and documents, while in some circumstances, there will be a cross-reference.

Figure 6.1 illustrates a typical network of documents surrounding a case note relating to a re-assessment in adult services. It shows the case note for this particular intervention nested within the service user's case record, which might span several years of interventions. From this case note (in reality there may be several case notes relating to the intervention over several days or weeks) there are connections to a range of documents that either inform the case note or are actions flowing from the case note:

- *Field notes:* these are unofficial aid memoirs competed by some social workers, often by hand during or just after a visit or discussion, which contain key information to be included in the case note and other documents flowing from the record.
- *Assessment report:* this intervention relates to an assessment, so the case note will make reference to actions relating to conducting the assessment, but will also be informed by the assessment report. For example, the case note may contain recommendations for next steps that flow directly from the assessment.
- *Funding application:* it is normal for additional paperwork to be competed in order to seek approval for funding for services. This may be more complex than a single document as it is common for service users' contributions to also be assessed.
- *Occupational health referral:* one of the next steps flowing from an assessment might be a referral for another service such as occupational health. The case note is likely to record the fact that an assessment has been made, as well as any further correspondence or discussions with professionals receiving the referral.
- *Emails:* in the course of any one intervention there are likely to be numerous emails sent and received by the social worker. These are not generally copied into case notes, but some agencies do require significant emails and even SMS texts to be copied across, and it would be common for the case note to record any important correspondence.

Figure 6.1: Network of documents surrounding case records

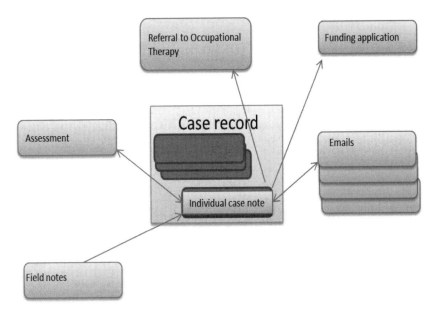

The case record, therefore, acts as a fulcrum for a diverse range of documents. *The Munro review of child protection: Interim report* (2011) suggests that recording has three functions, the first of which is to record:

> The activity undertaken and the information gathered by workers on an individual basis to assess, inform, understand, reflect and plan for individual children and families. The record should be the record for the child in the future that should illustrate what decisions were made and why. It should also clearly tell the child's story. Therefore, records should provide an accurate reflection of the child's experiences, history and observations. It also provides the evidence should the worker or agency be held to account for their work. (Munro, 2011: 58)

Munro's report also identifies the service planning, performance management and data collection functions of recording, but places particular emphasis on the important role of individual workers in the writing of case records. Although Munro is referring here to children's services, the essential functions are common to all service user groups. Her summary provides a reminder that case recording is not only about information gathering and accountability, but also that it provides a space for social workers to:

- understand and reflect
- assess and plan
- make and justify decisions based on evidence.

Recording is therefore not just a straightforward logging of information, but involves more complex writing than the term 'recording' seems to imply.

Increasingly case records are almost universally written, stored and accessed digitally using secure software systems which also allow information sharing between statutory agencies Prior to the introduction of digital storage, case records were kept in paper files, and individual records were either handwritten by the social worker or typed up by secretarial staff. The introduction of digital storage, together with changes in requirements around accountability and centralised quality assurance of services, has had a major impact on the nature of case recording. At the time of writing, case recording is yet again undergoing a period of change. Recent reviews of social work practice (Social Work Reform Board, 2010; Munro, 2011) and changes in government have called into question the effectiveness of current methods of measuring the quality of social work practice through key PIs, and also the fitness for purpose of digital systems developed to facilitate the recording, storing and sharing of information. These developments and debates have thrown a spotlight on professional social work writing and its close association with the quality of practice. Some of these changes are outlined in this chapter, and in doing so, some of the challenges involved in effective case recording are highlighted, as well as offering some suggestions for developing best practice in case recording, drawing on illustrations from practice.

Historical development: the shift towards digitally mediated systems

Social work recording 20 years ago was a very different activity from what it is today. Social workers did not have access to computers and recorded information, either by hand or using Dictaphones, some of which would have been typed up for them. Virtually no information was kept on digital databases. Information was held within a specific service, making sharing across professional boundaries a time-consuming and sometimes difficult issue. The move from paper to digital files in social work has been driven by both the availability of new technologies and concerns about how well information is shared between agencies, concerns that have attracted particular attention with regard to children's services. This move was also underpinned, particularly in England, by an interest in using recording as a tool for performance management and audit.

This concern in part led to the development of ICS, a national digital method of recording and undertaking assessment used in England and Wales until extensive criticism of it led to a de-commitment from a nationally uniform system, as discussed further below (Ince, 2010; Wastell and White, 2013). Scotland and Northern Ireland did not follow suit in adopting a uniform system, but allowed the development of new technologies to be on a more piecemeal, localised basis. From 2006 in Scotland the sharing of digital data was encouraged through the setting up of 14 data sharing partnerships (DSPs) across services for children and adults. In 2007 this was taken further with the introduction of eCare, a system for securely sharing information between agencies and raising child protection alerts. Digital recording in healthcare was introduced in Northern Ireland in 2012, but this does not as yet apply to social care. The trend therefore is broadly towards more extensive use of digital technologies in social work recording, with many agencies attempting to establish a paperless working environment.

Although digital recording has developed across the UK, developments in England provide a particularly interesting example of the way in which concerns about social work practice generally have influenced the ways in which professional writing has changed. The introduction of ICS in England and Wales marked a significant shift in the way in which social workers recorded their interventions with service users. It was introduced in 2007 in England (2006 in Wales), and was intended to provide a digital record of social workers' (and other childcare professionals') involvement with children. The Department for Children, Schools and Families described it as:

> A conceptual framework, a method of practice and a business process to support practitioners and managers in undertaking the key tasks of assessment, planning, intervention and review. (DCSF, 2008, in Hall et al, 2010)

The ICS was therefore much more than a digitally mediated system for making case records. It was also a system of assessment, a decision-making tool where managers reviewed and approved (or otherwise) decisions, and also a tool for audit and performance management. One of the features of performance management was that the system imposed time limits on specific activities, such as the length of time in which assessments should be completed. The resulting highly complex piece of software was based around a mixture of exemplar paperwork to be uploaded and prescriptive 'tick box' style forms mapped against time-limited targets. In her review of social work, Eileen Munro commented that:

> Many social workers ... reported that their locally procured computer systems were substantial obstacles to good practice. (Munro, 2011: 111)

Overall the system attracted considerable criticism due to the fact that information collected was fragmented, and content added by users of the system was restricted by the predetermined boxes that only allowed a certain number of characters. In addition, entering data to the system, and consequently the completion of key tasks such as assessments, was driven by externally imposed timescales that did not take account of individual family circumstances (Hall et al, 2010). Shaw et al comment on ICS, suggesting that:

> It is a superhuman task to ensure that social workers complete all this information comprehensively, accurately and according to the same definitions or that families understand the information held on them. So, social workers skip questions and answer others based on varying assumptions. There are costs in the lack of accuracy, missing data, time and family engagement. (Shaw et al, 2009: 623)

The Social Work Task Force reported in 2010, and acknowledged the growing dissatisfaction about ICS that arose in part due to concerns and criticism about the amount of time social workers were spending in front of computer screens, and the impact of building in monitoring of work against national PIs into recording practices (White et al, 2009). Although ICS was primarily introduced as a response to the recommendations of the Laming report (2003), which identified interprofessional communication as a key area for development in children's services in England, it had the effect of fragmenting information on families, rather than viewing them as a system, and disrupting the story or narrative of events which made assessment more difficult. There was also concern that it was overly driven by the political desire to monitor performance, and that the time being spent by social workers on ICS was taking them away from direct contact with families. A further important criticism of ICS was that it fragmented families. Research undertaken by Hall et al:

> Shows the struggles faced by practitioners who try to manage systems which separate children from their familial, social and relational contexts. As a consequence, we suggest, the work has become increasingly fragmented and less mindful of children's life within families. (Hall et al, 2010: 393)

The disjointed nature of case records therefore made it very difficult for practitioners to map family connections across individual members' case records, that enable a systemic approach, noted by Munro to be vital to effective child protection (Munro, 2011: 111).

As a consequence of these concerns, the Social Work Task Force, in consultation with the Department for Children, Schools and Families, recommended reform of the system to simplify the national specifications for ICS, and to clarify the local authority's responsibility for ensuring that systems support effective professional practice (Social Work Reform Board, 2009: 10). Eileen Munro, in her review, went further, offering three principles to underpin the development of ICT systems:

> Recording systems for child and family social work should meet the critical need to maintain a systemic and family narrative, which describes all the events associated with the interaction between a social worker, other professionals and the child and their family
>
> ICT systems for child and family social work should be able to adapt with relative ease to changes in local child protection system needs, operational structures and data performance requirements
>
> The analysis of requirements for ICT-based systems for child and family social work should primarily be based on a human-centred analysis of what is required by frontline workers; any clashes between the functional requirements that have been identified by this process and those associated with management information reporting should normally be resolved in terms of the former. (Munro, 2011: 111)

The developments and debates surrounding ICS discussed above relate to children's services in England, but given the general move towards the use of IT-mediated recording systems, the issues raised are of direct relevance to all services and national contexts. In the current development of such systems, there continue to be problems, some of which are discussed below, but there is also a greater awareness of some of the pitfalls in earlier systems, such as ICS, and there are ongoing attempts at improving these.

Furthermore, there is a strong awareness that the use of digitally mediated systems inevitably changes the way in which recording is done and how documents interconnect. Case recording in a digitally mediated system, for example, does not refer to a single document but a network of related documents linked to a service user. This network also commonly links documents relating to specific service users with family members and to other professionals involved in providing services for them. A key challenge within these newly reconfigured systems is to ensure that they facilitate (rather than constrain) frontline social work practice in ways that can best serve the needs of service users, and that enable social workers to carry out the kind of recording that is essential to meet this goal. One of

Munro's concerns about writing practices emerging from the use of digital recording systems was that the dominance of tick box formats restricted or even prevented the use of story-telling, or narrative, in case recording (Munro, 2011).

Case recording as narrative

One of the criticisms of ICS in England and Wales was that by breaking case recording into discrete chunks of information, the requirements of the digital system disrupted the story-telling or narrative function of social work writing, thereby losing both meaning and continuity. In the past, in paper-based practices, narrative was used extensively with 'story-telling' in some form, underpinning much social work practice (White and Featherstone, 2005); however, this aspect of social work communication seems to be largely missing in digitally mediated systems. White et al (2009) suggest that case recording using the digital-based Common Assessment Framework (CAF):

> May disrupt the traditionally storied child welfare professional accounts, in which facts and observations/perceptions are assembled in a temporal sequence typical of the narrative format. Professional texts have been found to be arranged in terms of story structures that link characters and events and address specific audiences. (White et al, 2009: 1200)

The use of menus, boxes and fragmented associated documents risks parts of the story being lost or hidden in repetitive or irrelevant information. White et al (2009) argue that social work recording is chronology and narrative-based, and that the use of forms such as those introduced by the *Framework for assessment* and ICS are in antithesis to the everyday experience of the social worker, where narrative plays a very important part.

One illustration of this is the lack of the systematic inclusion of case summaries that provide an opportunity for social workers, at a point of pause or transfer, to create a summary of 'the story so far' for the reader. Such summaries may also be selective and lack comprehensive detail, but they are based on key information at a particular point, which is based on the professional judgement of a specific worker. Broadhurst et al (2010) undertook research into the nature of case recording in ICS and commented on:

> The scantness of the information, compounded by the difficulties of piecing together fragments of narrative scattered across multiple

boxes, made it very difficult for the reader to glean a holistic picture of the child and his/her family. (Broadhurst et al, 2010: 363)

Even where information is not missing, it can be very difficult for the reader to build a narrative of events or, for example, a rich picture of a child within a family where information is so disjointed. The loss of narrative in case recording was not entirely unintended, and arose as a consequence of a move to more prescriptive recording systems. Of course narrative accounts in the past were not without their limitations – criticisms had been made of social work recording that it was too rambling and lacked focus and clarity, and this was a major driver behind the introduction of the *Framework for assessment* records in England, which pre-dated ICS, and was intended to introduce a more analytic approach through prescribed information fields (Cleaver and Walker, 2004). A specialist report (commissioned for the Social Work Task Force) investigated the computer systems developed in social work, and concluded that the development of software systems that have a heavy 'management reporting' function 'virtually eliminates' 'narrative forming' elements, knowledge, observations and experience of case recording (Ince, 2010: 15). Ince suggests that:

> The narrative part of an ICS form had to be shoe-horned into a database more used to dealing with fixed length text: those found in industrial applications such as banking. It also betrays a misunderstanding of the day-to-day work of a social worker. (Ince, 2010: 10)

While rambling, unfocused linear accounts are clearly not helpful as a tool for analysis and decision making, the imposition of overly structured data entry systems appears to have taken case recording too far away from the important narrative function of social work recording. One question is whether digitally mediated systems inevitably fragment the narrative aspect of case recording, or whether systems can be devised so that this important function can be supported. It is important that case records do tell a coherent story without the reader needing to move between fragmented windows or documents. This fragmentation arises from the design of the software itself, and also from the competing demands of gathering data to monitor performance and as a practice tool. The creation of effective case notes, therefore, is a shared responsibility between the agency that commissions software and designs the policies for recording and the individual social worker. The most skilled writer will be unable to craft effective texts within the constraints of prescribed documentation, be it paper or digitally based, which do not facilitate the core functions identified by Munro and cited above. Narrative is an important aspect of effective recording, but so also is the ability to synthesise information and to present summaries and chronologies that enable practitioners to reflect, assess, plan, make and justify decisions.

Ongoing challenges for social workers writing effective case records

The introduction of technology to social work recording has both created difficulties and put a spotlight on this important area of social work practice, which has enabled researchers to think about the inherent challenges involved in case recording more generally. Case recording, as indicated above, is both a running account of events and a tool for analysis and decision making. Balancing these functions is not easy for the writer, and where recording has also become a tool for audit and performance management, its effectiveness in practice has become threatened. The remaining part of this chapter focuses on the key elements of writing case records that should be applicable in developing systems of data creating and storage that will inevitably vary from service to service. The first of these is the role of fact and opinion.

Fact and opinion

Historically, one of the key elements of good practice in case recording has been the inclusion and demarcation of 'fact' and 'opinion'. Students training in the 1980s were drilled in the importance of focusing on the facts, and where 'professional opinion' was included, it had to be clearly marked as such. Both of these elements remain important in case recording. Factual information must be substantiated with evidence, and be objective and relevant. Opinion refers to the professional opinion of the social worker, and the difference between these elements should always be clear. Social workers may also find that expectations of where and how they express such views varies depending on the service they are working in or the context of the recording, so this is an area which is important to explore at the point of induction and as an ongoing issue in supervision.

Professional opinion should not, however, be confused with personal opinion. As trained and qualified professionals social workers are expected to make judgements based on their professional knowledge, observations and judgement. It may also be relevant for such professional opinions to be backed up by evidence that provides justification for opinions expressed, decisions made and next steps that may be recommended. Providing a professional opinion can be daunting as it requires social workers to commit on record a judgement based on their training and experience in the knowledge that they may in the future be called on to justify their recommendation. Case recording can be drawn on for evidence in court, and also as a key source of evidence where the actions of the individual worker or the agency are called to account.

It would be an oversimplification to suggest that case notes contain only reported facts and the professional opinion of the social worker. In reality, case notes can include information from many sources, and may include any of the following:

- observations of the social worker;
- professional opinion of the social worker;
- verbal accounts given by the service user and reported by the social worker (these may be factual or opinion);
- verbal accounts given by a carer or family member and reported by the social worker (these may be factual or opinion);
- verbal or written accounts given by another professional and reported by the social worker (these may be factual or opinion).

Where there are potentially so many voices in a case record, it is important for the social worker writing the text to be very clear about whose views they are reporting. This is illustrated in the following short extract from a piece of case recording taken from an adult services context:

> Jerry [service user's son] and Adam [service user] are managing really well and Adam is happy to be at home. The lunch time and tea time calls are not really required during the week as Jerry is managing to transfer Adam to the toilet and change his pad.

In this extract there are several statements where the writer is not explicit about whose views are being reported. This can make the case record misleading, both as a tool for decision making, and as evidence of the social worker's practice. Here is the same extract with the sections that have an unclear attribution of view underlined:

> Jerry [service user's son] and Adam [service user] <u>are managing really well</u>.

Is this the reported view of both Adam and Jerry? Do they agree with each other? Or is it the view of the social worker, in which case, is it based on a discussion with the family or on the social worker's own observations?

> <u>Adam is happy to be at home.</u>

Again, is this the reported view of both Adam and Jerry? Do they agree with each other?

> <u>The lunch time and tea time calls are not really required during the week</u> as <u>Jerry is managing to transfer Adam to the toilet and change his pad.</u>

Is this Jerry's reported view and does Adam agree? Or is it the view of the social worker, in which case, is it based on a discussion with the family or on the social worker's own observations? If this is the professional opinion of the social worker, what is the evidence to support it? This may appear a relatively uncomplicated extract of case recording, but the lack of clarity could create significant problems if concerns or disputes arise in the future, or even in the context of a handover to a new worker. The text could make more explicit whose views are being represented, as indicated by the text in brackets:

> [It is my view that] Jerry and Adam are managing really well. [There have been no calls to the emergency duty team, Adam's GP reports that he has gained weight and is in better health and both appeared more relaxed on my previous two visits] and Adam [says that he is] happy to be at home. [I have confirmed with Adam and Jerry that they no longer want the] lunch time and tea time calls [and it is my view that the risk has dropped sufficiently to mean that they] are no longer required during the week. [This is because I have observed that Jerry is managing to transfer Adam to the toilet, change his pad and prepare meals so they now only need support at each the end of the day to assist with getting out and into bed.]

In this example, additional detail clarifies whose views are expressed, and additional evidence is provided as to how the social worker arrived at their professional opinion. But of course it is not always the case that adding details is what is required; longer does not necessarily mean better. The information included should be concise and relevant to enable the reader to access key information quickly, as identified by the following example from the WiSWAP Project in which Nicky, a social worker in a long-term children's team, talks about writing concisely:

> 'Well I think the audience needs to get the key points in a very quick and easily accessible way, and while the detail is important, if you could write it in a slightly more condensed, style, manner, then it would kind of easier to pick out the key points. And that is difficult....'

One of the skills involved in effectively using fact and opinion, therefore, is getting the balance right between enough detail for a case note to accurately reflect events, perspectives and supporting evidence, without making it inaccessible through too much information. Despite the challenges and complexity of balancing facts and professional opinion, these core components of case recording are both routine (in that it is carried out day in, day out) and undertaken under significant time pressures in which it may not seem like the most pressing task when compared with face-to-face contact with service users or other professionals.

Evidence and the use of theory

Swain (2009) illustrates that although it is important to include professional opinion in case notes, they will be significantly more authoritative where relevant evidence is provided. Evidence can be very simple; for example, it may be sufficient to just provide a clear description of what was observed or said during a visit to a service user:

> There must be evidence (facts, observations and the like) to substantiate conclusions although in some instances it may be the facts themselves that may be of greater worth (for court purposes) than the conclusion. Thus the file note that "Mr Jones was drunk at the interview" will be of less value for evidentiary purposes than the note "When Mr Jones arrived at the interview he was unsteady on his feet, slurred his words and said that he couldn't remember where he had been since the night before." In such a situation the social worker may not need to add the conclusion (regarding drunkenness) as any court would reach the same conclusion from the observations noted by the social worker – the facts will speak for themselves. (Swain, 2009: 72)

The ability to both make and record relevant observations is a central social work skill, as discussed in Chapter One (HCPC, 2012), and its value should not be underestimated. There are also times when it will be important to explicitly draw on and apply theory to observations to inform professional judgements made, although the explicit inclusion of theory to support an observation or professional opinion is not routine in writing case notes. An example would be where a professional judgement was made about recommending the removal of a child, based on the social worker's understanding of child development. This would underpin the recommendations made, but would be unlikely to be cited directly in a case note. More commonly, therefore, the knowledge base and theory of social work will inform observations (and therefore recording). A social worker should therefore observe and record the significance of behaviour or actions that are inconsistent with expectations based on normal development. The following illustration of a case note is based on a mother and her sons, aged 18 months (Ryan) and 3 years (Mark).

> I visited Kathryn at home and saw Ryan and Mark. I observed Ryan standing and moving around the room more confidently although he was still holding on to the furniture at times and occasionally 'bottom shuffles'. I talked to Kathryn about the concerns raised at the review meeting at the nursery about Mark's language and social development and also the need to encourage him to develop more independence with his toileting. Kathryn said that she is not worried about Mark or Ryan's development as she was also a late developer and she doesn't find the nappies a problem. Mark was curled up on the sofa wearing a nappy and t-shirt only playing with a plastic action figure. He was making some verbalisation but the words were indistinct and he did not make eye contact with me. I informed Kathryn that based on my observations of both children and the report from the nursery on Mark I remain concerned about their development.

The concerns about the development of these children are based on a theoretical knowledge of child development, and also arise from a wider knowledge of the family based on previous contacts and information from other services (the nursery). In a case note a social worker would not normally be expected to include evidence in the form of a reference for this theoretical knowledge, but it is possible that they might be asked to provide this if questioned in court about the basis for their judgement. Evidence, therefore, commonly refers to informed observations that are accurately recorded and pertinent to the case record.

Chapters Three and Four explored academic writing, and one of the commonalities between academic and professional writing is the importance of the use of evidence. Evidence in academic writing is usually from published sources based on research such as books and scholarly articles (Rai, 2006) or, in some vocational academic writing such as social work, illustrations from practice.

Familiarity with the rigour of academic writing should enable students to develop a good understanding of the importance of providing evidence and referencing sources systematically, and this also applies to professional writing. This kind of theoretical evidence also has a place in some professional writing, particularly court reports, but is probably not the kind of evidence that social workers use most frequently. The use of evidence is addressed again in Chapter Seven in the context of report writing, but here the focus is on case recording, and so evidence mainly refers to information provided by service users, carers, family members or other professionals. The reason that evidence is important is that it demonstrates that written comments are not based on unsubstantiated assumptions or subjective opinions. The use of facts and opinion is discussed below, but such personal opinion is different from professionally formed judgements that are grounded in research-based theory and evidenced by observed facts about circumstances or behaviour.

It is common for social workers to receive and coordinate evidence from many different sources that may not be consistent, each carrying a different weight or significance. It is therefore always vital that the source of evidence is made clear, and that social workers present any differences in views in a fair and balanced way. One of the challenges of writing in social work is this collation of information, presenting it clearly and offering a summary or recommendation that takes account of information from each source. It is also very important to clearly indicate where evidence comes from, just as in academic writing, where it is required that original sources are acknowledged. The importance of identifying sources when writing case notes is more to do with providing accurate information trails on which both current and future decisions can be based. Details that may not seem important now could become very significant in the future, and a paper trail that clearly identifies the sources of evidence may be crucial.

Audience

One of the skills required for case recording is retaining an awareness of the different people who will need to read and respond to what is written based on their role and current circumstances. The importance of retaining an awareness of the intended audience was introduced in Chapter One. This is not an easy task in the context of professional writing, as it involves writing for future readers and circumstances, and requires the writer to ensure that records are clear and to make logical links to information stored elsewhere in the network of documents. Some agencies require occasional summaries to be written, particularly for more complex work and at key points such as a handover to a new worker. Effective intervention requires case records to include a chronology of significant events that flag up serious problems when reading a file (*Re E and Others [Minors] [Care Proceedings: social work practice], The Times*, 10 May 2000). A chronology for a court report should not contain a professional judgement but focus on a concise sequential account of facts (Seymour and Seymour, 2011: 108).

Involving service users: ethical and legal responsibilities

The involvement of service users in case recording is both an ethical and legal responsibility. Service users have had the right to read their case records prior to the transfer of systems to digital databases; this move has, however, added a layer of legal duty to all service providers. Guidance is contained in the Department of Health's *Recording with care*.

In the following quote from the WiSWAP Project, 'Angela', a service user, talks about her experience of social work writing. Her children were subjects of statutory intervention due to concerns about their welfare over several years:

> 'Because my family was large and the issues were complex, I needed time to read the reports through a few times. My understanding of why things were happening got clearer the more times I read it.... I needed to process the information over and over again ... remember I was personally attached to the information written about me and my children.... It was like an emotional rollercoaster.'

Practice writing, whether case recording or more sophisticated report writing, should not be considered as an isolated or discrete social work task. The example above reminds us that involving service users in writing case records is often an important stage in the ongoing dialogue about their circumstances. This is also true of sharing reports with service users. Involving service users in practice writing can lead to very challenging and emotive discussions that will require the social worker to draw on a number of other interpersonal skills in order to guide the discussion, to support the service user and to encourage conversations that may begin to bring about the potential for change and growth.

> 'At one time I didn't have faith in anyone believing in me, the child protection report acknowledged that there was faith in me to do well. I never thought that I could have another chance to parent.' (Angela)

The written word, either in the form of a case record or a report, can be a useful tool to engage with service users about difficult issues. Practice writing can also be used as a way to explore what future possibilities might look like. However, it is essential to think about the professional use of language within case recording, and what message this conveys to the audience, and in particular, the service user. The impact of what is recorded about service users can be far reaching and leave a legacy about them for years to come. Adults accessing their childhood case files years after social care involvement often find the information written about them and their families very challenging to read. Not only is the detail often painful and emotive, but social workers should remember that for many service users, this may be the only record of the detail about the decisions made about them and their lives, and so it may then become their narrative about who they are, and how they were viewed and valued by others.

> 'I found it really offensive being described as a drug user when I didn't see myself in that way. Nobody made me feel like a junkie with what they said ... but when I saw this written down ... it made me feel worthless. Professionals need to remember that individual circumstances are different and you can't tar everybody with the same brush. This can take away people's strength to overcome their difficulties.' (Angela)

Best practice involves working in partnership with service users, and collaborating with them in compiling case records can help to address issues of power imbalance. However, it is a complex social work task and it may not be possible to always arrive at an agreed joint viewpoint about a service user's circumstances. The very process of collaborating in the case recording involves an open discussion with service users that should include conversations about what language they feel best describes their situation. As in the example above, the professional term 'drug user' to the service user meant 'junkie', and so greater detail or clarity may have been more useful. It can also be helpful to use the service user's own language and to double-check that both are using the same language to describe the same things. A case record detailing this might have included:

> Angela has used class B drugs on a daily basis for around a year. She states that she smokes one 'spliff' (cannabis) before she goes to bed in the evenings to help her sleep as she finds the anxiety about her children not living with her difficult and subsequently disrupts her sleep.

This version describes what was observed by the social worker more precisely, and also indicates which information the service user provided. The extract avoids language that could be interpreted differently by different readers, and where colloquialisms are used ('spliff'), these are clearly defined.

Good practice requires social workers to strive for partnership with service users. Achieving a genuine partnership, however, is often unrealistic in statutory contexts, for example, child protection and some mental health work, due to the inherent imbalance of power between service user and social worker. The principle of consultation and involvement remains, and the challenge of achieving a true partnership should not detract from the responsibility of social workers to involve service users as fully as possibly in decision making (Rai and Stringer, 2010). Social workers can be required to include the views and wishes of service users in reports, and are frequently required to share reports with service users, for example, prior to child protection review meetings. Involving service users can pose a challenge for social workers, most obviously in negotiating disagreements and potential hostility to unwelcome information or judgements, but also in the act of writing itself. And there are practicalities around sharing or writing in partnership away from the office when documents are designed to be completed digitally via online software.

Guidance for social workers providing services to children and adults was produced in 2008 (DCSF, 2008: 11). This guidance sets out seven golden rules for sharing information:

1. Remember that the Data Protection Act is not a barrier to sharing information but provides a framework to ensure that personal information about living persons is shared appropriately.

2. Be open and honest with the person (and/or their family where appropriate) from the outset about why, what, how and with whom information will, or could be shared, and seek their agreement, unless it is unsafe or inappropriate to do so.

3. Seek advice if you are in any doubt, without disclosing the identity of the person where possible.

4. Share with consent where appropriate and, where possible, respect the wishes of those who do not consent to share confidential information. You may still share information without consent if, in your judgement, that lack of consent can be overridden in the public interest. You will need to base your judgement on the facts of the case.

5. Consider safety and well-being: Base your information sharing decisions on considerations of the safety and well-being of the person and others who may be affected by their actions.

6. Necessary, proportionate, relevant, accurate, timely and secure: Ensure that the information you share is necessary for the purpose for which you are sharing it, is shared only with those people who need to have it, is accurate and up-to-date, is shared in a timely fashion, and is shared securely.

7. Keep a record of your decision and the reasons for it – whether it is to share information or not. If you decide to share, then record what you have shared, with whom and for what purpose.

This guidance refers to the Data Protection Act 1998 that, along with the Freedom of Information Act 2000, requires social workers to make personal information held on record available on request, usually within 20 days. There are some circumstances in which information may be withheld, but the spirit of the legislation is to favour openness and access to information. The Human Rights Act 1998 also sets out the right to respect for a private and family life which includes the right to have access to records kept by professionals intervening in their lives. Social workers also have a duty to keep personal information confidential under common law, and this has been re-enforced by the *Code of practice for social care workers* (GSCC, 2010).

The *Code of practice* (GSCC, 2002) also sets out the accountability of social workers, and this includes the way in which their practice is represented through their case recording and other professional writing. Social workers are both held to account and judged on the reports and other written documents that are scrutinised in the courts and other multi-agency settings. Specific agencies will have their own policies for governing access to records for service users, so it is important for new social workers to familiarise themselves with local procedures.

The legal duty to make records available to service users belies the challenge for social workers of writing in such a way as to enable them to be genuinely accessible. Case notes are primarily read by other social workers and their managers, and even where the writer remains mindful of service users as potential readers, they will not be the primary audience. Guidance issued by the Department of Health and contained in *Recording with care* suggests that 'Children and families should be encouraged to contribute to and see their records' and that 'Written records should be written in a manner that conveys respect, irrespective of the background or culture of the individual' (Goldsmith, 1999). While seeing case records is covered in the legislation, the requirement to contribute to them relies on practice guidance, but is nonetheless very important and commonly included in local agency policies. Where social workers are aware of a difference of view at the time of the interview, it is important that the view of the service user is clearly recorded alongside the social worker's own professional opinion.

Representing the views of other professionals

In addition to clearly presenting service users' views, case records need to include selected information provided by other professionals such as education and health colleagues. Social work intervention with all service user groups involves working closely with other professions and agencies. In some services professionals work together in multiprofessional teams, and case notes may be completed by practitioners who are qualified as, for example, occupational therapists or nurses, but who undertake the same care management role alongside their social work colleagues. The professional training and culture may have a significant impact on how case recording is undertaken; this may pose a challenge, but it might also offer an opportunity for professionals to learn from each other.

Research conducted by the authors with adult services in one local authority in England illustrated that the introduction of occupational therapists to a group of care mangers resulted in the managers noting some differences in recording practices in the context of there being a concern expressed by management that there was sometimes a lack of detail and of professional opinion within case notes. As a professional group, the occupational therapists were more accustomed to providing their professional opinion based on very clearly identified evidence that informed their assessment. This practice was carried over to undertaking assessments and writing up case notes as part of their care management role, and was notably different from the writing of some care managers who had qualified through other routes, including social work. The existence of differences between professional cultures, knowledge bases and priorities has long been recognised in social work (Huntington, 1981; Pietroni, 1994; Mackay et al, 1995; Irvine et al, 2002; Manthorpe and Iliffe, 2003; Richardson and Asthana, 2005; Edwards, 2011), so it should not be a surprise that differences also exist in the ways in which practitioners from different professional backgrounds write case records. Whether working within multiprofessional teams or across agencies, it is important to be aware of these professional differences, so that practices can be improved and differences understood.

The voices of professionals from other agencies will be included in case recording at the point of referral, during the process of assessment and during service delivery. Each of these is important and has an impact on the assessment of needs and risk, the quality of service and indeed, whether a service is offered at all. Social workers are frequently the central point for information from many sources of information. Some recording systems enable other agencies to add or access information on a read-only basis. Most commonly, however, social workers will be gathering information from many sources and writing up a summary of key information in the case note. This 'orchestration' of voices (Lillis and Rai, 2012) through the representation of many professionals is a very important aspect of recording which enacts multi-agency communication in social work practice, as illustrated by 'David', a newly qualified social worker in the WiSWAP Project:

> 'I am very surprised about the amount of information that is passed through ourselves, either coming through or going out. I knew that as a qualified social worker you would be open to a lot of

information and you would be making a lot of decisions … and there is a lot of information put past you and particularly about decision making.'

As with service users' views, it is important that case records are explicit about whose observations, evidence or views are being expressed. The social worker not only needs to clearly attribute contributions, but also to select and edit information so that it is relevant and accessible. Including information from other professionals may only require very brief but accurate facts, for example:

Date

Call to Ward 7 at the General Hospital, Sister Jane Dunn informed me that Mr Philips is reportedly very unwell and on IV and antibiotics.

Call to Dale Rogers (Emergency Duty Team) who is aware of situation and informed me that day care services are also aware and has called Mr Timms, grandson, who is also aware and in touch with his mother who is away at the moment. Dale has passed my contact details on to ward staff and to Mr Timms.

In this example professionals are identified by name and role, and the information that they have provided is clearly stated. As with information from the social worker completing the case record, other professionals may also offer both facts and professional opinions, so it is important that these are clearly distinguished. Factual information may contain details that are vital for other workers following up on action, for example:

Date

T/C to William Grace, Area Care Manager – not available. Spoke with Nancy Korfman, Duty Care Manager, who informed me that William had spoken to Sister Lea on Ward 7 yesterday and arranged re-instatement of Mr Phillip's care package from Wednesday PM call on 29/11/2006.

Professional opinions from other professionals will contribute to assessments and decision making and so should also include any evidence offered:

Date

T/C received from Mr Philip's physio, Donna Hill. She has spoken to Kim Jones, physio on Ward 7, and her view is that the original discharge fell down because Mr Philips was unable to stand in the standing hoist. She wondered if Mr Philips could be managed at home with an ordinary hoist. This has implications on the care package and on her attendance at the Resource Centre. Message left for Tim Lore (Care Manager).

Some information from other professionals may need to be included as a direct quotation, copied over from an email or transcribed from a telephone message. Individual agencies may have their own policies on copying emails or phone messages into case notes, but where information is complex, detailed or connected to concerns about risk, it is important to include adequate detail.

Recording analysis and recommending action

As discussed above, there is no single format for case recording, and each agency will use its own software, policies and guidance on case recording. Some will require, or suggest as good practice, the use of headings to help organise the information to be included. Many case notes will be very brief and take the form of running lists of action taken, as in the examples above. This will largely depend on the nature of the work being undertaken. The extracts above, for example, were taken from an adult services team working with a service user who was receiving short-term crisis intervention following treatment in hospital. In this context there was intensive activity over a relatively short period of time, with daily contact with the service user, his family or other professionals. In contrast to this, some interventions may be over a much longer period and involve longer, but less frequent, contact with a service user. In this context case records may include more extensive entries. Both contexts will require analysis and recommendations of action or decisions made to be recorded, but these may be either in the form of periodic summaries or included in the recording of contacts. The following extract is from a case record written in a Youth Offending Team (YOT) in England, which provides recommended headings for its case notes to include the plan for the session, an evaluation/analysis and next action:

YOIS CASE DIARY

Case ID: xxxxxxxxx

21/10/20xx   14yrs 8m   Author: Duncan Mills
Youth Offending Team: West Town

Diary subject: Contact

………
………………………………………………………………………

PLAN: Discuss breach and restorative justice

Session: Met with C at home, she seemed in a relatively good mood. She explained that she had not made her reparation appointment as initially she did not want to. She explained that she finds the sessions boring and did not get on with the workers. I explained that this was not good enough and that if an appointment was arranged she needs to attend, and that if she did not like something on a session she needs to talk to me about this. C apologised and agreed this is what she would do in the future. I explained she had also missed one of my appointments and she explained she had gone out and forgotten about this. I again reiterated the importance of attending sessions. C agreed this was not acceptable and I explained I would give her one more chance but the next missed session she would be back in court.

We had a discussion around school and C explained that she had been having difficulties with other young people and had become annoyed about this. We had a short discussion around appropriate ways to act. C explained her tag off on the weekend and was pleased as she would be able to stay at friends' homes. I explained to C that her Mum would determine which were suitable and which were not and she needs to respect this. I aslo talked about the importance of retruning home when her curfew is in place set by Mum. C agreed she would.

YOUNG PERSON'S ENGAGEMENT: Good, seemed to listen to the necessity of attending appointments.

YOUNG PERSON'S VIEW: Apologised for missing sessions. Pleased that tag is coming off.

EVALUATION: C did seem to understand the importance of attending the sessions; unfortunately the pull of her friends appears to outweigh the sessions. She understands she must attend and the consequences of returning to court. I do not feel she has the full requisite skills to make the right decision if spending time with friends. She still gives little regard to consequences at the time and only reflects on these when she is presented with them much later.

I feel when her tag comes off we will see resulting problems. I think she may struggle to return home when requested and place her self in vulnerable situations. C does understand she needs to stick to these but as explained I still feel she will not be able to make the correct decision at the time.

SAFEGUARDING/RISK: When tag comes off I feel she may place herself in more vulnerable situations, This may also be linked to further offences if she had opportunities around substance misuse.

NEXT ACTION: Monitor tag being removed.

DATE OF NEXT APPOINTMENT: 11/11/20XX

The use of headings, as seen here, can be helpful, even if just used as a guide rather than a prescriptive layout. Prescriptive layouts can be problematic in that, as illustrated above, case recording will vary depending on the nature of the service and the current context of the service user, so the level of detail in the example above will not always be helpful. This case note also illustrates the level of repetition that arises where prescribed headings/sections are used. It is important for social workers to keep in mind that case recording is not only about documenting factual information. Whether in periodic summaries or in the body of a record of contact, recommended actions and the analysis that underpins them should be included. Some agencies will require that summaries that include these elements be completed on the transfer of a case, when a worker goes on leave, and at periodic intervals to enable colleagues to quickly apprise themselves of the current situation. This can be a very useful practice as it not only benefits co-working, but also creates a reflective pause where analysis and planned action can be recorded.

Applying the concepts of purpose, voice and audience

Throughout this chapter references have been made to the purpose of case recording, the voices that they contain and the audience that notes are written for. In this final section these ideas are drawn together with reference to the discussion in Chapters One and Two in order to offer some thoughts on how an understanding of purpose, voice and audience can assist in creating more effective records. As indicated above, case recording has multiple purposes that are influenced not only by individual agencies and service user groups, but also by government policy. The individual social worker's writing, therefore, takes place in a very broad institutional and political context, although the impact of this may not be overtly apparent. The policy changes in the use of ICS, for example, illustrate the way in which changes in academic thought, based on research, and political ideology, can have a direct impact on writing undertaken at the grass roots. As a social worker these debates and developments may seem very distant, but an understanding of broader policy issues may help in understanding how to use the systems to create more effective case recording. From the perspective of effective practice, the enduring purposes of case recording will always include documenting information for assessments, services provided, analysis of risk and need, decisions made and actions recommended and taken. Not all these purposes will be relevant to every entry to a case note, but they should appear at some point, either in the case record itself, or in associated documents.

The audience for case recording is closely associated with its purpose, and policy changes can influence for whom case records are written, for example, a greater emphasis on measuring performance criteria could result in management becoming the primary audience. One enduring audience, however, is that of colleagues within the same agency who might use the records to review actions and decisions when the allocated worker is unavailable or transfers the work. It is also common for case records to be reviewed when a referral is received in relation to someone who has received a service before, or who is related to someone who has received a service before. As communication systems facilitating multi-agency working become more interconnected, professionals accessing records become more diverse, although some agencies may only have partial access. This has implications for how social workers write, as the use of social work-specific jargon or abbreviations could lead to confusion or misunderstanding. Clarity and the avoidance of jargon is also important where case records are used as evidence, and may therefore be accessed and read by solicitors and other court officials and for service users who may access case records. When writing case notes it is always important to explicitly indicate whose views are being reported. It is often unhelpful therefore to use the passive tense in case recording as this can leave the reader unclear about whose view is being expressed. See, for example, the following case note:

Kathryn was visited at home and Ryan and Mark were seen. Ryan was observed standing and moving around the room more confidently although he still holds on to the furniture at times and occasionally 'bottom shuffles'.

Is less clear and less explicit than if it had been written in the passive tense:

> I visited Kathryn at home and saw Ryan and Mark. I observed Ryan standing and moving around the room more confidently although he was still holding on to the furniture at times and occasionally 'bottom shuffles'.

The views of the mother in this example are stated and attributed to her:

> Kathryn said that she is not worried about Mark or Ryan's development as she was also a late developer and she doesn't find the nappies a problem.

Where there are differences in opinion between the social worker and a service user, it is particularly important to represent these and to obtain agreement from the service user that their views have been accurately reflected. Although enabling service users to check and ideally contribute to case recording can pose a practical difficulty where it is undertaken digitally, this should not be a barrier to good practice.

Handwritten drafts can be written with service users that are later entered digitally, or a printed version can be taken back for agreement after an entry had been made, as long as the system allows for amendments to be made if the service user does not think that their views are represented accurately. Both methods are time-consuming, but where there are important differences of opinion, it is vital that these are recorded precisely as they may be contested in court at some future date. Involving service users in the creation of case records in this way can also ensure that recording is part of the overall communication with the service user – it is an integral part of social work practice rather than a record of it. Putting observations or professional opinions on paper is very powerful, and reading them can be an uncomfortable experience for service users. The needs of service users as a potential audience also raises more complex professional issues. Language used should be accessible to all service users who need to be involved, and this may include children and people with limited or no literacy skills or with impairments that effect reading or writing. Committing information and judgements to paper also removes 'wriggle room' which may exist when communicating verbally, requiring a level of honesty and clarity that can be challenging in complex or compulsory interventions.

The significant range of audiences referred to above means that social work case recording differs from many texts that are written for one specific purpose and audience. Writing effectively for all of these audiences is a challenge, and it is not realistic for social workers to keep this range of readers in mind when writing all case records. An awareness of audience can be helpful, however, as a reminder of the importance of creating accounts that are accessible for a reader who is potentially unfamiliar with the discourses of social work. Although case records will primarily be written by the allocated worker, there are commonly many voices represented in them. As outlined above these include both service users and other professionals from the same and other agencies. Some of these voices will appear as extracts of texts written directly by another professional or, occasionally, a service user, but more frequently it will be the task of the social worker to collate key information provided by others. This is referred to above as the 'orchestration' of texts (Lillis and Rai, 2012), a process through which the social work writer coordinates incoming information and crafts it into a text that meets the institutional purpose of case recording. This process draws on many skills common to academic writing such as selection, using evidence, analysis, accurate referencing of sources of information and clarity.

Conclusion

Case recoding is probably the writing task that occupies more of social worker's time than other forms of writing. It does not have a high status and can be seen as an unwelcome chore (BASW, 2012). Effective case recording is, nonetheless, an essential element of safe social work practice and performs several important functions. Without it social workers would be unable to plan, review previous actions or undertake assessments, and management would be unable to monitor performance or supervise practice. At its best, recording can be an invaluable reflective tool for social workers and service users. In a pressurised profession such as social work, however, it is too easy to overlook the significance, value and complexity of case recording, and to treat it as merely an administrative task (Holmes et al, 2009). Case records sit within multifarious paper and digital documents that constitute a network of, sometimes duplicated, sometimes linked, information. Using such networks effectively requires more than competence in literacy, and the responsibility for good quality recording does not lie with individual social workers alone; it is an agency-wide or even an inter-agency responsibility. At the heart of this complex network of information is, or should be, the service user. The service user should, in some form, contribute to the creation of records, be a key potential audience when records are written, and the welfare and safety of service users should underpin decisions made about what is recorded, when and how. As discussed above, there is a risk that the focus for recording can get diverted to managerial priorities, or indeed that the status of recording can become so low that only cursory attention is given to anything other than very minimal, factual recording of information. Retaining an awareness of the purpose of recording, the potential audience and the writer's voice offering a skilled professional opinion is one way in which both the individual worker and management can enhance the value of recording and, hopefully, make it a more rewarding task for the writer.

7

Writing reports as a tool of professional assessment

Lucy Rai, Theresa Lillis, Guillermo Garcia-Maza and Amanda Harrison

Introduction

This chapter provides guidance on report writing, specifically in the context of assessment and court work. All reports draw on assessments in some form, but the contexts and purposes differ, and this has an impact on the way in which the report is written. Within a statutory context, the two most common contexts within which reports are written are when undertaking an assessment of need and risk and when reporting to the court.

Reports in social work are very powerful documents that can have a life-changing impact on the service users involved. Reports may recommend that children are removed from the care of their parents, that young people receive a custodial sentence or that someone's liberty can be restricted as a result of risks arising from mental health needs. A weak report can fail to secure the outcome that the writer recommends, and this can also have a major impact on the lives of service users, their families and their communities. Getting reports right is therefore very important and relies as much on effective writing skills as on effective social work practice skills.

References to writing skills throughout this chapter should be understood in the context of the discussion in Chapter One where the problematic nature of a simplistic skills approach was introduced. Writing effective reports, as with other forms of writing, relies on the writer developing an understanding of the context-specific nature of writing and the importance of thinking about the audience, their own voice as a writer and the purpose of the text. While court reports are common in statutory social work, assessment reports are undertaken on a regular basis, and are therefore a form of writing that all social workers will be involved in. Both court and assessment report formats vary considerably depending on the service user group and agency, as do all forms of writing, but there are common lessons contained here that should support social workers in writing not only assessments but other forms of report.

Reports are probably the most common text types in social work, after case recording, but can be challenging to write as they differ from other forms of writing that social workers may be familiar with from previous contexts, including the writing carried out for courses as a student. The format, content and style of reports can also differ significantly from agency to agency. Effective and safe assessments lie at the heart of social work practice across all service user groups. This chapter explores the contribution of report writing to assessments, planning and decision making through the ways in which an understanding of voice, purpose and audience can enable social workers' writing to support best practice.

This chapter is divided into two main parts. The first part deals with the nature of reports in social work and some of the features of an effective report, including the importance and challenges involved in expressing a professional opinion. It also explores the 'orchestration' role involved in social work writing (Lillis and Rai, 2012: 60) through which information from many sources is drawn together and combined into key texts that drive decision making. Assessment, planning and decision making are closely aligned activities, and all of them should be guided by effective assessment (and review) reports. In the second part of the chapter reports are considered in three statutory settings: children's services, youth offending teams and mental health services. This part draws on data from the WiSWAP Project (outlined in Chapter One). Extracts from authentic reports and social workers' views on the challenges they face in writing these are used to illustrate the professional dilemmas involved in writing assessments.

What is a report?

A report, whether for assessment or the court, is a structured piece of factual writing that is written for a specific purpose and usually offers some sort of recommendation. Decisions that have been made based on reports are commonly made by groups of people, such as a case conference or a court. Relatively straightforward assessment reports, for example, may also be intended for use within the agency and be acted on without wider discussion, for example, simple assessments of need undertaken by care managers in adult services. In social work reports are frequently based around a rigid structure or may even involve populating data fields in an electronic template. This is not always the case, and some reports allow more flexibility or are based on loose subject headings to organise the structure and content. Assessment reports represent one of the formal ways in which statutory duties are evidenced by the agency and contain required fields for essential information, and must also be completed in specific timescales. Court reports may allow the writer a little more freedom in organisation and content, however. Completing a report can therefore vary, from inputting data within very limited word counts through to documents that are constructed as 'free text' (that is, spaces for writing with no word limit or specific categories) that require considerable organisation to be drafted by the writer.

Skills developed from writing in other contexts, particularly those by social work students such as writing essays, can be very helpful in preparing them to write reports. But there are many differences between different types of texts. The key differences between a report and an essay are outlined in Table 7.1.

Table 7.1: Contrasting reports and essays

A report	An essay in social work
Is a highly structured document	Is structured by the writer based on academic conventions
Draws on evaluative and analytical skills and should end with a clear judgement	Draws primarily on analytical skills and the end point is the quality of the discussion
Is usually written using headings with clearly marked and labelled sections	Headings are less common, and where used, this is generally at the discretion of the writer. There are commonly, however, broad sections, such as the introduction and conclusion
Includes few, if any, citations	Commonly contains direct citations and references to published sources
Uses factual evidence from observations, testimony and reported information which is then analysed to build recommendations for action	Builds an argument based on evidence from (usually) published academic sources
Is written to support decision making in a specific context	Is written for the purpose of demonstrating learning, often for purposes of being assessed
Is written for a complex audience, both immediate and longer term	Is often written for one person, such as a tutor or assessor
Occasionally makes reference to theory, but this is very purpose-specific	Usually makes reference to theory and published research

Although reports differ from academic essays in several ways, they also have commonalities, and when these are understood, they can help student writers use these skills, from writing essays to writing reports. As with essays, reports are primarily descriptive, build an argument based on evidence and should generally offer a concluding evaluative judgement based on analysis of the information presented. The following are potentially common skills, although there will be differences in how they are used in reports and essays:

- selection and appropriate use of supporting evidence
- writing in a clear, concise style
- analysis of information.

These three key aspects of writing are considered in the following sections.

Selection and appropriate use of supporting evidence

The selection and use of evidence is key to both essay writing and report writing, although there are some important differences. Essays are intended to enable students to demonstrate their knowledge and understanding of their subject, which involves selecting and analysing information from different sources for the purpose of presenting a coherent argument, supported by evidence. Evidence in the context of essay writing or academic writing usually means citations and quotations from published, authoritative sources, such as books and journal articles. These citations can refer to factual information, but also to theories and arguments arising from research or learned thinking. Writing an essay, therefore, develops the writer's ability to seek out sources relevant to the topic, select those that best support the argument being made, and then to weave in the ideas of others appropriately while writing in their own words, and giving credit to citations and quotations where they are used.

A report also requires the writer to seek out and select information to build an argument or a case in order to make a recommendation. The difference with a report is that the sources of information are not generally in published works, such as books and journal articles (although theory might occasionally be referred to), but gathered by the writer from conversations, observations and written information provided by the service user, their family/carers and other professionals. Selecting the information to use is driven not by the crafting of an academic argument, but by the social worker's professional judgement as they seek to arrive at a recommendation that furthers the best interests of the service user in the context of available resources. Citations and quotations are not generally used other than in court reports, but it might be appropriate in some reports to provide some verbatim quotes from those contributing to a report, particularly the service user. It is important to clearly indicate the sources of information, as it is not uncommon for a report to contain conflicting views or even versions of events. It is the job of the social worker to use their professional judgement to decide how to manage such conflicting information, and to use this to reach a conclusion. In some reports it is beyond the remit of the social worker to provide a decision on outcomes, but they would generally be expected to offer a recommendation that would then be considered by a wider group, such as at a case conference. Selecting and using appropriate sources of evidence are therefore skills required in both essay writing and report writing, but the specific nature of the evidence used in each case is different.

Writing in a clear, concise style

There are strong institutional and professional expectations that writing, particularly assessment reports, should be 'clear and concise'. Achieving this is a challenging task, not least because people have very different understandings and expectations about what 'clarity' and 'conciseness' are. Some of the complexities arising from differences in interpretation between writers and readers are dealt with below.

Academic writing is usually governed by word limits, and practice writing should convey key information to the reader effectively, without the inclusion of unnecessary detail. Writing within a word limit is one of the greatest challenges of essay writing for many students, and these limits are there partly to encourage students to develop their skills in writing concise, focused essays that do not contain irrelevant content or unnecessarily wordy language. A report should also be concise, and the reason for this is that reports are professional documents that are read by very busy people. The effective use of sub-headings, which are essential in reports but not always used in essays, can assist the reader in navigating a document swiftly, and searching for the key information that they need. Academic writing and reports may contain technical or subject-specific language, but this should not make them difficult to understand, and the writer should always try to use vocabulary that it would be reasonable to expect their reader to understand. Even in published academic books and articles, it will sometimes be important to provide a footnote or comment in parentheses (brackets) to explain the meaning of a word where it is used in a context that would make it unfamiliar to the reader.

There are two other skills that academic writing should develop which are invaluable to the social workers when they are writing, and these are: an awareness of the audience or reader (as discussed in Chapters One and Two) and the concept of the writer 'voice'. Neither of these concepts is generally explicitly included in the study skills taught at university, although many students will implicitly have become skilled in adapting their writing according to the required audience and voice, and these skills are important to develop further in the context of report writing.

Analysis of information

Analysis is an important skill, in both academic and professional writing. In both contexts the writer is required to make sense of a potentially large body of information and to use this to construct a discussion or argument. Such information in academic writing will be theoretical discussion from published sources. In practice, information comes in many forms, including face-to-face discussions, notes on telephone conversations and written reports. Analysis involves more than just collating information; the writer also needs to interpret, evaluate and make a professional judgement. This involves the social workers applying their theoretical knowledge and experience to information gathered. As in academic writing, such analysis involves weighing up potentially conflicting perspectives and information to reach a balanced and well-argued conclusion. In social work practice reports, conclusions are associated with recommendations to inform decision making. Such decision making is at the heart of social work practice, and the ability to use analysis to form and present a professional view is a skilled activity developed over time.

There is complexity at all stages of undertaking an assessment, but the analysis of information is perhaps one of the most challenging. Students and newly qualified social workers should be able to expect support from line managers and senior colleagues in analysing information and forming judgements and recommendations. The focus here, however, is on *writing* analytically. Some elements of assessment reports should rightly contain factual, descriptive information, and the tightly controlled content arising from some software used in report writing makes such information very prescriptive. The analysis underpinning a recommendation should be supported by factual information, but by its nature needs to be informed by the professional insight of the writer. It is possible for social workers to shy away from expressing a view due to anxiety about being accused of bias or including personal opinion in reports. There is a difference, however, between unsubstantiated personal opinion (which has no place in professional writing) and a professional judgement based on soundly argued analysis. The importance of forming a professional judgement and making a recommendation in assessments is discussed below.

Writing for a complex audience

As indicated above, it is common for there to be more than one intended reader of reports. Many reports are written to advise case conferences or court hearings, and in these contexts the reader will include not only the service user, but also a range of other professionals with varying familiarity with social work. As a professional tool it is important that everyone involved in decision making based on a report is able to understand it. This creates a challenge for social workers – writing for a specific audience is considerably more straightforward when there is only one intended reader who is known to the writer, yet social work reports have readers, with very different interests and ways of talking about the subject being discussed.

Hall and Maharaj (2001) suggest that all communication, whether written or verbal, involves interpretation. This is because there are always cultural and experiential differences between (in this context) the writer and reader that inevitably result in an imperfect communication of meaning. They use the concept of 'culture' very broadly, suggesting that every individual has unique cultural or social experiences that have an influence on the ways in which they interpret language . The concept of cultural interpretation is particularly interesting in the context of reports, as it could be argued that there is more cultural commonality between social workers than between social workers and other professions, or indeed between professionals and service users. This can make it easier for social workers to understand the intended meaning of other social workers, and they have more shared understanding of the meaning lying behind the language used. This connects with the discussion of discourse in Chapter One – familiarity with the discourses of social work lends a particular meaning to language used that in other contexts might convey a very different meaning.

Many professionals, and some service users, will have such extensive experience of working with social workers that they will have developed a familiarity with their discourses; some may have been developed through service user groups themselves. One example of this would be the discourse around disability referred to as the 'medical' or 'social' models of disability. The social model of disability was developed from within the disability rights movement, but also within academic debates about disability. A key element of this shift in paradigm involved challenging the language historically used in relation to disability and disabled people, offering not only new ways of thinking about disability in the context of society, but also a new vocabulary that represented these perspectives (Campbell and Oliver, 1996; Oliver, 2009). Language – including specialist language – is an important tool for social workers who, like all other professional groups such as doctors and psychologists, rely on written and verbal communication when carrying out their professional duties.

When writing a report, therefore, social workers need to maintain an awareness of the needs and perspectives of readers in order to use language that will be useful in articulating a particular issue or problem, but at the same time, will neither be inaccessible nor misleading. For service users this will often mean that time is needed to explain the meaning of the report. Other professionals who routinely work with social workers, such as the police and health practitioners, should be sufficiently familiar with the language and concepts used to understand specialist terminology, but where very specialist terminology or theoretical references are made, it will be important to explain these. This is even more important where a report is intended for use in court, as court officials may have less familiarity with social work, and a misinterpretation could have serious outcomes for the service user. Although there will be times when social workers rightly use specialist language to communicate their expert knowledge, where possible, reports should be written using non-technical language that could be understood by a lay person. Where it is important to use specialist language, this should be clearly explained so that the report is accessible. It can be unhelpful to use shorthand phrases that can be used to refer to issues that are commonly understood within the profession but actually signal something relatively complex. Examples would be phrases such as 'good enough parenting' or 'failure to thrive', both of which signal a complex set of ideas around parenting and child development that may not be evident to the lay reader.

Awareness of voice in writing

The concept of voice refers to the way in which writers present themselves in their writing. It is a concept closely aligned to 'writer identity' (Clark and Ivanič, 1997) or the way in which a writer's identity is conveyed through their writing. Clark and Ivanič argue that the identity of the writer is multiple and shifts, depending on context and their experience as a writer (Ivanič, 1998, p 23). To illustrate this, when writing an informal email or a letter to a friend it would be normal to use a very personal voice – the writer may use colloquialisms, abbreviations and even words that have a special meaning shared between the writer and reader. Such very personal words are common within families and peer groups, but may also be specific to geographical regions and potentially baffling to those outside of these communities. Just to illustrate, words used for 'savoury bread roll' across the UK include 'bap', 'cob', 'batch', 'breadcake', 'barm cake' and 'teacake'. These differences may seem unimportant, but similar regional terms can potentially lead to real misunderstanding in the context of social work writing; for example, if there were concerns about the diet of a child, such regional terms might not be immediately understood by a reader who was not familiar with these terms, and the reader might interpret a 'teacake' as a sweet bun rather than a savoury roll.

The content and style of language used, along with the particular formats and layouts used, all reflect the voice being used by the writer. In a professional context a social worker will normally be expected to use a voice that reflects their professional role, rather than their personal perspectives or style. Likewise, they will usually be expected to adopt a more formal style, although the balance of formality/informality will vary depending on the specific written communication, and the writer may even alternate between levels of formality depending on the subject matter. An example of the way in which the formal and informal voice can appear in a single text is in the email in Table 7.2 from a social worker to a colleague in the health service.

Table 7.2: Email illustrating formal and informal voice

Example email comments	Level of formality used
Hi Mark – good to see you at the meeting last week ... looking refreshed after your leave lol!	The email opens using an informal, personal voice – this indicates a level of familiarity between writer and reader. The content and language used is informal and friendly, for example, the use of 'Hi' and 'lol! [laugh out loud]'
I have now been to visit the Kirby family, as agreed, and discussed with them Mr Kirby's request for additional services to support him in his care of Mrs Kirby. Their daughter, Miriam, was able to attend also and contribute to our discussion. I completed an initial assessment and have passed a referral to OT for them to action. I will be in touc h again as soon as this has been completed and the assessment finalised.	As the email moves into the 'business' of the message, a more formal, professional voice appears here, such as the use of full sentences and the use of some more formal phrases, including 'request for additional services' and 'completed an initial assessment'.
Let me know is there is any more info that you need. Cheers Kate PS Did you manage to catch that programme we talked about? I thought it was fab, can't wait for next week!!! J	The content focuses just on the professional role, and the language used includes technical terms ('initial assessment' and 'OT') that would have a particular meaning within the professional community.

Although this example contains a mixture of professional and personal voice, it retains a more professional voice than a personal correspondence. Reports do not usually contain any of the indications of a more personal/informal voice that might be appropriate in an email communication, even if the intended immediate readers of the report are well known to the writer.

The use of voice is generally an unconscious process, particularly for more experienced professional writers. Inexperienced social work writers can sometimes slip into an inappropriately informal voice, and this usually stands out to an experienced colleague who is in a position to offer support and guidance as part of their junior colleague's professional development. It is helpful to consult with senior colleagues in order for the more novice professional social work writer to gain a more conscious awareness of their use of voice, so that they can take more control of their writing through both the content and language used. For example, there may be times in correspondence with some service users where it is helpful to adopt a more informal voice, but equally others could experience this as disrespectful or overly familiar. As discussed above, writing is a complex form of communication between people, and the writer needs to consider how they write in order to communicate most effectively with the many potential readers.

One important reason why assessment reports are written in a formal voice is that the professional social worker is writing on behalf of the agency they are working for. This means that the personal voice is even more distant, both in terms of the content and the language used. One way in which the agency voice is reinforced is through the gatekeeping of reports. This is a process through which a document needs approval by a senior colleague before it can be used or circulated. It should meet the agency responsibility for quality assurance, and also be a source of support and professional development for social workers. The following example, taken from the WiSWAP Project, is drawn from a youth offending team (YOT), and illustrates the way in which reports written by a social worker in this particular context are mediated by the required agency voice:

> 'It wouldn't be acceptable to write quite profound swearing words in a professional report, so the report really played down the seriousness of this young person's confrontation with me and another professional. If you did report profane speech directly it wouldn't get past the gatekeeping process so the report wouldn't get to court. My line manager keeps an eye on all written reports that go to court and makes sure you're following any written regulations or guidance on what these reports should look like. It's not exactly written down that you shouldn't use profanity or you shouldn't use direct speech, it's not as plain as that. There's a little bit of discretion there, but you have to have a professional etiquette in terms of your writing, the management don't want any slang being used within the court arenas, or any unprofessional.' (Chris, social worker, YOT)

Chris' comments here illustrate several challenges around writing assessment reports. First, that finding the best way of accurately representing accounts of incidents or events is not straightforward. In this case, Chris was clear that he wanted to use swear words to emphasise the aggressive behaviour of the young person, whereas his manager did not consider this necessary. Chris seems to indicate that his manager's gatekeeping activity is not helpful. Second, Chris feels that there may be serious consequences arising from him not using the language that he wants to include – diminishing rather than accurately reflecting the young person's behaviour.

Of course, court reports have to be written in a style acceptable to agencies, and what is an acceptable to one agency may differ for another (for example, witness statements can be written more colloquially). But in Chris' case above, perhaps a compromise could have been found, for example, by using quotations so that the voice of the social worker – and therefore indirectly the voice of the agency – can be clearly distinguished from the voices of those being represented in the report. In some contexts quotations are used so that the impact and force of language used can be taken into account when making assessments and judgements. This case illustrates one of the challenges of report writing which is representing the many voices involved and implicated in any report: the voice of the individual social worker, the voice of the agency and the voices of those being written about. Many reports contain the views of a range of people, and this is particularly true of assessment reports. In addition to the social worker, a typical safeguarding assessment would include views from:

- parents
- the child
- school teacher or nursery worker
- GP, health visitor or school nurse
- the police.

In some cases the report would also include the views of a:

- psychologist
- housing officer
- specialist health service
- child minder/foster carer
- previous social worker or social worker from another service such as mental health.

These voices all form a large part of the 'evidence' that the social worker uses to build a case for a particular recommendation. The social worker has responsibility for weaving together all of these voices and, in doing so, ensuring that the views are correctly attributed, either directly by naming contributors for particular sections, or by using quotation marks.

Presenting the evidence

Reports are built around the development of a recommendation based on evidence, and much of this evidence is gathered from both direct contributions and information from other professionals. Third party contributions may come in different forms, and collecting and collating evidence is a large part of undertaking an assessment. Information from other professionals, such as colleagues from health, education or other social work services, may be provided in writing, but the nature of this writing can vary greatly. For example, it may arrive as an email, a more formal report (either hard copy or attached to an email) or even as a telephone message taken by a colleague. More formal written documents may provide content that can be quoted directly and then clearly attributed to the original author. Evidence from parents, foster carers and child minders may be collected through face-to-face conversations in which nothing is written down other than notes taken by the social worker. These informal 'field notes' then become very important sources for the social worker to represent faithfully the views of others, but unless verified by the person whose views they represent, they cannot be used as quotes and would require the social worker to capture the views of the person concerned.

The nature of evidence from a child can vary greatly, partly depending on their age, development and communication needs. Social workers may be involved in observations, communication through play and even discussions with specialist therapists in order to gain an understanding of the needs and wishes of the child. This then needs to be written into the report alongside other evidence.

Lillis and Rai (2012: 60) suggest that social workers have an 'orchestration' role, pulling together many voices and weaving them into a single report. Part of the skill of writing a report is presenting conflicting views and drawing them together to form a well-reasoned recommendation based on a professional judgement.

Involving service users

It is essential that service users are involved in the writing of reports, and this can happen at several stages. As discussed above, service users and their carers or relatives are a key source of evidence; gathering information about both their wishes and needs is a central aspect of assessment. Depending on a service user's ability to make a direct contribution to writing, it will often also be important for social workers to share and discuss reports prior to decisions being made in a wider professional context, such as a case conference. The nature of this consultation depends on the specific practice context. Some reports are not used for discussion at broader meetings, and are used to make relatively simple assessments of need and recommendations for service provision. Many of these reports are largely written with service users, and copies are shared on completion.

Reports written for the court or to assist in decision making in statutory case conferences may make recommendations that the service user does not agree with, and may be very emotive. It is important, therefore, that time is taken to ensure that service users understand the evidence and recommendations before reports are discussed formally, and this requires empathy, clarity and communication skills. Sharing contentious or emotive reports can be made a little easier, however, where they are written in an accessible style and where evidence is presented clearly. The use of some technical terms is sometimes unavoidable, but where possible, language used should not disguise meaning through terminology unfamiliar to service users. It is also important for social workers to remember the huge impact that information in print can have – reading information in a printed format can convey meaning in a much more forceful, and potentially intimidating, way than spoken communication. For this reason it is helpful, where possible, for service users not to encounter distressing information for the first time in print, but rather for there to be opportunities for discussion at different stages of the report writing process. This is even more complex where the service user has learning difficulties or there is a need to work through an interpreter, and in these situations, planning and time is needed to ensure that service users are able to understand what has been written about them.

The other sources of evidence sometimes used in a report are references to the law and to theory or research. Caution needs to be taken about when to use these, particularly in the context of court reports, and advice should be sought from line managers and, where appropriate, county solicitors, as such references can cause difficulties where social workers are cross-examined in court. Social work reports are effectively expert witness statements, so it is important for social workers to stay within the limits of their knowledge and experience so that they are able to talk authoritatively about any references within the report.

Making a recommendation

All reports should contain a recommendation based on the social worker's professional judgement. Report writing is not just about collating and selecting relevant evidence; it also requires the writer to use their professional knowledge and skill to evaluate the information available and to provide a recommendation that takes account not only of the needs and risks involved, but also of available resources. Taking account of resource limitations can make the writing of assessments challenging for social workers as they may find that they are not able to make recommendations that they believe are the ideal outcome for the service user. Making recommendations with an understanding of the writer's role within the agency requires a high degree of professionalism and often a separation of professional and personal views. In the following example from the WiSWAP Project, 'Samantha', a social worker in a child protection team, talks about the way in which she tends to adapt her writing style when offering a professional judgement depending on the document:

> 'In child protection conference reports it tends to be written along the lines that "it is recommended that the children…" not "I recommend…". In my case notes I would write in the first person like "I think this", "I think that", but in reports it is not really done in the first person because you represent the view of the local authority in child protection conferences. A core assessment is meant to be a multi-agency assessment where you include views from health, school and everybody involved, including the parents and the children. So in terms of your opinion I think they are in case notes rather in actual report.'

Samantha demonstrates here that the professional view is always important, but it might be expressed slightly differently depending on the context of the writing. She differentiates between case recording, discussed in Chapter Six, and a report, suggesting that she is less likely to use 'I' in a report than in case recording for a number of reasons: the report represents not just her view but also the view of the local authority, and the report is intended to represent views from a range of people in addition to the social worker, including other professionals, as well as parents and children.

Assessment reports and the digital environment

The purpose of an assessment report in all contexts is to document an assessment that is then used to draw up plans for further action. They are often documents that guide the initial phases of practice with service users or at key decision making points, and that provide an important point of reference for future assessments and reviews. Assessment reports have several purposes:

- they identify need and risk;
- they collate information from the service user, carers/family and key service providers/specialists;

■ they are a tool to measure the social work agency performance;
■ they standardise the information that should be sought;
■ they regulate activities that the social worker should complete.

Assessment reports do vary across service user groups, but there are common purposes for all assessments in statutory social work. The regulatory purposes are not always explicit, but they are nonetheless important when thinking about the audiences for a report. As with most social work writing, assessment reports are frequently aimed at a complex readership. The intended readers are multiple and not fully predictable at the time of writing as reports are frequently used retrospectively. The key readers, however, include:

■ service users/carers/family/advocate
■ colleagues within the social work agency
■ line managers and auditors within the social work agency
■ colleagues from other agencies such as health, education, housing
■ court officials.

The purposes and audience for assessment reports, therefore, are not straightforward, and it can be difficult to manage the tension between working with service users and the influence of managerialism, although auditors draw on assessment reports as a key source of data to evaluate performance against Performance Indicators. Managerialism in social work was introduced in Chapter One, but relates here to the influence or even dominance of management or bureaucratic priorities on social work practice.

As with case recording, discussed in Chapter Six, the introduction of digital systems has had a profound impact on practices surrounding writing assessment reports. Munro's review of social work (2011) identified significant problems associated with the use of ICT in social work, with practitioners suggesting that the timescales placed on the completion of assessments were unhelpful, and that 'locally procured computer systems were substantial obstacles to good practice' (2011: 111). Munro does not argue that ICT is generally unhelpful, but that systems have been allowed to disrupt frontline practice by focusing on measuring institutional targets and failing to respond to feedback from practitioners:

> The impact of technology on human performance is complex. As Woods et al point out, the conventional view is that new information technology and automation creates better ways of doing the same tasks. However, it is more accurate to say that any new technology is a change from one way of doing things to another. It alters the tasks that humans are expected to perform and it can,

in subtle and unexpected ways, influence and distort the way they carry out their part of the process. (Munro, 2011: 111)

Broadhurst et al (2010) explored initial assessments in children's services, and concluded that the software systems devised for assessment reports foregrounded measuring workflow at the risk of inhibiting direct work with service users and also effective decision making. This auditing function of assessment has become possible as a result of software designed to regulate assessments, such as the Common Assessment Framework (CAF) and ASSET (the assessment profile used by YOTs across England and Wales). These software systems have had a major impact on the experience of writing assessment reports, which were previously based on looser frameworks providing indicative content rather than the more restrictive format of systems such as ICS and ASSET.

There are significant differences between writing a report using software with pre-designed spaces for writing, and writing a report without a pre-set structure and content. It is increasingly common in social work for assessments to be highly structured with required information, without which the report cannot be formally completed. The rigid structure of this kind of report does remove the challenge for the writer of devising a structure, but it does also present other challenges such as required fields that are not relevant to a particular assessment and repetition. The design of software can therefore place unhelpful restrictions or demands on the writer. One example from a WiSWAP participant was the requirement to enter the last dental check for a looked-after child – failing to enter this information meant that the form could not be finalised. In most cases this would be relevant and important information, but the child in this example was less than six months old, and so the required field could not be completed. This kind of overly rigid design of software is ultimately in the hands of the agency that commissions it, and where such glitches are identified, it is the responsibility of senior managers to request changes in the design of the electronic forms.

Similar frustrations arise from the requirement for the same information to be repeated within and across documents. There is an argument for some very limited and essential information, used to identify a service user, to be repeated on all paperwork. Problems have arisen as a result of repetitive requests for information arising in part from separate files on each child that do not effectively cross-reference to other members of the family. Technology certainly offers potential benefits, but only if people using it are able to influence the design. It is also important that uniformity created by systems does not inhibit the use of professional discretion.

Software systems should ideally be developed in partnership with managers, frontline social workers and technology professionals taking account of both technical and social requirements. This is referred to as a 'socio-technical' design by Wastell and White, and facilitates a user-focused design process that benefits both the organisation and the individual end users (Wastell and White, 2013: 2).

There is important learning, therefore, for senior managers and frontline social workers about the use of ICT for writing assessment reports. The move from paper documentation to digital tools is one that is likely to be translated to these local procedures, so it will be the responsibility of each local authority to commission software tools that are effective, both in terms of practice effectiveness and usability for social workers. Localising systems offers an opportunity for developing electronic tools that are more effective if commissioners of new software are able to learn lessons from research into the shortcomings of the eCAF. Alongside this opportunity there is also a risk that local control will result in social workers and their colleagues in other services encountering an unhelpful regional diversity.

Court reports

Court reports, along with assessment reports, are perhaps the most important documents that are written by social workers working in a statutory context. Although both play a key role in decision making about service users' lives and the allocation of resources, there are important differences between them, and these are driven by their purpose and intended audiences. Holland (2004) illustrates the way in which social workers adapt their writing when the primary audience is the court, drawing on the observations of one social worker, 'Valerie':

> Valerie, here, neatly summarises some of the decisions that child welfare practitioners make, consciously or unconsciously, in how they present their assessment analysis and recommendations to others. She suggests that in assessment reports for court she tried to stick to verifiable facts, "what is in front of me", to write about that which is "backed up" by evidence and to check her report with her manger. She suggested that her style is more guarded, neater and more circumscribed. In doing so she is responding to the expectations of the courts for digestible, evidence-based assessment conclusions. (Holland, 2011: 43)

Here, Holland illustrates the different ways in which a court report is written specifically with the audience of the court in mind. This has an impact on both content (Valerie tried to stick to verifiable facts) and also style of writing (her style is more guarded, neater and more circumscribed). The court is essentially a lay audience, in other words, magistrates and judges are not trained childcare professionals, and so do not have an intimate understanding of the terminology, theory and research that guides social work practice. The use of language that enables the intended reader to access and understand what is written is one of the most important aspects of a good court report. As discussed throughout this book, writing is highly context-specific, and achieving such clarity for a range of audiences is not straightforward. Feedback from court has criticised social workers for using specialist terminology, euphemisms, jargon and acronyms in reports that make the meaning opaque for the reader. All of these linguistic devices are used extensively in social work, however, and it requires a careful eye to recognise the words and phrases that may confuse or even irritate a court – for example, the use of abbreviations, such as LA (local authority) and CSA (child sexual abuse), shorthand phrases used without explanation, such as 'challenging behaviour', and phrases that have a particular meaning within the agency or profession, such as 'eligibility criteria' and 'dysfunctional'. Care is needed where such words and phrases are used to ensure that the meaning is explained to the reader. There many examples of these terms which, although having an important role within social work discourse may not be welcomed by a judge for example inappropriately clothed eligibility criteria, challenging behavioural and empower. Seymour and Seymour (2011) cite the views of one family court judge:

> I would like social workers to tell me in plain English what they really think. Far better to say that they found the mother "fed-up and difficult", and describe the facts which led to this conclusion, than some bromide expression like "Mrs Smith's co-operation was a little lacking".
>
> "Behavioural issues" could mean anything from a tendency to fidget to a propensity to arson.
>
> "Kevin has difficulty relating adequately to his peer group" just means he hasn't go any friends. (Seymour and Seymour, 2011: 112)

What is clear from these examples is that there are very strong views about what counts as 'plain English' or 'imprecise language', and that social workers have to engage with such views even if at times they are unhelpful. In this example it could be argued that the judge's own interpretation of what phraseology is helpful language in a report conflicts with the kind of pejorative language social workers strive to avoid. As already discussed, communication through writing involves interpretation, and there is complex work for the writer in striving to ensure that the intended meaning is taken up. One strategy is for social workers to aim to succinctly and accurately describe what they have observed, and to provide descriptive examples. Taking one of the phrases above, 'Inappropriately clothed' does not provide the reader with any specific information on which to judge whether this concern is reasonable. It is more effective to describe the facts, and for the writer to lead the reading to support the conclusion they have made on the basis of clear evidence and argument. This may necessarily involve the use of some specialist terminology, albeit with further explanation or clarification where the terms used may not be familiar to the reader.

The role of the social work report is to present information in such a way as to enable the court to make a decision based as far as possible on facts, but social workers are also expected to present evidence based on their own expertise. Reports should not contain all information available, but rather a selection of *relevant* information presented in a logical order. For example, risks should be presented in order of priority, as evaluated by the social worker. The court will also expect the social worker to be able to present a recommendation based on their professional knowledge and judgement,. An effective court report, therefore, should provide a recommendation based on evidence presented, and the social worker's own professional judgement. Reports should avoid overly long descriptive passages that may make accessing key information more difficult for the reader. Care should be taken in only using specialist terminology that is necessary to convey meaning, and these should be explained within the document for those readers not familiar with them.

Reports in three statutory contexts

The second part of this chapter focuses on statutory reports in three areas of practice: assessments of risk and need in children's services, assessments of risk in youth offending and assessment reports in adult mental health. In each of these areas there are particular challenges but also some commonalities, such as the impact of digital formats on the social worker's role in writing assessment reports. These three areas have been selected as examples of practice contexts as they all involve a statutory role in which changing judgements are made, based on written reports.

Assessments of risk and need in children's services

Assessments of risk and need in children's services are frequently undertaken using standardised electronic forms, and these pose some of the same challenges as those for case recording, as discussed in Chapter Six. The reason that standardised forms were introduced was to ensure that all reports included what was seen as 'essential' information, but as with case recording, the introduction of electronic systems for writing assessment reports made it possible to monitor practice based on PIs. The standardisation of assessment in children's services was seen as an important way to drive up standards in the protection of children, but also in the service offered to children in need. The *Framework for the assessment of children in need and their families* was originally introduced by the Department of Health in in England in 2000, and represents statutory guidance issued under Section 7 of the Local Authority Social Services Act 1970. The purpose of assessment under Section 7 is to determine whether a child is 'in need of support' (Section 17, Children Act 1989) or 'in need of protection' (Section 47, Children Act 1989). It is based on a framework which addresses the three domains of: parenting capacity, child development and the wider family/environment (see Figure 7.1).

Figure 7.1: *Framework for the assessment of children in need and their families* **(England and Wales)**

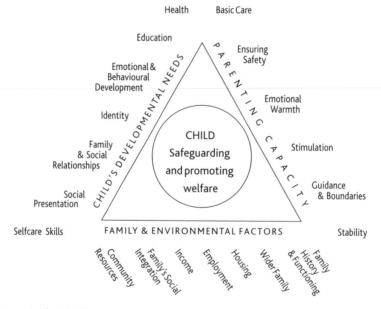

Source: DH (2000: 17)

This framework remains the basis of assessment in England and Wales, and in Scotland it has been developed to focus even more clearly on the child's perspective (see Figure 7.2).

Figure 7.2: *Integrated assessment framework* **(Scotland)**

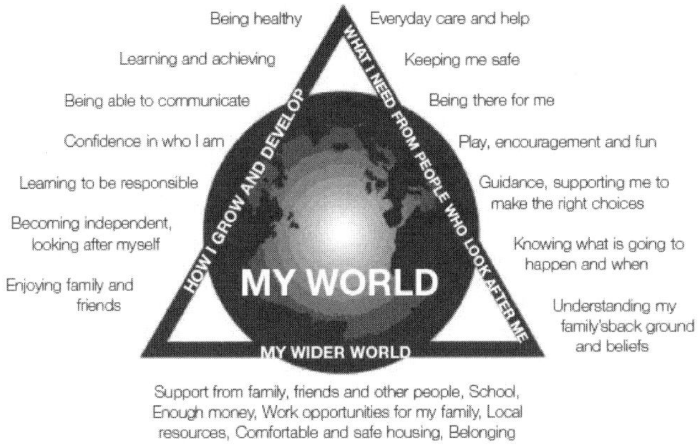

Source: The Scottish Government (2005)

This guidance has remained essentially unchanged, but in 2006 CAF was introduced in England and Wales. It was based on the *Framework for assessment*, but was intended to offer a tool for all agencies to undertake an assessment of any child in order to determine whether they were receiving suitable services. It was not intended to replace more specialist assessments, such as initial and comprehensive assessments of children in need of support or protection. The *Framework for assessment of children in need and their families* continues to be the key reference point for assessments, but it is now the responsibility of individual local authorities to develop documentation for all assessments. CAF became a digital tool in 2008 (eCAF), and was used nationally until 2012, when it was decommissioned following criticism of the model by Munro in her review of social work (2011), in which she recommended that the government remove constraints on local innovation and professional judgement:

> This review recommends a radical reduction in the amount of central prescription to help professionals move from a compliance culture to a learning culture, where they have more freedom to use their expertise in assessing need and providing the right help. (Munro, 2011: 6)

As in all social work writing, the essential skills that are needed for writing assessments using digital tools or paper-based documentation are social work practice skills. What should underpin any written assessment is an understanding of the needs of service users and of potential risks – the software is only the medium through which this assessment is communicated. What can be very challenging is 'telling a story' within the confines of a system that essentially requires small bits of factual information, restricted by character limits. Munro refers to this as a 'family and systemic narrative' to enable social workers to tell a story through their report. Her suggestion is that the development of uniform software systems has reduced the influence that frontline practitioners can have on the design of reports, and she urges the development of local systems that are driven by the needs of frontline social workers rather than information reporting (Munro, 2011: 111). Social workers should be confident, therefore, in reporting any difficulties that arise as a result of conflicts between using their professional skills (collecting, interpreting and analysing information and expressing an evidence-based judgement) and the tools provided by the agency to record their assessments.

Lessons can be learned about the most effective format and design of reporting systems from frontline practitioners, for example, the differences between writing assessments at different points of interventions. Initial assessments may need to be completed quickly in order to assess immediate risk, and are also often undertaken by social workers who do not know the child and who have little time to develop a relationship. Initial assessments therefore require social workers to gather key, factual information from a range of sources in a relatively short period of time. In comparison, core assessments and reviews of children receiving long-term services are more likely to be undertaken by social workers who know the child very well or at least who have the opportunity to gather information over a longer period of time. These differences will have an impact on the style of writing as well as on the content. The following quote is from Nicky, an experienced childcare social worker from the WiSWAP Project, illustrating the shift needed between initial assessment work and long-term teams:

> 'When I spent some time in the initial assessment team during my first placement I had to adjust the way I wrote and then when I came back I had to readjust again and not write so much. I tend to just write what happened why it happened, be very analytical rather than explicit to what conversations we had. But you can see the different styles of writing, so the writing is certainly adjusted for each department.'

This quote illustrates the way in which the focus of the specific team has an impact on the kind of writing that is needed. In this example Nicky found that the initial assessment team that she worked in required her to include a greater amount of detail to support her assessments, while in the long-term team the expectation was that the social workers provided a judgement based on their own analysis, but not necessarily including as much factual detail. This is not necessarily universal practice across intake and long-term teams, but one reason for the difference might be that in the initial stages of work with a family, the priority is in gathering new information in order for a group of professionals to make a decision on the next steps. Once a family or child is well known to a social worker, the emphasis can shift to professional judgements based on an established, in-depth understanding of needs and risks. It is important, therefore, to be aware of the purpose and context of the assessment report, and the balance required between factual information and analysis. However, assessments will require some elements of managerialism and professional judgement.

Assessments of risk in youth offending

In youth offending the purpose of an assessment is to inform and advise the court so that a judgement can be made about levels of risk to the public and also to the young person. As a result, primary audience is in some senses clearer than assessment reports in children's services. There is an added complexity, however, in that social workers in YOTs are working in a profession represented by practitioners with very different disciplinary training. As already discussed (see above; see also Chapter Two), social workers develop specific ways of thinking, talking and writing that arise from the discourses of the profession, but in youth offending, they need to communicate such discourses with colleagues from a range of professional backgrounds, including probation, the police service and youth and community workers. Although there is some commonality arising from undertaking a common role, there can also be considerable differences. These differences in theoretical and philosophical training, alongside the inherent challenges of the task, as well as potentially different discourses and ways of talking about an issue, can result in potentially competing objectives in assessment, as illustrated by Briggs (2013: 25):

> It is clear that YOT practitioner assessment and intervention is a complex process which utilizes a number of, often competing, rationales, belief systems and ways of working to inform practice with children and young people. Perhaps this is unsurprising since contemporary youth justice practice is set against a milieu of different philosophies and ideologies including: restoration; rehabilitation; retribution and punishment.

The complexity of writing an assessment in youth offending arises, therefore, from being a document that has the potentially competing purposes of assessing risks to the public from re-offending, and also needs and risks posed *to* the offender as a vulnerable person. These two priorities are relevant for any YOT workers, but differences in workers' professional background and therefore training may lead them to analyse and respond to each of these areas of risks differently. This can be particularly challenging for YOT workers who are qualified social workers with a line manager who is qualified in, for example, probation, who may not share the same theoretical and philosophical perspective. Whatever the professional background of the writer in youth offending, the primary audience is the same – the court, as discussed above. Youth offending assessments are intended to provide a professional opinion to enable the court to reach a judgement and disposal.[1] This does not mean that others do not read the report – court reports are read by service users, their families and other professionals involved – but they are very clearly written for this primary audience. The etiquette of the court or that perceived by management in the youth offending service can have an impact on how an assessment report is written, as illustrated by the following quote from the WiSWAP Project in which Colin, a social worker (qualified as a youth offending worker) suggests:

> 'You have to have a professional etiquette in terms of your writing. Management don't want to see any slang being used within the court arenas, or any unprofessional words that can be seen as a lot of profane swear words. I'm almost mindful that the Crown Prosecution Service when the witness statements are written up and presented to the Crown Prosecution Service, they're quite vocal in how they describe what's happened to the victim, quite open in terms of their language. But the youth offending service and children's services haven't got this discourse, I think there's a big difference in the way they discuss cases in court with ourselves.'

This example illustrates how the writer felt that he had to temper the way in which he expressed his assessment of the offending behaviour and attitude of the young person in order to meet the agency expectations of 'professionalism' and writing style. This approach is not necessarily representative as there can be important reasons why the exact words of service users should be included in recording. Professionalism in this context, therefore, is a disciplinary-specific concept; it refers to the expectation within this service that professionals should not use profane language in a report, even where quoting the words of a service user. This view of professionalism is not necessarily shared across agencies or even between individual workers and managers. Of course, exactly what counts as 'professional voice or language' can vary from context to context; the profane language that this YOT worker felt would more accurately convey the level of risk was unacceptable within his own agency, but might be acceptable in another, for example, within the Crown Prosecution Service. Louise (a social worker with the children's services intake team) illustrates that in her team, the use of profane language was accepted as long as it was clearly marked as a quote:

> 'I will use quotation marks to show the language used, obviously if it's abusive language.'

A social worker writing an assessment in youth offending needs to balance the priorities of risk to the public and the needs of the offender, and also be aware of the specific writing conventions of the service. These issues of content and style arise from the mixed disciplinary nature of the youth offending service, and the potentially conflicting roles in protecting the public and meeting the needs of young people. In his research into the experiences of youth offending officers, Briggs concludes that:

> While practitioners employed the technical language of risk and risk factors their decision making was underpinned by concerns with welfare. Interviewees believed welfare needs to be at the heart of assessment and viewed children and young people as presenting with such needs rather than solely as posing risks. Despite the use of official language, therefore, practitioners were uncomfortable in assessing and dealing with children and young people as objects of risk. (Briggs, 2013: 25)

Practitioners appear to be able to use the assessment tool to achieve both objectives; the scoring provides the apparently technical assessment driven by the managerial agenda, while the narrative provides an opportunity to focus on the underpinning welfare issues. This is illustrated from the following extract from an ASSET report for 'Craig'. The social worker has scored the highest level of risk here (4), but the narrative provides a context that assists the court to understand the reasons for this level of risk (see Figure 7.3).

The narrative elements of assessment are evident in this report, such as the description of key events (for example, 'Craig's father passed away…'), a strong attention to what has happened over time ('when he was aged 9…') and description of present circumstances ('the rocky relationship…'). Narrative remains a crucial aspect of assessment reports, regardless of the tools that are required by the agency or the overlaid managerial functions such as risk scoring. It is within these narrative elements that social workers are able to use the information gathered to offer an analysis informed by their professional training.

Figure 7.3: Section of ASSET report

(0 = not associated, 4 + very strongly associated with offending behaviour)

Family and personal relationships   Section rating 4

The same concerns are apparent from the previous assessment carried out on 22/12/xx –

There is clearly a very rocky relationship between his family which results in being rejected

by family members. It has also been suggested by his social worker that grandmother has

recently told Craig that his father, who passed away a few year ago, was not his father and

his natural father is in fact grandfather. It is unclear if there is any truth behind this as his

grandmother suffers from mental health issues.

Craig's father passed away when he was aged 9, from cancer after a lengthy battle, this hit

the rest of the family very hard. This, his mother tells me, is when Craig became

unmanageable in the family home. Prior to his father death his parents had been travelling

around the country to find suitable medical treatment for his father. During this time his

siblings were passed from family member to family member, it is believed that this is the

time when Craig started getting attachment issues and his behaviour became difficult to

handle.

Craig is currently living at home with his mother, older sister. Craig is very close to his

mother and finds it difficult to accept that she is unable to have him live at home on a

permanent basis. Craig does not get along with his 13-year-old brother and often hits and

assaults him, causing him distress and to be fearful of Craig.

Assessment reports in adult mental health

Mental health, as with most social work services, uses standardised electronic forms in order to complete assessment reports. The role of the social worker in writing these reports is complex. In some of the assessment reports their role is clearly visible and defined, and the social worker often has a sense that they are making an important professional contribution; however, as outlined below, this is often not so in the case of a mental health assessment of need.

Social workers, under the role of approved mental health practitioner, conduct Mental Health Act assessments. These assessment reports are the ultimate area where mental health social workers' professional judgement is centrally significant, and determine whether service users are detainable under the Mental Health Act (1983, 2007). While the social worker works with other professionals, GPs and a psychiatrist, they must come to an individual professional judgement that the person is detainable, and provide evidence for the reasons for this judgement. A number of other reports, for specific sections of the Act, may also be produced, including reports for Mental Health Tribunals, where social workers' professional judgements are central to the assessment reports:

> John was uncommunicative throughout the assessment, not speaking at all. He remained in the same position throughout, and displayed some evidence of waxy flexibility, with his arm remaining raised for several minutes before gradually dropping to his side. He made no eye contact with anyone in the room. (Extract from Mental Health Act 1983, Section 2 assessment)

Safeguarding is an area where the professional judgement of social workers is also at the forefront. It is the responsibility of the social worker to gather information, investigate and provide assessment reports. Given the varied nature of these investigations, there is no structured format, and there is clearly scope for professional visibility. As Michael, a social worker (in the mental health team) in the WiSWAP Project stated, it involves taking responsibility by presenting information and advocating for someone:

> '... fits quite nicely within social work without being bureaucratised. I do not actually mind it. For me as a writer, it feels more open and respectful than other reports. Very positive.')

Michael here is indicating the freedom and status accorded to his role, both in terms of the assessment reports not being constrained by either electronic or bureaucratic frameworks, and also by social workers feeling respected while undertaking these tasks.

The mental health assessment of need in England and Wales falls under the Community Care Act 1990. The main activity of mental health social workers is to assess the eligibility of residents of a local authority for social care by the application of Fair Access to Care Services guidance (2003) and the raising of a budget to pay for the care provided. Three developments have had a profound effect on the writing of assessment reports: the introduction of service user electronic records; the introduction of self-directed support from the national policy, *Putting People First* (2007); and co-funding policies.

The introduction of *electronic systems of record keeping* have a built-in logic that must be followed, and this imposes a specific sequencing on the writing of assessment reports. It also gives considerable control to the designer of the system, who standardises the structure and the questions and the sequence of questions to be asked.

The main purpose behind the introduction of *self-directed support* is the identifying of personal budgets for eligible service users that they can use to meet their needs in the best way they think, effectively putting the service user at the centre of the assessment. A positive outcome of digital systems is that assessment of needs now contains a formula to calculate the budget – this is intended to standardise the content and form of the assessment as well as to eliminate any localised inconsistencies in the assessment process by individual social workers. The goal is to ensure that service users receive the same budget for similar needs, and are provided with the minimum budget to meet their needs. To be able to do this, the assessment reports in mental health, like those in children's services and youth offending, are designed with a mixture of tick boxing and free text boxes that demand responses to particular questions.

Service users' *co-funding of their packages of care* has led to assessment reports being inspected more closely, and being more frequently disputed.

While these three developments were not introduced at the same time, together they have dramatically changed the writing of assessment reports in mental health.

The process of assessment reporting in mental health is still in development, and so far it has not been a smooth ride. Cumbersome, unwieldy, time-consuming and repetitive to start with, it is still evolving in an age of financial crisis. Assessments can be done in a single document or in a succession of documents to capture different elements – eligibility, mental health risk, simple or complex needs, personal budgets, capacity, professional involvement – with structured formats including tick boxes. Formats have changed according to the historical development of the software systems, the requirements of the local authority and feedback from practitioners and users of the documents. Some local authorities, following the logic of self-directed support, require their mental health social workers to write the assessments in the first person as if written by the service user, as illustrated below. While recent official discourse has been to re-enhance the role of the mental health social worker and their professional input, the actual assessment process and systems have tended to remove their professional input from the mental health assessment reports. All this has created difficulties for social workers. As Michael, a social worker in a mental health team, puts it:

'The system is bureaucratic, with constant change of electronic forms in structure. It is budget led. A uniformed system, despite social worker and training, the system tries to take out all interpretation and judgement and takes away the holistic approach, as it is system that determines level of care and amount of time. It asks you about times. I find it difficult and problematic the way the assessment is geared.'

Even with the best intentions, structured digital assessments, requiring tick box answers, diminish opportunities for the expression of professional judgements. Through both this tick box design and the required use of the first person on behalf of services users (who are able and want to take an active role in the assessment process) there is a real danger that the professional role and voice disappears from the assessment report, with the social worker effectively taking on the role of scribe. It appears at this point that there is very little room for manoeuvre for mental health social workers, apart from going through the succession of steps in an administrative way until the personal budget for the service user has been raised.

Assessment reports for those mental health service users who are not able to engage or who are reluctant and hostile due to their mental health conditions pose interesting dilemmas for social workers having to use the first person. Michael describes a particular situation:

'Mel has paranoia, psychotic symptoms. [Due to all this, the assessment was a] stilted conversation [with him] so I gleaned information from other people, but I have written in first person, expanded, not verbatim. This type of assessment is geared to older people. The conversation has to be interpreted so that is going to get a budget and support the person. Social work intervention comes at this point of interpretation of the conversation, certain way of expressing things so we can get people money, which equals service. When writing, the main thing is the bottom line, the bottom line figure for the budget.'

Michael is aware that his priority is to get a budget for a service user who may mistrust the assessment process due to their condition, and who may mistrust any assessment report, thus not wanting to cooperate with this process. He is also aware that the conversation, the questions asked and the assessment report may affect the mental health condition of the service user. Nevertheless, he needs to write a report in the first person voice of the service user, and ensure that it includes the adequate triggers for a budget, so that the service user gets some support to assist in reducing the effect of their mental health condition.

The assessment report appears to quote the service user, 'Mel':

> "'I wish to remain in my flat and establish new routines that support me to keep mentally well. I like being on my own, but would sometimes like to go out –for this I need the support of others to minimise my anxieties.
>
> "My medication is vital to keeping me well, and I need support to ensure that I take this regularly.
>
> "I would like to establish new routines that assist me with maintaining the condition of my flat.'"

However, this is the social worker's writing, adding information from other sources, including his own professional judgment about what 'the service user wants' to remain independent. The social worker has to camouflage his professional opinion under the first person in the writing of assessment reports, thus creating tensions for social workers. Assessment reports in mental health are skilful pieces of risk management work, and social workers have to navigate the changes imposed on them to get the right outcome for their service users while attempting to maintain their professional identity.

Conclusion

In this chapter the purpose and challenges involved in writing assessment and court reports have been explored. There is no doubt that in all statutory settings assessment reports are vital tools in the decision-making process, and that writing them entails social workers using a range of professional as well as writing skills. Newly qualified social workers do not come to report writing as novice writers, however, and there are many skills that will have been developed in other contexts, particularly writing for academic courses that they will be able to draw on in developing their practice writing. Academic writing, such as essays, develop the writer's ability to source, select and critically evaluate information, or evidence, and to craft it into a persuasive argument. The professional judgements that underpin such arguments can only come from developing competence in a broad range of practice skills, and so for students and novice social workers, the availability of good quality supervision that acknowledges the importance of report writing is essential.

The context, purpose and intended audience is perhaps even more significant in assessment and court reports than for case recording, discussed in Chapter Six. These reports more commonly involve the social worker pulling together evidence and potentially conflicting information and opinion from a range of sources – a challenging process of orchestrating a number of voices within one coherent text. Perhaps one of the most difficult aspects of report writing in statutory social work relates to the professional voice of the writer in an institutional context, for example, where a difference of opinion relating to content or presentation arises between the individual practitioner and their agency. In all cases, however, a key skill in report writing is the ability to craft a persuasive text that presents information in such a way that it can be understood and relatively easily assimilated by the many potential readers, even when it contains conflicting opinions and complex information. Achieving this involves careful use of language based on an awareness that meaning in writing is rarely transparent or straightforward.

The introduction of digital systems appears to have created additional tensions in all of the three service areas considered, but the direction of travel, particularly in children's services, is for social workers to re-claim some control over the way in which they 'tell the story' which underpins many assessments. This narrative form needs to find a way to sit alongside the now inevitable managerialist requirement to standardise the assessment and decision-making process. Whatever the inevitably changing political and policy influences on social work, reports will remain key documents for effective practice. An awareness of the purpose, context, audience and voice used is one way in which social workers can be more purposeful in their writing, to ensure that reports are as effective as possible in supporting best practice.

Note

[1] 'A disposal is an umbrella term referring both to sentences given by the court and pre-court decisions made by the police. Disposals may be divided into four separate categories of increasing seriousness starting with pre-court disposals then moving into first-tier and community-based penalties through to custodial sentences' (Youth Justice Board/Ministry of Justice, 2013: 7).

8

Embedding writing as best practice

Introduction

This concluding chapter draws together the key principles of effective writing, which have been introduced and illustrated throughout the book. It highlights the themes, such as maintaining a greater awareness of voice, audience and purpose, in order to make writing as effective as possible. In addition, it draws together some of the issues introduced that will continue to challenge academic and practice writing in social work for students and qualified staff, including effective use of new technologies, professional accountability, involving service users and orchestrating complex texts. In drawing together the themes of the book, this chapter considers the contribution that educators can make to ensuring that writing in social work practice supports and enhances best practice. Finally, it concludes by reflecting on the way that writing in social work has changed, and offers some thoughts on possible future developments in academic and professional writing in social work.

Learning to write: purpose, context, audience and voice

Chapters One and Two suggested that learning to write effectively in academic and practice domains is a complex, context-specific activity, with the demands of each type of text varying and influenced by a range of factors. It is unhelpful, therefore, to reduce advice on learning to write to the development of incremental skills that can simply be transferred from writing task to writing task. It is for this reason that *Effective writing for social work* has not attempted to map out how to write generally in social work, but rather to provide writers with the questions to ask in order to better understand the most effective way of writing a specific text. Such interrogation and reflection on individual writing tasks begins with the purpose and context of the document, for example, a report written to advise the court in the context of youth offending (see Table 8.1).

Table 8.1: Purpose, context, audience, voice

Type of document	Report
Purpose	To advise the court about the context of the offence and the risks of re-offending, risks to the community and risks/needs of the young person involved
Context	YOT
Audience	The court, defence and prosecution solicitors, the service user and the service user's family, the police, line manager and colleagues in the YOT
Voice	Professional social work voice, representative of the YOT and mediated voice of the service user and the service user's family

The concepts of purpose, context, audience and voice have been discussed throughout this book in relation to both academic and practice writing. Table 8.1 summarises the elements involved in one type of writing, discussed in more detail in Chapter Seven. Although the voices represented in the report include those of the service user and the service user's family, these are mediated through the social worker's lens. This means that there is inevitably some modification of the service user's perspective, if only through the selectivity that the social worker employs when compiling a report based on extensive assessment and discussion with a range of contributors. Put simply, although the service user's voice may be represented in the report, it is unlikely to be represented in the way in which the service user might have presented their own voice if they had written the report themselves, as the social worker has to balance several voices within the text.

Once there is clarity about the purpose and context, the writer then needs to think about the audience, and, as identified in Chapters Five to Seven, this may be very complex in social work where it is common for there to be many readers with different needs, potentially at different times. Reflecting on the audience is one reminder that writing is an act of communication rather than purely an administrative task or even a tool to document practice. There are elements of social work writing that are administrative, such as completing expenses claims or routine requests for ongoing services such as transport, but these do not make up the major part of social work writing. Documenting practice (providing factual information about events) is also one function of writing, particularly in case recording, but it is not a simple task as there is a need for selectivity and discretion in which events are documented and how. Alongside these purposes sit several more complex functions, such as planning, assessing, expressing a judgement and communication.

Communication is an omnipresent aspect of writing, but despite social work education rightly placing significant emphasis on the development of communication skills, these are rarely applied to writing. Communication in all forms involves two parties, a speaker and a listener, a writer and a reader. Just as in all communication, both parties need to be aware of both their own communication and the needs of the receiver. Hence, just as the writer needs to be aware of the reader, they also need to be aware of their own voice in writing.

Social work practice writing is also complex in this respect as the social worker may be representing their agency, the voice of the service user or their own voice as a social work professional. Combining these, often disparate, voices can be challenging, and requires not only sophisticated writing skills, but also the ability to negotiate with other contributors and to think critically about the way in which different views are presented. A focus on the writer's voice and the audience is one way in which to retain an awareness of the communicative function of practice writing. Social workers already have well developed communication skills, and where these are applied to writing, it becomes a dynamic and integral part of their practice rather than an administrative task.

Institutional context for writing

Social work writing takes place within an institutional context in both academic and practice domains. This means that the writer needs to be aware of the explicit and implicit rules that govern whether a piece of writing is considered to be 'successful'. In the academic domain this judgement is in the form of assessment, and meeting the success criteria is likely to be a significant consideration for the writer. However, the criterion against which student work is assessed is rarely straightforward, as illustrated in Chapters Two and Three. There should be explicit assessment criteria for all assignments, but implicit criteria are also applied, and these frequently differ between assignments, disciplines, tutors and universities. This means that experienced students, such as graduates joining postgraduate programmes, can also be caught out by unexpected module or university-specific criteria that have not been made explicit to them. Differences can include anything from the acceptability of using the first person, such as 'In this essay I will discuss…', through to the style of referencing or use of footnotes. One of the most important areas of potential confusion, however, is the expectation of the marking tutor in relation to the use of personal or practice experience, which is a particular feature of much academic writing in social work. The diversity of both explicit and implicit requirements in academic writing mean that it is impossible to provide definitive advice on writing a good assignment, even within one discipline such as social work. Students therefore need to be able to seek out guidance and support on each course studied, and in particular, when they move to a new institution.

The institutional context is no less relevant in practice, although the issues are different. Practice writing is not 'graded' as such, but success criteria do exist and practice writing is evaluated in several ways. It has been argued throughout this book that the most important success criteria is the effectiveness of the writing to support best social work practice, or, in other words, supporting the welfare of the service user. This can become hidden with more explicit measurements of success, such as entering key data that measures PIs, overshadowing best practice as judged by the social worker. The impact of digital systems in recording and report writing, discussed in Chapters Six and Seven, has been one factor in distorting the emphasis of practice writing from a social worker-led activity that supports best practice, to a managerial, systems-driven tool for measuring performance. Reclaiming writing as an important tool for social work practice involves re-focusing on it as an integral part of practice.

The physical environment for writing in practice, discussed in Chapters Five and Six, is another important influence that the institution has on writing. While in academic writing the student has a fair degree of control over their tools (such as a laptop or pen and paper) and the environment in which they write, in practice the environment and tools are largely prescribed by the social work agency. Large open plan offices with hot desking and frequent interruptions and distractions are the norm in social work, and this is not an environment that most people find conducive for undertaking complex writing. The experience of this physical environment is also socially determined – in other words, it can be mediated by the behaviour of other people sharing the space – and in Chapter Five it is argued that there are ways in which a team (with the support of a manager) can organise an open plan space to allow quiet times and spaces for writing. Achieving a suitable writing environment, therefore, is a shared responsibility between social work team members and their managers.

Implications for educators: enhancing best practice

Students and recently qualified social workers clearly have a responsibility to develop their own writing skills alongside a range of capabilities taught on social work programmes. This responsibility is shared, however, with educators in the university and with practitioners involved in supporting students during practice placements. Within the academic context there are many ways in which practice writing could be developed before students begin their practice placements, such as through:

- designing the curriculum
- designing the assessment strategy, including assessment outcomes and associated clear guidance on writing
- support and feedback.

Curriculum development

As discussed in Chapter One, the social work curriculum currently and historically has only obliquely referred to writing in practice, and this is mainly within the broader context of communication. Greater emphasis should be placed on teaching practice writing, and there would be significant benefits in doing so, particularly within a broader framework of social work skills. The area that students in the WiSWAP Project identified as lacking in their preparation for practice writing was an understanding of the complex and demanding context for writing in practice. They also suggested that writing skills developed through their academic assignments benefited them when they came to write in practice, but that there was very little attention given to specifically teaching practice writing. Both essays and reflective writing require rigour, planning and scholarly skills that social workers valued and, in many cases, recognised as contributing to their professional writing.

The transfer of learning was not necessarily explicit for social workers, but experience in thinking critically about changes in how they positioned themselves in the text (reflective writing) and the use of evidence (both essays and reflective writing) to build an argument appeared to be relevant and valuable to their professional writing. The value of reflective writing was explicitly considered by social workers, partly due to the challenge it posed them. While its value in developing their ability to reflect critically on their practice was evident, it was less clear whether this necessarily transferred to any specific areas of professional writing. The curriculum on social work programmes is a space with many competing demands, particularly with the development of shorter postgraduate programmes with shorter periods available for academic study. The interconnected nature of social work writing, however, provides possibilities for it to be considered alongside a range of other topics, such as assessment, planning and decision making.

One approach to directly teaching practice writing is offered by Leon and Pepé (2010), who draw on an evaluation of a project that developed a bespoke module within a social work programme in which writing 'documentation' was directly taught to undergraduate students. They suggest that students learn to write practice texts more effectively in the context of their broader social work practice. 'Documentation' is used here to refer to all forms of professional writing in social work. The researchers' interest was in the way in which social work students are taught how to write in the professional context during their qualifying training. The project arose from a concern that social work students did not receive any guidance on professional writing until they moved into the practice context. They suggest that:

> To adequately prepare undergraduate social work students on documentation skills, educators and social service agency field instructors must continue to independently and in collaboration with each other provide documentation and record-keeping training from the very beginning of the student's academic career. Schools of social work must integrate documentation/recordkeeping training in their curricula if students are to be fully prepared to participate in agency settings that demand documentation accuracy and accountability. (Leon and Pepé, 2010: 373)

This research poses the challenge to educators to think about to what extent they can directly teach aspects of practice writing in university, rather than just focusing on writing in the context of scholarship skills, and relying on the practice environment to teach practice writing skills.

Assessment

Assessment is a complex area and it goes beyond the remit of this book to explore it in any great detail. Higher education is grappling with the challenges of assessing students in a meaningful way that supports them in becoming independent learners and addresses both content and skill development. In practice-based disciplines such as social work, there is the added complexity of addressing both scholarly and practice skills.

The assessment of practice writing is generally only located within the practice portfolio and, as discussed in Chapter Four, this does not usually involve the quality of the writing itself being judged, but rather the practice writing provides evidence of other social work capabilities. It may be possible for aspects of practice writing to be assessed through academic assignments, or indeed, for specific practice tasks to be incorporated into the practice learning assessment that brings together academic and practice assessments. As discussed above, this book has not advocated trying to 'teach' how to write specific kinds of texts, or even tried to define what 'good' writing is, but rather, it has attempted to illustrate the ways in which social workers, with support, can approach each new writing task (or kind of writing) through asking questions that will help them reflect on and understand what is required. This interrogation of the context and purpose of texts can be taught and assessed, and students should be supported to take this learning with them into practice.

Support and feedback

Novice writers in both academic and practice contexts need support and guidance in developing their ability to write effectively. Study skills guides and generic study support have their place, but learning to write is a very personal experience, and so there are benefits in offering support that is individually tailored. From the perspective of academic literacies just focusing on the student or novice social worker, this is also problematic as the 'problem' is focused on the individual writer and their level of 'skill' rather than on the broader and more complex disciplinary, institutional, cultural and inter-relational factors. The approach taken in this book, therefore, has been to offer suggestions for the individual writer, and also for others who have a role in supporting writing, such as educators and managers.

As discussed in Chapter Three, it can be helpful for students to undertake a language and educational history that they share with their tutor. Reflecting on past writing experiences in this way can be beneficial for the student in recognising specific needs or anxieties around writing. It is also very valuable for this to be a conversation with a tutor so that a dialogue is opened up about writing that is broader than the assessment criteria, and that recognises the student as an individual with a relevant history and identity. Ideally this dialogue should also flow into feedback on writing in assignments, although this may be difficult where there is little consistency in markers across a programme. Feedback on written assignments provides an important opportunity for students to learn about their progress in developing writing skills that they can then apply to future assignments and, ideally, to incremental development of their practice writing skills.

Social work as a practice-based discipline has always strived to achieve the difficult balance between the academic and practice domains, and its partnerships with practice agencies are a deeply embedded element of all programmes of study. Despite this, the area of teaching practice writing appears to have fallen between these domains, with neither the university nor practice agency having a clear responsibility or focus on teaching and supporting students (and newly qualified social workers) in developing their writing. In the WiSWAP Project, participants reported that they did not feel well prepared for the writing that they were required to do in practice, and that support with their writing appeared to be random and offered according to the individual enthusiasm of particular supervisors, manager or tutors rather than through a systematic or consistent approach (Rai and Lillis, 2013: 9). Responsibility for supporting students in developing writing skills does not lie with practice agencies alone, and the WiSWAP Project also identified that there was also no clear role played by university staff or practice supervisors in supporting practice writing.

Le Maistre and Paré (discussed in Chapter Five) suggested that social work writing is not only about recording and transferring information, but involves complex skills such as hypothesizing and interpreting information (Le Maistre and Paré, 2004: 83). This complexity was reflected in the WiSWAP Project in which participants suggested that practice writing involved a diversity of text types that differed from team to team, multitasking and managing competing demands. Social workers also need to navigate the software (and paper) systems within a particular team, and there is considerable research (cited in Chapters Six and Seven) to support the assertion that the introduction of digital systems to social work writing has not been unproblematic. Dias and Paré's research in Canada (discussed in Chapter Five) also suggested that social workers did not learn how to write in practice from any direct teaching in university, but rather through an informal and implicit apprenticeship (Dias and Paré, 2000). There is, therefore, a role for those experienced colleagues in practice to support and guide students on practice placements, novice qualified social workers and also those transferring to a new team or agency in developing their writing.

Reflecting back and looking to the future

When I completed my social work training and began my first professional role in 1989, all of my assignments were handwritten. There was no teaching delivered through digital technologies, and no expectation that I would have to use any resources that were not in print. In the child protection team where I began my professional career, all of the files were hard copy. There were no computers in the social workers' office, and records were either handwritten by social workers or typed up secretarial staff from notes or recordings on Dictaphones.

Both of these institutional writing contexts are unrecognisable just two decades later, with an increasing number of social work agencies being entirely paperless, and universities making increasing use of the virtual learning environment (VLE). Most students will only encounter writing by hand in examinations, with developments in software also likely to bring computers into examination rooms, even virtual examination rooms. The VLE, electronic submission of assessments and plagiarism software are standard components of learning at university, and educators routinely expect students to access digital reading and teaching resources. Some lecturers are also exploring the use of web-based commination, such as social media, to supplement their teaching and to engage students in wider debates such as Twitter. These changes have been significant and have brought both opportunities and challenges for students and social workers.

Digital technologies open up possibilities for gathering and sharing information in a radically different way to paper documents, and this has had an impact on both teaching in higher education and social work practice. Digital technologies have the potential to gather data on the behaviours and practices of both social workers' and students' such as when and for how long they are logged on to specific elements of the digital network. This has already been seen in social work practice, as discussed in Chapter Five, in the use of digital assessment tools enabling managers to audit and scrutinise not only the contents of assessments, but also the timescales that documentation was completed in. As teaching is increasingly conducted digitally, university educators will also be able to monitor and analyse the ways in which students participate in learning through interacting with teaching materials. In both examples, the technology has the potential to offer powerful resources to improve service delivery, but also poses the risk that audit will become the key driver rather than the effectiveness of the service itself. Concerns about the way in which a focus on audit may disrupt effective practice has indicated the need for practitioners, as the primary users, to be consulted about the development of software tools. Mobile digital tools create opportunities for service users to be involved in recording and assessment reports in new ways, such as through the use of tablet computers. The availability of digital resources, both online and downloadable to mobile devices, presents opportunities for students to access teaching in a more flexible way. As discussed in Chapter One, social media is also changing the ways in which students can participate in increasingly global conversations about social work. Digital technologies will continue to change the way in which we write and communicate with each other that may potentially facilitate greater participation and access to information.

Conclusion

Effective writing for social work has offered an alternative perspective on supporting writing development in social work to the traditional skills approach. Thinking about writing as a socially mediated, context-dependent activity sits comfortably within the broader discourses of social work, and the approach taken here should enable social workers to draw on skills, attributes and knowledge that they already possess, or are in the process of acquiring in the course of their qualifying studies. This does not mean that learning to write effectively will not pose challenges to the student social worker, but the discussions presented here illustrate that the effectiveness of social work writing in academic and practice domains does not rest on the shoulders of the individual alone. Universities have a responsibility for developing appropriate assessment strategies and for communicating marking criteria clearly to students. They also have a responsibility for ensuring that students are taught and supported in developing their writing, and this includes writing in practice. Practice assessors have a role to play through offering support and guidance to students, but line managers and senior management also share a responsibility for the quality of practice writing. It is only through agency policy and local arrangements to support writing that social workers can be provided with the systems, guidance, physical environment and working practices that will enable them to use the skills that they have developed to write effectively in support of best practice for service users.

References

Bakhtin, M. (1981) 'Discourse in the novel', in M. Holquist (ed) *The dialogic imagination. Four essays by M. Bakhtin*. trans. C. Emerson and Holquist, M., Austin: University of Texas Press, (1981), pp 259-422.

Barton, D. (1984) *Literacy: An ecology of written language*, Oxford: Blackwell.

Barton, D. and Hamilton, M. (1998) *Local literacies: Reading and writing in one community*, London: Routledge.

BASW (British Association of Social Workers) (2012) *Voices from the frontline*, May (http://cdn.basw.co.uk/upload/basw_23750-6.pdf).

Baynham, M. (1995) *Literacy practices: Investigating literacy in social contexts*, London: Longman.

Baynham, M. (2000) 'Academic writing in new and emergent discipline areas', in M. Lea and B. Stierer (eds) *Student writing in higher education: New contexts*, Buckingham: Open University Press, pp 17-31.

Bazerman, C. (1981) 'What written knowledge does: Three examples of academic discourse', *Philosophy of Social Sciences*, vol 11, pp 361-87.

Bazerman, C. (1988) *Shaping written knowledge: The genre and activity of the experimental article in science*, Madison, WI: University of Wisconsin Press.

Bazerman, C. and Prior, P. (2004) *What writing does and how it does it: An introduction to analyzing texts and textual practices*, Mahwah, NJ: Lawrence Erlbaum Associates.

Berman, J. (2001) *Risky writing: Self-disclosure and self-transformation in the classroom*, Amherst, MA: University of Massachusetts Press.

Berman, S. and Katoma, V. (2008) 'An elearning model based on collaboration and sharing', Paper given at 3rd International Conference on e-Learning, University of Cape Town (http://pubs.cs.uct.ac.za/archive/00000502).

Bhatia, V. (2004) *Worlds of written discourse: A genre-based view*, London: Continuum.

Bolton, G. (2003) *Reflective practice: Writing and professional development*, London: Paul Chapman.

Boud, D. (1999) 'Avoiding the traps: seeking good practice in the use of self-assessment and reflection in professional courses', *Social Work Education*, vol 18, no 2, pp 121-32.

Boud, D. and Solomon, N. (eds) (2001) *Work-based learning: A new higher education?*, Buckingham: SRHE and Open University Press.

Boud, D., Keogh, R. and Walker, D. (eds) (1985) *Reflection: Turning reflection into learning*, London: Kogan Press.

Bowl, M. (2000) 'Listening to the voices of non traditional students', *Widening Participation in Lifelong Learning*, vol 2, no 1, www.staffs.ac.uk/journal/Volume2(1)/contents.htm

Bowl, M. (2002) 'Experiencing the barriers: non-traditional students entering higher education', *Research Papers in Education*, vol 16, no 2, pp 141-60.

Briggs, D.B. (2013) 'Conceptualising risk and need: The rise of actuarialism and the death of welfare? Practitioner assessment and intervention in the Youth Offending Service', *Youth Justice*, vol 13, no 1, pp 17-30.

Broadhurst, K., Wastell, D., White, S., Hall, C., Peckover, S., Thompson, K. and Davey, D. (2010) 'Performing "initial assessment": Identifying the latent conditions for error at the front-door of local authority children's services', *British Journal of Social Work*, vol 40, no 2, pp 352-70.

Campbell, J. and Oliver, M. (1996) *Disability politics: Understanding our past, changing our future*, Abingdon: Routledge.

Carey, M. (2013) *The social work dissertation: Using small scale qualitative methodology*, London: McGraw Hill International.

CCETSW (Central Council for Education and Training in Social Work) (1995) *Assuring quality in the Diploma in Social Work: 1: Rules and requirements for the DipSW*, London: CCETSW.

Chelune, G.J. (1979) *Self-disclosure: Origins, patterns and implications of openness in interpersonal relationships*, San Francisco, CA: Jossey-Bass.

Clark, R. and Ivanič, R. (1997) *The politics of writing*, London: Routledge.

Cleaver, H. and Walker, S. (2004) 'From policy to practice: the implementation of a new framework for social work assessments of children and families', *Child & Family Social Work*, vol 9, issue 1, February, pp 81-90.

Cleaver, H., Walker, S., Scott, J., Cleaver, D., Rose, W., Ward, H. and Pithouse, A. (2008) *Integrated Children's System: Enhancing social work recording and inter-agency practice*, Research Brief, London: Department for Children, Schools and Families (http://webarchive.nationalarchives.gov.uk/20130401151715/https://www.education.gov.uk/publications/eOrderingDownload/DCSF-RBX-01-08.pdf).

Creme, P. (2005) 'Should student learning journals be assessed?', *Assessment in Higher Education*, vol 30, no 3, pp 287-96.

Creme, P. and Lea, M. (2008) *Writing at university*, Buckingham: Open University Press.

Curry, M.J. and Hewings, A. (2003) 'Approaches to teaching writing', in C. Coffin, M.J. Curry, S. Goodman, A. Hewings, T.M. Lillis and J. Swann (eds) *Teaching academic writing: A toolkit for higher education*, London: Routledge, pp 19-44.

Curry, M.J. and Lillis, T.M. (2003) 'Issues in academic writing in higher education', in C. Coffin, M. Curry, S. Goodman, A. Hewings, T. Lillis and J. Swann (eds) *Teaching academic writing, Volume 1*, London: Routledge, pp 1-18.

DCSF (Department for Children, Schools and Families) (2008) *Core assessment record exemplars* (http://webarchive.nationalarchives.gov.uk/20090813152455/dcsf.gov.uk/everychildmatters/safeguarding andsocialcare/integratedchildrenssystem/icspracticeresources/icsexemplarsdocuments/docs/).

Department of Health (2000) *Framework for the assessment of children in need and their families* London: Crown Copyright, p 17.

Dias, P. and Paré, A. (2000) *Transitions: Writing in academic and workplace settings*, New York: Hampton Press.

Edwards, A. (2011) 'Building common knowledge at the boundaries between professional practices: Relational agency and relational expertise in systems of distributed expertise', *International Journal of Educational Research*, vol 509, no 1, pp 33-9.

Eraut, M. (1994) *Developing professional knowledge and competence*, London: Falmer.

Etherington, K. (2004) *Becoming a reflexive researcher: Using our selves in research*, London: Jessica Kingsley Publishers.

Gast, L. and Patmore, A. (2012) *Mastering approaches to diversity in social work*, London: Jessica Kingsley Publishers.

Goffman, E. (1963) *Behaviour in public places: Notes on the social organization of gatherings*, London: Free Press/Collier-Macmillan.

Goldsmith, L. (1999) *Recording with care: Inspection of case recording in social services departments*, London: Department of Health.

GSCC (General Social Care Council) (2002) *Code of practice for social workers*, London: GSCC.

Hall, C., Slembrouck, S. and Sarangi, S. (2006) *Language practices in social work*, Abingdon: Routledge.

Hall, C., Parton, N., Peckover, S. and White, S. (2010) 'Child-centric information and communication technology (ICT) and the fragmentation of child welfare practice in England', *Journal of Social Policy*, vol 39, no 3, pp 393-413.

Hall, S. (1996) *Questions of cultural identity*, London: Sage.

Hall, S. and Maharaj, S. (2001) *Innovations: Modernity and difference*, London: Institute of International Visual Arts.

HCPC (Health and Care Professions Council) (2012) *Standards of proficiency: Social workers in England*, London: HSPC.

Hoadley-Maidment, E. (2000) 'From personal experience to reflective practitioner: Academic literacies and professional education', in M. Lea and B. Stierer (eds) *Student writing in higher education: New contexts*, Buckingham: Open University Press, pp 165-78.

Holland, S. (2004) *Child and family assessment in social work practice*, London: Sage.

Holmes, L., McDermid, S. and Jones, A. (2009) *How social workers spend their time: An analysis of the key issues that impact on practice pre and post implementation of the integrated children's system*, Loughborough: Department for Children, Schools and Families.

Horner, B. and Lu, M.Z. (1999) *Representing the 'other'. Basic writers and the teaching of basic writing*, Urbana, IL: National Council for Teachers of English.

Howe, A. and Collins, A. (2010) 'Unlocking the potential of the ePortfolio for work-based learning', *Learning and Teaching in Higher Education*, vol 4, no 1, pp 96-99.

Hunt, C. and Sampson, F. (2006) *Writing: Self and reflexivity*, Basingstoke: Palgrave.

Huntington, J. (1981) *Social work and general medical practice: Collaboration or conflict?*, London: George Allen & Unwin Ltd.

Hyland, K. (2006) *English for academic purposes: An advanced resource book*, London: Routledge.

Ince, D., Griffiths, A., Hall, W. and Keynes, M. (2010) *A chronicling system for children's social work: Learning from the ICS failure*.

Irvine, R., Kerridge, I., Mcphee, J. and Freeman, S. (2002) 'Interprofessionalism and ethics: consensus or clash of cultures?', *Journal of Interprofessional Care*, vol 16, no 3, pp 199-210.

Ivanič, R. (1998) *Writing and identity: The discoursal construction of identity in academic writing*, Amsterdam: John Benjamins.

Jasper, M.A. (2005) 'Using reflective writing within research', *Journal of Research in Nursing*, vol 10, no 3, pp 247-60.

Jourard, S. (1971) *Self-disclosure: An experimental analysis of the transparent self*, New York: Wiley-Interscience.

Kolb, D. (1970) *Learning in groups*, London: Croom Helm.

Laming, Lord (2003) *The Victoria Climbié Inquiry: Report of an Inquiry by Lord Laming*, Cm 5730, London: The Stationery Office.

Lavé, J. and Wenger, E. (1991) *Situated learning: Legitimate peripheral participation*, Cambridge: Cambridge University Press.

Lea, M.R. (1998) 'Academic literacies and learning in higher education: constructing knowledge through texts and experience', *Studies in the Education of Adults*, vol 30, no 2, pp 156-72.

Lea, M.R. (2004) 'Academic literacies: a pedagogy for course design', *Studies in Higher Education*, vol 29, no 6, pp 739-56.

Lea, M.R. and Stierer, B. (2000) *Student writing in higher education: New contexts*, Buckingham: SRHE and Open University Press.

Lea, M.R. and Stierer, B. (2009) 'Lecturers' everyday writing as professional practice in the university as workplace: new insights into academic identities', *Studies in Higher Education*, vol 34, no 4, pp 417-28.

Lea, M.R. and Street, B. (1998) 'Student writing in higher education: an academic literacies approach', *Studies in Higher Education*, vol 23, no 2, pp 157-72.

Lea, M.R. and Street, B. (2000) 'Student writing and staff feedback in higher education', in M.R. Lea and B. Stierer (eds) *Student writing in higher education: New contexts*, Buckingham: SRHE and Open University Press, pp 32-47.

Le Maistre, C. and Paré, A. (2004) 'Learning in two communities: the challenge for universities and workplaces', *Journal of Workplace Learning*, vol 16, no 1/2, pp 44-52.

Le Maistre, C., Boudreau, S. and Paré, A. (2006) 'Mentor or evaluator? Assisting and assessing newcomers to the professions', *Journal of Workplace Learning*, vol 18, no 6, pp 344-54.

Leon, A.M. and Pepé, J. (2010) 'Utilizing a required documentation course to improve the recording skills of undergraduate social work students', *Journal of Social Service Research*, vol 36, no 4, pp 362-76.

Lillis, T. (1997) 'New voices in academia? The regulative nature of academic writing conventions', *Linguistics and Education*, vol 11, no 3, pp 182-99.

Lillis, T. (2001) *Student writing: Access, regulation and desire*, London: Routledge.

Lillis, T. (2010) 'New voices in academia? The regulative nature of academic writing conventions', *Language and Education*, vol 11, no 2, pp 182-99.

Lillis, T. and Rai, L. (2012) 'Quelle relation entre l'écrit académique et l'écrit professionnel? Une étude de cas dans le domaine du travail social', *Practiques*, vol 9, no 12, pp 51-68.

Lyons, K. (1999) *Social work in higher education*, London: Ashgate/CEDR.

Mackay, L., Soothill, K. and Webb, C. (1995) 'Troubled times: the context for interprofessional collaboration?', in L. Mackay, K. Soothill and C. Webb (eds) *Interprofessional relations in health care*, London: Edward Arnold, pp 5-10.

Manthorpe, J. and Iliffe, S. (2003) 'Professional predictions: June Huntington's perspectives on joint working, 20 years on', *Journal of Interprofessional Care*, vol 17, no 1, pp 85-94.

Moon, J. (2004) *A handbook of reflective and experiential learning: Theory and practice*, London: Routledge Falmer.

Morris, K. and Featherstone, B. (2010) 'Investing in children, regulating parents, thinking family: A decade of tensions and contradictions', *Social Policy and Society*, vol 9, no 4, pp 557-66.

Munro, E. (2011) *The Munro review of child protection: Final report*, London: The Stationery Office.

NICE (National Institute for Clinical Excellence) (2012) *Service user experience in adult mental health: NICE guidance on improving the experience of care for people using adult NHS mental health services*, London: British Psychological Society and Royal College of Psychiatrists.

O'Rourke, L. (2010) *Recording in social work: Not just an administrative task*, Bristol: Policy Press.

Oliver, M. (2009) *Understanding disability: From theory to practice*, London: Palgrave Macmillan.

Paré, A. and Le Maistre, C. (2006) 'Active learning in the workplace: transforming individuals and institutions', *Journal of Education and Work*, vol 19, no 4, pp 363-81.

Pierson, J. (2011) *Understanding social work: History and context*, London: McGraw Hill International.

Pietroni, P. (1994) 'Interprofessional teamwork: its history and development in hospitals, general practice and community care (UK)', in A. Leathard (ed) *Going inter-professional: Working together for health and welfare*, London: Routledge, pp 77-89.

Pithouse, A., Broadhurst, K., Hall, C., Peckover, S., Wastell, D. and White, S. (2011) 'Trust, risk and the (mis)management of contingency and discretion through new information technologies in children's services', *Journal of Social Work*, vol 12, no 2, pp 158-78.

QAA (Quality Assurance Agency) (2008a) *Benchmark statement for social work* (www.qaa.ac.uk/Publications/InformationAndGuidance/Documents/socialwork08.pdf).

QAA (2008b) *The framework for higher education qualifications in England, Wales and Northern Ireland*, London: QAA.

QAA (2013) *Skills for employability* (www.qaa.ac.uk/AssuringStandards AndQuality/Pages/employability.aspx).

Rai, L. (2004) 'Exploring literacy in social work education: a social practices approach to student writing', *Social Work Education*, vol 23, no 2, pp 149-62 (http://oro.open.ac.uk/913).

Rai, L. (2006) 'Owning (up to) reflective writing in social work education', *Social Work Education*, vol 25, no 8, pp 785-97 (http://oro.open.ac.uk/22062).

Rai, L. (2008) 'Student writing in social work education', PhD thesis, Milton Keynes: The Open University (http://oro.open.ac.uk/25820).

Rai, L. (2011) 'Responding to emotion in practice-based writing', *Higher Education*, vol 64, no 2, pp 267-84 (http://oro.open.ac.uk/31060).

Rai, L. and Lillis, T. (2011) 'A case study of a research-based collaboration around writing in social work', *Across the Disciplines*, vol 8, no 3 (http://wac.colostate.edu/atd/clil/lillis-rai.cfm).

Rai, L. and Lillis, T. (2012) 'Effective practices? Re-connecting academic and professional writing in social work', Paper given at Professions and Professional Learning in Troubling Times Conference, Emerging Practices and Transgressive Knowledges, Stirling, 9-11 May (www.propel.stir.ac.uk/conference2012/papers.php).

Rai, L. and Lillis, T. (2013) '"Getting it write" in social work: exploring the value of writing in academia to writing for professional practice', *Teaching in Higher Education*, May, vol, 18 issue 4, pp 352-64.

Rai, L. and Stringer, D. (2010) 'Partnership or participation?', in L. Long, J. Roche and D. Stringer (eds) *The law and social work: Contemporary issues for practice* (2nd edn), London: Palgrave Macmillan, pp 40-45.

Rich, A. (2001) 'Teaching language in open admissions. On lies, secrets and silence: Selected prose 1966-1978', in K. Halasek and N. Highberg (eds) *Essays in basic literacy*, New York: W.W. Norton, pp 1-14.

Richardson, S. and Asthana, S. (2005) 'Inter-agency information sharing in health and social care services: The role of professional culture', *British Journal of Social Work*, vol 36, pp 657-69.

Rogers, C. (1962) 'The interpersonal relationship: the core of guidance', *Harvard Educational Review*, vol 34, no 4, pp 416-29.

Rosegrant Alvarez, A. and Moxley, D.P. (2008) 'The student portfolio in social work education', *Journal of Teaching in Social Work*, June, pp 37-41 (http://dx.doi.org/10.1300/J067v24n01_06).

Ruch, G. (2002) 'From triangle to spiral: reflective practice in social work education, practice and research', *Social Work Education*, vol 21, no 2, pp 199-216.

Schön, D. (1989) *Educating the reflective practitioner: Towards a new design for teaching and learning in the professions*, San Francisco, CA: Jossey-Bass.

Scottish Executive (2003) *The framework for social work education in Scotland*, Edinburgh: The Stationery Office.

Scottish Government, The (2005) *Integrated assessment planning and recording framework (IAF)* (www.scotland.gov.uk/Publications/2005/06/20135608/56144).

Seymour, C. and Seymour, R. (2011) *Courtroom and report writing skills for social workers* (2nd edn), Exeter: Learning Matters.

Shaughnessy, M. (1977) *Errors and expectations: A guide for the teacher of basic writing*, New York: Oxford University Press.

Shaver, L. (2011) 'Using key messages to explore rhetoric in professional writing', *Journal of Business and Technical Communication*, vol 25, no 2, pp 219-36.

Shaw, I., Bell, M., Sinclair, I., Sloper, P., Mitchell, W., Dyson, P. and Rafferty, J. (2009) 'An exemplary scheme? An evaluation of the integrated children's system', *British Journal of Social Work*, vol 39, no 4, pp 613-26.

Smith, K., Todd, M. and Valdman, J. (2009) *Doing your undergraduate social science dissertation*, Abingdon: Routledge.

Social Work Reform Board (2009) *Building a safe and confident future*, London: The Stationery Office.

Social Work Reform Board (2010) *Building a safe and confident future: One year on*, London: The Stationery Office.

Sticker, G. and Fisher, M. (1990) *Self-disclosure in the therapeutic relationship*, New York: Dormer Institute of Psychological Studies.

Stierer, B. (2000) 'Schoolteachers as students: Academic literacy and the construction of professional knowledge within master's courses in education', in M. Lea and B. Stierer (eds) *Student writing in higher education: New contexts*, Buckingham: Open University Press, pp 179-95.

Street, B. (1984) *Literacy in theory and practice*, Cambridge: Cambridge University Press.

Swain, P. (2009) 'Recording and social work practice', in P. Swain and S. Rice (eds) *In the shadow of the law: The legal context of social work practice*, Annandale, Australia: Federation Press.

Timms, N. (1977) *Perspectives in social work*, London: Routledge & Kegan Paul.

Waller, M. (2000) 'Addressing student writing problems: applying composition theory to social work education', *Journal of Baccalaureate Social Work*, vol 5, no 2, pp 161-6.

Wastell, D. and White, S. (2013) 'Making sense of complex electronic records: Socio-technical design in social care', *Applied Ergonomics*, volume 45, issue 2, Part A, March, pp 143–49.

Watson, F. (2002) *Integrating theory and practice in social work education*, London: Jessica Kingsley Publishers.

White, S. and Featherstone, B. (2005) 'Communicating misunderstandings: multi-agency work as social practice', *Correspondence*, August, pp 207-16.

White, S., Hall, C. and Peckover, S. (2009) 'The descriptive tyranny of the common assessment framework: Technologies of categorization and professional practice in child welfare', *British Journal of Social Work*, vol 39, no 7, pp 1197-1217.

Youth Justice Board/Ministry of Justice (2013) *Youth Justice Statistics 2012/13* www.gov.uk/government/publications/youth-justice-statistics

Index

Note: page numbers in *italic* type refer to figures; those in **bold** type refer to tables.